SUICIDE BY COP

Inducing Officers to Shoot

Practical Direction for
Recognition, Resolution, and Recovery

Compiled by
VIVIAN B. LORD

43-08 162nd Street
Flushing, NY 11358
www.LooseleafLaw.com
800-647-5547

This publication is not intended to replace nor be a substitute for any official procedural material issued by your agency of employment or other official source. Looseleaf Law Publications, Inc., the author and any associated advisors have made all possible efforts to ensure the accuracy and thoroughness of the information provided herein but accept no liability whatsoever for injury, legal action or other adverse results following the application or adoption of the information contained in this book.

©2004 by Looseleaf Law Publications, Inc. All rights reserved. No part of this book may be reproduced, stored in a retrieval system, or transcribed, in any form or by any means, electronic, mechanical, photocopying, recording, or otherwise, without the prior written permission of the Copyright owner. Requests for such permission should be addressed to Looseleaf Law Publications, Inc., 43-08 162nd Street, Flushing, NY 11358.

Library of Congress Cataloging-in-Publication Data

Lord, Vivian B.
    Suicide by cop--inducing officers to shoot : practical direction for recognition, resolution and recovery / Vivian B. Lord.
        p. cm.
    Includes bibliographical references and index.
    ISBN 1-889031-60-7
    1. Police shootings--United States. 2. Justifiable homicide--United States. 3. Homicide investigation--United States. 4. Criminals--Suicidal behavior--United States. I. Title.
HV8143.L67 2004
363.2'3--dc22

                                                        2004004131

> *The masculine pronoun is used herein only for ease of reading. It is important to realize that the female gender is assumed.*

Cover design by *Sans Serif, Inc.* Saline, Michigan

©2004 Looseleaf Law Publications, Inc.
All Rights Reserved. Printed in U.S.A.

TABLE OF CONTENTS

PART THREE - LEGAL ISSUES SURROUNDING SbC

PART FOUR - TACTICAL AND NEGOTIATION STRATEGIES

DEDICATION

To all law enforcement officers
who put their lives on the line,
never knowing what the next call might
actually require from them.

ACKNOWLEDGMENTS

This book is the result of the professional collaboration of several people at Looseleaf Law Publications, Inc. First, we wish to express our gratitude to Michael Loughrey, President , who had the faith in this project's coming to fruition, and that it would make a substantial contribution to the extensive and growing body of criminal justice literature. Also, we wish to acknowledge the efforts of our production editor, Maria Felten, whose expertise and efforts in all phases of bringing a book to fruition were certainly essential. Furthermore, our copy editor, Mary Loughrey, improved the final product immensely. The editor also wishes to acknowledge the invaluable assistance of Allen Cowan, whose reviews of the early manuscript resulted in many beneficial changes. Also, special thanks to all the police and sheriff personnel who provided access to their files so that we might in turn share with all law enforcement officers knowledge about the phenomenon of suicide by cop.

ABOUT THE AUTHORS

Scott Allen, Ph.D. is the supervisor of police health professionals for Miami-Dade Police Department and adjunct professor, Florida International and Nova University. He also serves as consultant to the FBI, ATF, and Customs in the areas of hostage negotiation, anti-terrorism, and post-trauma. Dr. Allen received his Ph.D. in Psychology from the University of North Carolina at Chapel Hill and is also a licensed practicing psychologist in Florida. He is the author of several journal articles and book chapters in the area of post-traumatic stress disorder and suicide.

John J. Cloherty III, J.D. is a Partner in the Boston firm of Pierce, Davis & Perritano, LLP. He is a graduate of Suffolk University Law School and Providence College. He is admitted to practice before the United States District Courts for the Districts of Massachusetts and Rhode Island; the United States Court of Appeals for the First Circuit; the United States Supreme Court; and the state courts of Massachusetts and Rhode Island. He formerly served as a Law Clerk to the Hon. Donald F. Shea of the Supreme Court of Rhode Island. Before entering private practice he served as an Assistant Public Defender for the State of Rhode Island and Assistant Corporation Counsel for the City of Boston. He has tried numerous civil and criminal cases in both state and federal courts in Massachusetts and Rhode Island. His practice is concentrated in municipal law, civil rights, employment practices, discrimination and products liability litigation.

Delmar E. Dickson, Jr. is Detective Lieutenant with the Baltimore City Police Department currently assigned to the Homicide Section. Sergeant Dickson has been a member of the Baltimore City Police Department since April 1986. In addition to his regular assignment, he is a member of the Crisis Negotiation Team, involved in more than 100 active negotiations. Sergeant Dickson is the Team's training officer and one of the technical assistance personnel on the team. Currently, Sergeant Dickson is working on his Criminal Justice degree.

Leonard Gigante currently holds the rank of Sergeant with the Charlotte-Mecklenburg Police Department. He is an experienced Crisis Negotiator and has been involved in the successful resolution of numerous crisis situations since 1988. After graduating from the University of Maryland at College Park, Len Gigante began his career with the Charlotte-Mecklenburg Police Department in Charlotte, North Carolina. In 1994, he started and supervised the first Domestic Violence Unit in a police department in North Carolina. He has lectured around the country on topics relating to crisis negotiation and domestic violence.

Robert **J. Homant** received his Ph.D. in Psychology from Michigan State University and is licensed for the independent practice of clinical psychology in Michigan. His career began as a psychotherapist with maximum security inmates. For the past 25 years he has primarily been involved in teaching and research at the University of Detroit Mercy, where he is chair of the Department of Sociology and Criminal Justice. He is the author of some 80 journal articles and has provided expert witness consultation in the area of suicide, police shootings, and corrections issues.

Mark **Lindsay, M.A.** until his recent retirement, was detective of violent crimes and negotiator for Baltimore City Police Department. In addition to intervening in more than 300 critical incidents, he also trained crisis negotiation to law enforcement officers. Detective Lindsay received his masters in clinical psychology from the University of Baltimore and is licensed as a psychological associate. He is the author of articles on crisis negotiation, suicide intervention and collaboration between police and mental health providers.

Vivian **B. Lord, Ph.D.** is an associate professor in the Department of Criminal Justice at the University of North Carolina-Charlotte with Adjunct Professor appointments in the Public Policy Doctoral Program and the International Studies Departments. Dr. Lord received her Ph.D. in Psychology from North Carolina State University and is also licensed as a practicing psychologist in North Carolina. Her career in policing began as a patrol officer and then detective in a municipal police department in North Carolina and subsequently instructed, then managed at North Carolina's state police academy. She is the author of journal articles, academic book chapters, and technical reports exploring topics primarily in law enforcement assisted suicide, women in policing, law enforcement selection, ethics, comparative law enforcement systems, occupational stress, and workplace violence

Richard B. Parent, M.A. is a police officer with Delta Police Department in British Columbia where he has general patrol, recruiting and training responsibilities. He also teaches part-time for Simon Fraser University. Officer Parent received his masters in criminology from Simon Fraser University and is currently a Ph.D. candidate at the same university. He is the author of several journal articles in the areas of police use of deadly force and suicide by cop.

Barry Perrou, Ph.D., now retired, was commander of the hostage/crisis negotiations unit of Los Angeles County Sheriff's Office. He was responsible for developing the Peer Counseling Program for the Los Angeles County Sheriff's Office, as well as assisting nine agencies in the development and training of their crisis negotiation teams. Dr. Perrou received his Ph.D. in Psychology from Ryokan College. His career began as a deputy with the Los Angeles County Sheriff's Office. He is the author of several articles on crisis intervention and mental illness issues. Dr. Perrou has provided assistance and training to the FBI, ATF and local agencies in the areas of suicide-by-cop, mental illness, crisis intervention, and hostage negotiation.

PART ONE

INTRODUCTION

2

Chapter 1

SUICIDE BY COP: THE ISSUES

Vivian B. Lord

Introduction

The area of Suicide by Cop (SbC) is controversial. There are differences in definition, and therefore how the term is operationalized in the research. Defense lawyers have discovered the term so legal cases are beginning to appear. Law enforcement agencies are attempting to identify potential SbC subjects and implement successful negotiation and tactical strategies. Of course, the term, "suicide by cop" is frequently used in the media so the public is curious. Finally the impact that these types of suicides have on a community is devastating. SbC subjects often include other innocent victims in their plan; the officer who commits the deadly act is left to deal with the fact that he or she has killed a person; and the public often questions the need for deadly force.

Many Suicide by Cop (SbC) articles begin with a short review of the literature, short because the area only has received attention since 1993 when Geberth (1993) first formally defined the term. It was another half a decade before studies appeared in academic journals. Most of the authors who appear in this book are the same authors who wrote the original articles, as well as still writing in the area.

Although now conceptualized and defined in a number of ways, SbC is not new. The editor of this book was introduced to the concept by police officers in a major North Carolina city. The officers believed that the SbC phenomenon became apparent after the deinstitutionalization of mentally ill citizens. They described homeless, depressed citizens who, possessing old handguns or replicas of handguns, would confront police officers with what appeared to be deadly force. Only later would the officer realize that the citizen had induced the officer to shoot. The editor then discussed these victim-precipitated acts with special-response teams and negotiators and discovered that it was a well-known phenomenon. Her research found that few studies had been conducted in this area so she communicated with those few researchers. From these informal conversations, facilitated further when the Behavioral Science Unit of the

FBI invited several of the researchers to present at one of their special-topic conferences, the researchers decided to contribute to a book on the topic of SbC. Thus *Suicide by Cop: Inducing the Police to Shoot* was born.

The reader will notice a diverse background among the authors. Although they all have a common interest, they are police officers, police psychologists, attorneys, and criminal justice professors. Such diversity gives the reader practical information from all angles-what the SbC subject looks like, intervention and negotiation techniques, legal defense strategies, training for all officers, and crisis intervention and incident debriefing for officers involved in SbC incidents. Although the authors are in different professions with different backgrounds, they are all interested in minimizing the number of SbC subjects who are injured or killed by police officers and keep police officers emotionally healthy and alive.

Terminology and Research Issues

Geberth (1993) is recognized as the researcher who first applied the term of SbC. He defined SbC as "Incidents in which individuals, bent on self-destruction, engage in life-threatening and criminal behavior to force the police to kill them" (105). Since Geberth's definition, several problems examining SbC have emerged.

Because most subjects engaging in SbC are killed, it is difficult to ever validate their intent, so researchers attempt to operationalize the concept through the subjects' behaviors and verbalizations before and during the SbC incident as documented by the police. For instance, Lord defines SbC as "those individuals who, when confronted by law enforcement officers, either verbalized their desire to be killed by law enforcement officers or made gestures, such as pointing weapon at officers of hostages, running at officers with weapons, or throwing weapons at officers" (See Chapter 2). Lord's definition provides specific verbiage and actions to use to determine SbC cases.

Hutson, Anglin, Yarbrough, Hardaway, Russell, Strote, Canter, and Blum (1998) established four criteria:

1. Stated a wish to die and asking police officers to kill them
2. Left evidence of written or verbal suicidal communication to a friend or family member

3. Possessed a lethal weapon or what appeared to be such, and
4. Presented evidence of intentional escalation of an incident or provocation for officers to shoot them.

These criteria also provide specific behaviors, although there is still room to debate whether certain behaviors or conversations establish the intent of the SbC subject, who is now dead and can't validate it.

Parent (1998) prefers the term victim-precipitated homicide, which was introduced by Marvin Wolfgang in 1957. Parent modifies the term specifically to include "the suicidal person confronting an assailant, with a real or perceived lethal weapon, forcing the assailant to respond with deadly force" (See Chapter 4).

Keram and Farrell (2001) argue that the terms "suicide by cop" and law enforcement-assisted suicide implicate the motivation of the law enforcement officer involved. "By" conveys an intent to harm the citizen by police officers, and represents the officers as an unfeeling instrument of the subject. "Assisted" implies an agreement entered into voluntarily by the officers and the subject with each fully understanding their roles. Although victim-precipitated homicide identifies the subject as the precipitator, he or she appears to be precipitating a homicide rather than suicide. Keram and Farrell (2001) believes that all these terms are inaccurate. They suggest the use of the "suicide-by-proxy." They define the term "suicide-by-proxy" as any incident in which a suicidal individual causes his/her death to be carried out by another person. They argue that "suicide-by-proxy" emphasizes that the officer (or another individual) and subject are harmed by the incident; the decedent is a victim of suicide, and the office is the victim of the subject's chosen method of suicide (2001: 4).

Given the different definitions of SbC and even what the phenomenon should be named, the scope of SbC is difficult to measure. SbC incidents are collected from within deadly force cases, so those individuals who are killed by officers can be examined for SbC behaviors; however, some SbC incidents are concluded with the subjects surrendering or captured with little or no injuries, so they must also be identified through other data sources. For example, Lord (Chapter 9) examined barricaded subjects, comparing those who exhibited SbC behaviors with those who did not.

The editor and authors of *Suicide by Cop: Inducing the Police to Shoot* want the readers to understand the limited nature of the research on SbC. This book is a pioneering venture, uncovering the first information on this subject.

Chapter Organization and Overview

Part One introduces the reader to the concept and discussion of the current research. Part Two consists of research on the subjects and circumstances surrounding the violent incident (Chapters 2 and 3). Part Three provides the readers with the legal ramifications of SbC (Chapters 4 and 5). Part Four will describe tactical and negotiation strategies used by law enforcement officers in SbC incidents (Chapters 6 through 8), and the book concludes with Part Five, the impact of SbC incidents on law enforcement officers (Chapters 9 and 10).

Chapter 2, *Suicide by Cop Incidents in North Carolina: A Comparison of Successful and Unsuccessful Cases*, describes historical, personality, behavioral, and situational factors of law enforcement-assisted suicides. These factors are then used to compare differences between SbC subjects who successfully forced officers to shoot them and those subjects who were unsuccessful.

Chapter 3, *Police Use of Deadly Force in the Pacific Northwest*, examines the underlying causes and prevalence of police shootings in the Pacific Northwest. Documented incidents in which lethal threats against police personnel in the states of Oregon, Washington and the province of British Columbia are directly attributed to incidents of "police assisted suicide" are analyzed. Through the examination of police investigations, coroner inquests, media reports and interviews with police officers, this chapter reveals that the phenomenon of police-assisted suicide is a significant factor in fatal-police shootings. The author concludes that police personnel in the Pacific. Northwest require further alternatives to the standard-issue firearm when dealing with individuals who are suicidal. Less-than lethal compliance tools such as the Taser, Arwen, Bean-bag shot gun and the Pepper-ball gun are discussed as possible alternatives to the standard-issue firearm when dealing with individuals who are suicidal.

Chapter 4, *Suicide by Police" in Section 1983 Suites: Relevance of Police Tactics*, discusses the courts' determination of "objective reasonableness" under the 4th Amendment, focusing on police shootings that led to excessive force civil rights litigation. It then examines how specifically identified SbC cases are handled by the courts.

Chapter 5, *Legal Defense of Law Enforcement Officers in Police Shooting Cases,* describes the post-SbC activities that need to be considered to defend successfully law enforcement officers involved in SbC. These activities begin with pre-lawsuit legal counsel, pre-lawsuit claim procedures, the defense of a use of deadly force and more specifically a SbC lawsuit, pre-trial tactics, and the trial itself. This chapter is written for lawyers using terminology readily understood by attorneys.

Chapter 6, *Negotiating with the SbC Subject*, outlines some of the negotiation strategies that have been found to be effective when communicating with SbC subjects. Special emphasis is placed on the SbC subject's desire to remain in control and to place continual stress on the law enforcement agency in order to have his or her death wish carried out.

Chapter 7, *Comparison of Situation and Tactical Strategies of Successful and Unsuccessful SbC Incidents*, describes the tactical and negotiation strategies used by police departments in North Carolina to intervene in SbC incidents. Although little differences were found in the characteristics of the SbC subjects, who were successful in forcing the officers to intervene with lethal force and those who were not, length of residency and duration of negotiation were significantly different and have negotiation implications. Also surprised officers are more likely to injure or kill subjects.

Chapter 8, *The Effectiveness of Less-Than-Lethal Force in SbC Incidents*, examines 143 SbC incidents for law enforcement officers' use of less-than-lethal force (LTL). The type of LTL force used, tactics used by law enforcement and the outcome of these cases in comparison with use of deadly force is described.

Chapter 9, *Comparison of Strategies Used in Barricaded Situations: SbC and Non SbC Subjects*, compares subjects, incidents and law enforcement strategies used by law enforcement officers among barricaded situations in one large southern city. As a subpopulation within the barricaded subject sample, those incidents defined as SbC are compared with non-SbC barricaded situations.

Chapter 10, *Antecedent Behaviors as Indicators of Imminent Violence*, explores the exact moment of lethal action, crisis. Case studies suggest when specific behaviors are present, individually or collectively, an act of self-termination is imminent. These behaviors include change in respiratory rate, hyper vigilance and counting down/up either verbally or with stereotyped movement. Suicidal individuals exhibiting these behaviors have subsequently attempted or completed suicide or aimed weapons at police officers. Certain behaviors may predict impending violence.

These behaviors are observed by law enforcement personnel and other emergency responders who act in the capacity of crisis interveners, as well as by special response team (SWT) long-rifle and spotter teams observing hostage-takers. In addition these acts are visually observable and /or audibly detectable by crisis workers, police dispatchers or crisis negotiators. Identifying these behaviors provides forewarning of danger or violence, and when detected, can give cause for personnel to seek safety or for SWT long-rifle teams to pre-empt a deadly act towards a victim or innocent bystanders.

Chapter 11, *Officer-involved shootings: case management and psycho-social investigations*, provides a number of information sources in the form of checklists that are useful to homicide investigators who must reconstruct the crime after a SbC has occurred.

Chapter 12, *Critical incident debriefing with officers involved in SbC Incidents*, outlines the post-shooting debriefings of SbC incidents. Usually SbC confrontation is a multiple-officer, if not, a tactical-team shooting. As such, there is an individual, as well as a "ripple effect" in terms of post-shooting sequelae. The dynamics of immediate, on-site debriefing for the police shooter(s) is delineated, along with the intervention techniques for follow-up team debriefings and debriefing session for communications staff.

Chapter 13, *Training Law Enforcement Officers to Identify, Intervene, and Cope with SbC incidents*, outlines training developed by a panel of "subject-matter-experts" for the California State Commission on Police Officer Standards of Training (P.O.S.T.). Nearly any "classic" suicide-in-progress can become a potential suicide-by-cop confrontation when police are summoned to the incident. Training provides understanding about the phenomenon of suicide, about suicidal subjects, and about suicide-by-cop subjects.

References

Geberth, V. J. (1993). Suicide by cop. Law and Order, July, 105-108.

Hutson, H.R., Anglin, D., Yarbrough, J., Hardaway, K., Russell, M., Strote, J., Canter, M., & Blum, B. (1998). Suicide-by-cop. Annals of Emergency Medicine, 32(6), 665-669.

Keram, E. A. & Farrell, B. J. (2001) Suicide by cop: Issues in outcome and analysis. In D. C. Sheehan & J. I. Warren (Eds). Suicide and Law Enforcement (587-599). Washington D. C.: Behavioral Science Unit, FBI.

PART TWO

CHARACTERISTICS OF SBC SUBJECTS AND INCIDENTS

Chapter 2

SUICIDE BY COP INCIDENTS IN NORTH CAROLINA: A COMPARISON OF SUCCESSFUL AND UNSUCCESSFUL CASES

Introduction

Suicide attempts using law enforcement officers, more commonly known as "suicide by cop," have received very little attention from researchers. Perhaps this sparsity is due to the perceived small number of cases as noted by Alan Berman, president of the American Association of Suicidology (Lewan, 1998)*. While his conclusion may reflect the perceptions of suicidologists, the limited research that has been conducted on law enforcement assisted suicides suggests that the phenomenon may be more prevalent than is generally realized. For instance, an examination of 384 officer-involved shootings in Los Angeles County between the years 1987 and 1997 found approximately ten percent of the victims met criteria for law enforcement assisted suicides, or "suicides by cop" (Scoville, 1998). These numbers do not indicate the impact that these types of attempts and completed suicides have on a community. Suicidal individuals often include other innocent victims in their plan; the officer who commits the deadly act is left to deal with the fact he or she has killed somebody; and the public often questions the need for deadly force. This form of suicide, and its involvement of the law enforcement community, clearly needs further examination.

In contrast to law enforcement assisted suicides, a great deal of research has been conducted on those individuals who, on their own, commit suicide. From the research, suicide victims have a number of characteristics in common. These factors include mental disorders, alcoholism and drug abuse, suicidal ideation, discussion of, and preparation for suicide, prior suicide attempts, lethality of method, social isolation, hopelessness, work problems, stressful life events, aggression and anger, and physical illness (Maris, 1992; Brown, Linnoila, & Goodwin, 1992; McIntosh, 1992; Roy & Linaoila, 1986; Weissman & Beck, 1981; Beck, Weissman, & Kovacs, 1976).

* *Criminal Justice and Behavior: An International Journal* 27: 401-418 (2000),Copyright © 2000 by Sage Publications, Inc. Reprinted with permission of the publisher

The suicide studies have also found distinguishing characteristics between fatal and nonfatal suicide victims. In a particularly well known study comparing nonfatal attempts with completions, Maris (1992) found that the primary reasons that suicide completers killed themselves were loss of job, children, or spouse. In contrast, the reasons for the nonfatal suicide attempts of individuals were mental illness, drug abuse, and interpersonal problems. Maris noted that attempting suicide might become a conditioned reaction. The attempter might endeavor to cope with stressful life events by self-destructive behaviors, and subsequent suicide attempts might be made with more lethal methods.

SbC subjects demonstrate through their actions or communications that they too are attempting suicide. However, they are enlisting another person to assist in their death, which could be an important difference from solo suicides and might lead to unique characteristics. To expand our limited knowledge on individuals who use law enforcement officers in their attempts to kill themselves, the current study examined the characteristics of SbC subjects, and the tactical and negotiation strategies used in the intervention of their incidents.

Method

Law Enforcement Assisted Suicides Defined

For the purpose of this research, law enforcement assisted suicides, or "suicides by cop"(SbC) were defined as those individuals who, when confronted by law enforcement officers, either verbalized their desire to be killed by law enforcement officers and/or made gestures, such as pointing weapons at officers or hostages, running at officers with weapons, or throwing weapons at officers. This study included completed law enforcement-assisted suicides *and* attempts in which the officers averted the shooting of the subject, bringing him or her out of the situation alive. The study also contained a few subsequent suicides, but only in which the initial gestures and/or verbalizations were observed, and the officers were able to prevent the subject from initiating an assault on them. After an extended period of time, the subject ended his[1] own life.

SbC victims are considered successful in their attempt to have the officer shoot them if they are killed or injured by officers; the subjects were able to carry out their intentions. Subjects who killed themselves during the SbC incident are also considered successful. If the SbC subjects were apprehended by the officer or the officers effected a surrender, they were categorized as unsuccessful.

An example of one of the SbC cases was a white male subject, age thirty-seven, who had a mental health history. Six months before the SbC incident, he was terminated from his job and began abusing alcohol. Then three days prior to the SbC incident, the subject bought a weapon. On the day of the SbC incident, the subject drove approximately one hundred miles from his home on a major interstate highway and then began shooting at cars with his weapon. When a deputy appeared, the subject shot at the officer and then raced in his vehicle down the highway. After approximately fifty miles, law enforcement officers were able to block his passage. The subject continued shooting until he was killed by a sniper, who was with one of the law enforcement departments. The family later provided the information that the subject had been diagnosed as bi-polar and was diabetic. He had attempted suicide before, although without the attempted use of law enforcement.

Selection of Cases

Thirty-two local North Carolina county and municipal law enforcement department administrators were personally contacted by the researcher. The officer responsible for the department's tactical unit or the department's negotiator(s) was interviewed. The researcher provided the definition of SbC to the responsible officer, and the officer was asked to select cases between the years of 1991 and 1998 that met this definition. To maintain the anonymity of the subject and officers involved, the interviewed tactical officer or negotiator read information from the selected case files to the researcher. The researcher was able to ask for clarification and additional information. Although some variation of information may exist among departments, overall the law enforcement departments studied kept extensive records on any case that involved use of force or apprehension.

Sample

Sixty-four SbC cases from 32 law enforcement agencies were examined. The departments represented a variety of different size towns and cities, as well as both police and sheriff agencies from across North Carolina. As described in Table 2-1, SbC subjects were primarily white males between the ages of 25 and 40. The SbC cases included 16 subjects killed by officers, 5 suicides committed during the standoff with police, and 43 attempts in which officers either negotiated a surrender or managed an apprehension. These attempts can be further categorized by action taken after the SbC incident. Eighteen subjects were committed to a mental hospital, 15 were arrested for assault on officers or other family members, and 9 were injured by officers. As noted within the definition of SbC, subjects killed or injured by officers are considered successful and are merged in the current study's analysis.

Table 2-1

Demographic Variables of All SbC Subjects

Variable	Number	Percentage
Sex		
Male	60	93.8
Female	3	4.7
Race		
White	48	75.0
Black	14	21.9
Latin American	1	1.6
Unknown	1	1.6
Age		
Under 25	9	14.1
25-39	36	56.3
40-59	18	28.1
Over 60	0	0
Unknown	1	1.6
Outcome		
No action	1	1.6
Committed to hospital	18	28.1
Arrested	15	23.4
Injured by officer	9	14.1
Killed by officer	16	25.0
Suicide during SbC incident	5	7.8

Results

The characteristics of the SbC subject and incident are categorized by the suicidal risk factors found in the literature. As noted earlier, mental disorders, alcoholism and drug abuse, suicidal ideation, discussion of, and preparation for suicide, prior suicide attempts, lethality of method, social isolation, hopelessness, interpersonal problems, work problems, stressful life events, aggression and anger, and physical illness are all risk factors for suicide (Maris, 1992; Brown, Linnoila, & Goodwin, 1992; McIntosh, 1992; Roy & Linnoila, 1986; Weissman & Beck, 1981; Beck, Weissman, & Kovacs, 1976). With the exceptions of the more affective areas such as hopelessness and stress, data on these factors were gathered on the current SbC cases.

Additionally the variable, "signs of planning," is included. William, Davidson, and Montgomery (1980) divided suicide attempters into two groups, impulsive and nonimpulsive. Those individuals who reported less than a five minute premeditation of their suicidal action were defined as impulsive. These impulsive attempters were more likely to tell someone about the act and think someone would find them within a short period of time. A high proportion of the impulsive attempters thought they would live. If those subjects who are more likely to attempt, but not succeed, are impulsively making their decisions to cope with their problems by SbC, there should be some differences in indications of planning.

Mental disorder. In the current study, mental illness was recognized either informally by family members or formally through an out-patient or in-patient commitment history in about 54% of the subjects (Table 2-2). A large percentage of individuals with mental commitment histories (28%) were successful in their attempts to have officers shoot them. Usually the actual diagnosis was not provided to law enforcement, but when known, the subject was often labeled schizophrenic or bi-polar. If the subject was not known by law enforcement officers to have a mental health problem or there were no family members available to supply such information, the subject was categorized as mentally healthy. It is therefore possible that more of the subjects had mental problems than were so identified by law enforcement.

Table 2-2

Comparison of Personal and Social Characteristics of the SbC Subjects

SbC subjects who were successful in their attempt to be shot by officers are compared with those who were unsuccessful in their attempt.

Variable	Successful % (n)		Outcome Unsuccessful % (n)		Total % (n)	
Mental Disorder						
None	45	(17)	48	(12)	46	(29)
Symptoms, but no diagnosis	18	(7)	12	(3)	16	(10)
Psychiatric history	18	(7)	12	(3)	16	(10)
Commitment history	18	(7)	28	(7)	22	(14)
Total		**(38)**		**(25)**		**(63)**
Lambda=.00						
Substance Abuse by Subject						
None	50	(16)	40	(8)	44	(24)
Alcohol	19	(6)	15	(3)	17	(9)
Prescribed	9	(3)	0		5.5	(3)
Marijuana	6	(2)	10	(2)	7	(4)
Alcohol + marijuana	0		5	(1)	2	(1)
Hard drugs	12.5	(4)	30	(6)	18.5	(10)
Alcohol + hard drugs	3	(1)	0		5.5	(3)
Total		**(32)**		**(20)**		**(54)**
Lambda=.15						
Substance Use during Incident						
None	23.5	(8)	26	(6)	26	(14)
Alcohol	62	(21)	48	(11)	59	(32)
Proscribed	3	(1)			4	(2)
Marijuana	3	(1)	4	(1)	2	(1)
Alcohol + marijuana	0		0		0	
Hard drugs	0		0		5.5	(3)
Alcohol + hard drugs	0		13	(3)	4	(2)
Total		**(31)**	9	**(2)**		**(54)**
Lambda=.13				**(23)**		

Variable	Successful % (n)		Outcome Unsuccessful % (n)		Total % (n)	
Social Isolation						
No Support	10	(4)	4	(1)	8	(5)
Partner	20.5	(8)	21	(5)	21	(13)
Parents	26	(10)	25	(6)	25	(16)
Extended Family	33	(13)	50	(12)	40	(25)
Friends	8	(3)	0		5	(3)
Professional	3	(1)	0		2	(1)
Total		**(39)**		**(24)**		**(63)**
Lambda=.00						
Length of Residence						
Not a resident	3	(1)	23	(5)	11	(6)
Resident< one year	16	(5)	4.5	(1)	11	(6)
Over one year	81	(25)	73	(16)	77	(41)
Total		**(31)**		**(22)**		**(53)**
Lambda=.182						
Work Issues						
Employed	39	(11)	35	(6)	38	(17)
Unemployed	61	(17)	65	(11)	62	(28)
Total		**(28)**		**(27)**		**(45)**
Lambda=.00						

Substance abuse. The variables, use of alcohol or drugs either during the incident or habitually used by the subject, have weak relationships with the outcome (Lambda=.13; Lambda=.15 respectively). Over half of the subjects were considered substance abusers (64%), and well over half used alcohol and/or drugs (74%) during the actual SbC incident. Proportionately over twice as many subjects who were successful in their attempt (30%) were addicted to hard drugs such as cocaine, while a greater number of unsuccessful subjects abused alcohol during the incident (62%) (Table 2-2).

Although it is not possible to determine the subject's judgment, or the lack thereof, Beck, Weisman, and Kovacs (1976) concluded that subjects under the influence of alcohol overcome their inhibitions and are more impulsive and more lethal.

Social isolation. With few exceptions, SbC subjects have other people in their lives; only five of the subjects (8%) did not have any close family or friends. In addition, over half of the subjects (77%) had resided in the area for over a year, with many living their entire life in the area in which the incident occurred. Overall, these subjects were not transient or loners, but rather individuals who were connected to their communities.

The subject's length of time in residence in the town in which the SbC incident occurred does have a weak relationship with the outcome of the incident (Lambda=.182). Nonresidents had a much higher rate of success than residents who had lived in the area for at least a short period of time (Table 2-2). If the subject is known to them, the level of danger that officers perceive might not be as high as with somebody they did not know.

Work problems. For those subjects whose employment status was known, over half were not employed (62%). Specific work problems were not likely to be an issue, though there were notable exceptions. For instance, Case #17 involved a 37 year old man who had received a promotion on his job, but was terminated soon after the promotion for embezzlement. The termination, in addition to mental and family problems, is attributed to his suicidal actions. The subject was first reported for shooting at cars traveling on a major interstate highway. When approached by a county law enforcement officer, the subject shot at the officer and then raced down the highway in his own car. After a high-speed chase through two counties, the subject was blocked. At which point, he continued to shoot at the officers, refusing any form of communication. A law enforcement sniper finally shot and killed him.

Stressful life events. The SbC incidents are categorized around three major stresses–domestic disturbances, mental illness, and criminal activity. In general, most of the subjects were experiencing what could be perceived as a stressful event prior to the SbC incident (Table 2-3). The largest percentage of individuals had either just lost significant people in their lives, or they were experiencing a major family problem (41%). The family problems included the parents' lack of understanding of one subject's homosexual orientation and another subject's attempt to stop his girlfriend from terminating their relationship. The mental illness of some SbC subjects constituted another large percentage of stressors (16%). Six individuals (9.5%) were experiencing multiple stressors that included domestic, financial, and/or consequences of criminal activity.

There is a weak relationship between stressful life events and the outcome variable (Lambda=.125). Subjects without an identified problem and those subjects with financial problems appear to be distinguishing elements. Three subjects who were primarily concerned with money were all successful in their SbC action. While approximately twice as many subjects without an identified problem were unsuccessful in their attempt (13%).

Table 2-3

Comparison of Stressful Life Events of the SbC Subjects

SbC subjects who were successful in their attempt to be shot by officers are compared with those who were unsuccessful in their attempt.

Variable	Successful % (n)		Outcome Unsuccessful % (n)		Total % (n)	
Stressful Life Events						
None	13	(5)	8	(2)	11	(7)
Termination of relationship	31	(12)	29	(7)	30	(19)
Family problems	20.5	(8)	17	(4)	19	(12)
Money problems	0		12.5	(3)	5	(3)
Mental illness	15	(6)	17	(4)	16	(10)
Criminal Warrant	10	(4)	8	(2)	9.5	(6)
Multiple	10	(4)	8	(2)	9.5	(6)
Total		**(39)**		**(24)**		**(63)**
Lambda=.125						

Subjects with personal relationship problems were more likely to be unsuccessful; however, it is important to notice that roughly equal numbers of individuals did succeed. While in many cases it might have been used more as an attempt to coerce the significant other into remaining in the relationship, in others as noted by Brown, Linnoila, and Goodwin (1992), murderous revenge is one reason for suicide. As an example, one subject returned to North Carolina from Florida after discovering his ex-wife had a boyfriend. The subject was killed by law enforcement after the subject killed his ex-wife's boyfriend and attempted to kill his wife and their two children. After the SbC incident, an audio-taped message was found in his car. On the audio-tape, he described his plan to kill the boyfriend, his family, and himself explaining, "no son-of-a-bitch is going to raise my kids."

Although only two subjects with outstanding arrest warrants were killed, criminal warrants were stressful events in a number of SbC subjects' lives. Many attempted to provoke their deaths after they had told a significant other that they would die before returning to prison. A subject in one case was wanted for breaking and entering. When the law enforcement officers arrived with a warrant, he attacked them with a knife. After his arrest, he informed them that he had a daughter and that he would rather die than return to prison. Another subject wanted for a number of breaking and entering and robberies shot a handgun at law enforcement officers, ensuring his death. His associates informed law enforcement that he had told several people that he would not be taken alive to prison; he would kill somebody or be killed.

Suicidal ideation or prior suicide attempts. Thirteen subjects (20.3%) possessed prior suicide histories, and previous suicide attempts did have a weak relationship with the outcome (Lambda=.125). Subjects who had attempted suicide once before were three times as likely to be injured or killed by officers as those who had never attempted suicide. This trend changes with multiple attempts (Table 2-4). As noted by Maris (1992), attempted suicide might become a conditioned reaction used to cope with stressful life events.

Over half of all the SbC subjects (58.5%) had made some sort of statement or changes in behavior that were interpreted by their significant others (friends or family members) as pre-suicidal gestures. Such behaviors included the subject in Case 28 writing a suicide note preceding the SbC incident, and the individual in Case 30 telling his therapist that he was going to force the police to kill him. More subtle indications were also noted, such as Case 39 where the subject stopped taking medication for schizophrenia, began giving away some of his possessions, and burned some of the items that he had made. Slightly more successful SbC subjects (65%) than unsuccessful (54.5%) gave indications of suicidal thoughts. Also in general, very little planning occurred with half of the subjects, although a slightly higher percentage of successful individuals planned (56%).

Maris (1992) found that as many as 75 to 80% of the suicide victims in his study gave presuicidal clues of their intentions. The current research only provides weak support for Maris' study. However, unless the subject's family members or the officers specifically stated that the subject had mentioned thoughts of suicide, displayed changes in behavior, or attempted suicide before, prior suicide ideation or activities were not included, but rather listed as missing information.

Table 2-4

Comparison of Suicidal Ideology of the SbC Subjects

SbC subjects who were successful in their attempt to be shot by officers are compared with those who were unsuccessful in their attempt.

Variable	Successful % (n)		Outcome Unsuccessful % (n)		Total % (n)	
Previous Suicide Attempts						
None	81	(25)	6	(17)	76	(42)
One	6	(2)	21	(5)	13	(7)
More than one	13	(4)	8	(2)	11	(6)
Total		**(31)**		**(24)**		**(55)**
Lambda=.125						
Suicidal Ideation						
No	45.5	(15)	35	(7)	45	(22)
Yes	54.5	(18)	65	(13)	58.5	(31)
Total		**(33)**		**(20)**		**(53)**
Lambda=.00						
Signs of Planning						
No	54	(21)	44	(11)	50	(32)
Yes	46	(18)	56	(14)	50	(32)
Total		**(39)**		**(25)**		**(64)**
Lambda=.00						
Lethality of Method						
None	2.5	(1)	0		2	(1)
Gun			92	(23)	73	(47)
Knife	61.5	(24)	8	(2)	22	(14)
Other	31	(12)	0		3	(2)
Total				**(25)**		**(64)**
Lambda=.00	5	(2)				
		(39)				

Lethality of method. Involving law enforcement officers guarantees a high degree of lethality. In addition, a majority of the subjects possessed either a gun (73%) or knife (21%) at the time of the incident, increasing the probability that lethal force would be utilized (Table 2-4). As might be expected, subjects with firearms were much more likely to be shot by officers (92%) than individuals who possessed knives(8%).

Aggression and anger. Aggression and anger were quantified in a number of different ways. Previous history of assaults and domestic violence, initial complaint to law enforcement, and conversation and actions of the subject during the actual SbC incident that were homicidal were included as measurements of the subjects' hostility and pugnacity toward other people. Conversation and actions of the subject were found to relate to the outcome variable (Lambda=.20). (See Table 2-5).

Over half of the subjects had no criminal record (51%). Of those individuals with records, domestic violence was most prevalent (18%). Drug related offenses were the only crimes that seemed to be more prevalent among those individuals who were successful (14%).

Only 13 of the subjects (21%) had actually been arrested for domestic violence or another personal crime; however, 20 of the incidents (31%) began with a domestic dispute complaint to law enforcement. Although less frequent than domestic violence or suicide attempts, criminal activity was most likely to end in the subject's death or injury by an officer.

Thirteen subjects mentioned the desire to kill another person in addition to themselves (20%). Individuals who chose not to negotiate with officers, or who surprised the officers so that the officers felt their lives were in immediate danger, were likely to be shot by officers. For some SbC subjects, their suicidal actions appear to include a desire to hurt others, as well as themselves. This scenario is also true in cases that the individual spoke of homicide and suicide (36%). In many cases the homicide conversation was directed at the officers. Such talk probably increased the danger awareness level of the officers.

Table 2-5

Comparison of Indicators of Aggression and Anger of SbC Subjects

SbC subjects who were successful in their attempt to be shot by officers are compared with those who were unsuccessful in their attempt.

Variable	Successful % (n)		Outcome Unsuccessful % (n)		Total % (n)	
Criminal History						
None	54	(21)	45	(10)	51	(31)
DWI	10	(4)	9	(2)	10	(6)
Domestic	18	(7)	18	(4)	8	(11)
Property crimes	8	(3)	9	(2)	8	(5)
Other Personal crimes	3	(1)	4.5	(1)	3	(2)
Drugs	8	(3)	14	(3)	10	(6)
Total		**(39)**		**(22)**		**(61)**
Lambda=.00						
Officers' Initial Role						
Suicide Intervention	44	(17)	36	(9)	41	(26)
Domestic Violence	31	(12)	32	(8)	31	(20)
Criminal Activity	23	(9)	32	(8)	27	(17)
Other	3	(1)	0		2	(1)
Total		**(39)**		**(25)**		**(64)**
Lambda=.00						
Conversation of Subject						
None	18	(7)	28	(7)	22	(14)
Direct suicide talk	72	(28)	36	(9)	58	(37)
Homicide + suicide	10	(4)	36	(9)	20	(3)
Total		**(39)**		**(25)**		**(64)**
Lambda=.20						

Physical illness. Physical illness, considered a risk factor for suicide, would have been listed in the "stressful life events" category. Illness was not considered a major reason for the SbC attempt in any of the cases; however, in two cases in which there were multiple stresses, the individuals had lost an arm or leg.

Summary. SbC victims and suicide victims in general appear to share several risk factors. A large percentage have identified mental health issues, abuse drugs and alcohol, suffer from stressful life events, and have talked about suicide.

Maris (1992) found significant differences between those individuals who succeeded in their suicide attempts and those who failed, and the current study detected some differences in the characteristics of the SbC subjects who were successful in their attempt in forcing officers to use lethal force, and those subjects who were unsuccessful. Substance abuse (especially hard drugs) previous suicide attempts, stressful life events, length of residency in the location of the SbC incident, and homicidal conversation during the SbC relate weakly to a successful SbC attempt.

Social isolation, a risk factor for suicide, was not a characteristic of SbC subjects; a majority of subjects possessed a support system. However, it is important to note that the termination of a relationship or family problems was quite often the stressful precipitating event for which officers were called out. The subjects may perceive that they have lost their social support.

Discussion

As the data of this study reveal, SbC victims in general do share a number of characteristics with individuals who commit suicide on their own. SbC appears to be unique from other types of suicide, primarily due to the involvement of other people. In Maris' Chicago study (1992), fifty percent of the completed suicides had no close friends. In the current study, only eight percent did not have any social support. Social isolation increases the risk of suicide both because of the human need for interaction with others and because of the diminished chances of rescue. Individuals who attempt suicide, but fail to complete the act, quite often believe that they will be rescued (William, Davidson, & Montgomery, 1980; Stengel & Cook, 1958). Similarly, in the current study, many SbC subjects began the attempt on their own, but quickly turned the responsibility of the act over to law enforcement officers when they arrived.

Within SbC subjects, there is some evidence of differences between those SbC subjects, who succeed in their attempt to manipulate law enforcement to use deadly force, and those SbC subjects who are not successful. History of mental institution commitments, abuse of hard drugs, nonresidents, financial problems, one previous suicide attempt, possession of a gun, criminal history of drugs, involvement in criminal activity, and homicidal conversation during the incident are more likely to be characteristics of individuals who were successful in their attempt to be injured or killed by law enforcement.

In the current study, SbC subjects with mental health problems were most often labeled as schizophrenic or manic-depressant. In contrast, Maris (1992) limited suicide victims' mental health problems to difficulties coping with depression and anger. Monahan (1992) found persons who met the criteria for a diagnosis of schizophrenia, major depression or mania/bi-polar disorder to be six times more likely to be violent than people who had received no diagnosis. The fact that a large number of SbC subjects who had histories of mental institution commitments were shot by officers is useful information; however, more data need to be collected about the prevalent types of mental illnesses SbC subjects possess.

While subjects who are under the influence of alcohol may become more impulsive (Beck, Weisman, & Kovacs, 1976), use of hard drugs(such as the stimulant, cocaine) appears to be more lethal in the current research. Again Monahan's results (1992) support the relationship between substance abuse and violence. He found that the prevalence of violence among persons who had been diagnosed as abusing drugs was 16 times that of a person who had not received such a diagnosis.

The high percentage of successful SbC subjects who had attempted suicide once, supports the consideration of previous suicide attempts as a risk factor. On the other hand, the lack of success of those SbC subjects who had a history of multiple attempts, also supports Maris' (1992) contention that suicide attempts may become a conditioned reaction to stress. Communication between law enforcement and treatment providers is needed to help identify suicide attempters in order to provide them alternative means to deal with stress.

The length of time the subject had lived in the area in which the incident took place appears to be a significant variable and demonstrates the need to consider the influence of the officer on the outcome of the SbC event. Those subjects who did not reside in the area in which the incident occurred were much more likely to be successful in their attempt than those who lived in the area even for a short period of time. It is possible that these nonresidents felt more isolated; however, in all probability the very element brought into play to kill them, the law enforcement officer, was one of the controlling factors of the outcome. Although the SbC subject is attempting to provoke officers to kill him or her, the officers' interaction with the subject, as well as the skills and tools available to them, will influence the final result. A large number of SbC subjects had previous contact with the law enforcement department through past, usually minor disturbances; so the subject was not an unknown assailant and the officer was not just a uniform. The level of danger that officers perceive might not be as high with an individual with whom they have dealt on more minor, nonlethal offenses.

The need to consider the law enforcement officers' reactions to the amount of danger the subject presents also becomes evident in a number of other variables: the weapon the SbC subject possesses, the initial complaint, and the conversation of the SbC subject during the incident. SbC subjects who had firearms, were wanted for outstanding criminal warrants, or included homicidal threats in their conversations with officers were more likely to be shot. It is not clear if these SbC subjects' intentions were more lethal than the nonsuccessful SbC subjects, but officers certainly perceived them as more deadly and acted accordingly.

Law enforcement officers are becoming more aware of individuals who attempt to use police to kill them. Tactical officers and negotiators also are beginning to comprehend the need for some subjects, especially in barricaded situations, to maintain control. Understanding these subjects will continue to help officers successfully intervene. It would be helpful for officers to expand the interview of SbC attempters who live to include information that would help law enforcement's understanding of the motives behind SbC incidents. Future research focusing on successful intervention strategies, particularly in the area of negotiation approaches, will also be helpful.

Notes

The current study only discovered male SbCs who ended their own lives.

References

Beck, A. T., Weissman, M. A., & Kovacs, M. (1976). Alcoholism, hopelessness and suicidal behavior. Journal of Studies on Alcohol, 37, 66-77.

Brown, G. L., Linnoila, M. I. & Goodwin, F. K. (1992). Impulsivity, aggression, and associated affects: Relationship to self-destructive behavior and suicide. In R.W. Maris, S.L. Berman, J.T. Maltsberger, & R.I. Yufit (Eds.), Assessment and Prediction of Suicide (pp. 362-380). New York: Guilford Press.

Dowdall, G. W., Babbie, E. & Halley, F. (1997). Adventures in Criminal Justice Research. Thousand Oaks, CA: Pine Forge Press.

Geberth, V. J. (1993). Suicide by cop. Law and Order, July, 105-108.

Kennedy, D.B., Homant, R. J., & Hupp, R.T. (1998). Suicide by cop. FBI Law Enforcement Bulletin. August, 21-27.

Lewan, T. (1998, April 26). Standoffs with police can be a death wish. The Charlotte Observer, pp. 1,18.

Maris, R.W. (1992). Nonfatal suicide attempts and completed suicides. In R.W. Maris, S.L. Berman, J.T. Maltsberger, & R.I. Yufit (Eds.), Assessment and Prediction of Suicide (pp. 362-380). New York: Guilford Press.

McIntosh, J. L. (1992). Methods of suicide. In R.W. Maris, S.L. Berman, J.T. Maltsberger, & R.I. Yufit (Eds.), Assessment and Prediction of Suicide (pp. 362-380). New York: Guilford Press.

Monahan, J. (1992). Mental disorder and violent behavior: Perceptions and evidence. American Psychologist, 47, 511-521.

Parent, R. B. & Verdun-Jones, S. (1998). Victim precipitated homicide: Police use of deadly force in British Columbia. Policing: An International Journal of Police Strategies and Management, 21, 432-448.

Roy, A. & Linnoila, M. (1986). Alcoholism and suicide. Suicide and Life-Threatening Behavior, 16, 162-191.

Scoville, D. (1998). Getting you to pull the trigger. Police, November, 36-44.

Stengel, E. & Cook, N. (1958). Attempted suicide: Its social significance and effects. London: Oxford University Press.

VanZandt, C. (1993). Suicide by cop. The Police Chief, 15, 24-30.

Weissman, M. E. & Beck, A. T. (1981). Cognitive approaches to understanding and treating suicidal behavior. In S.J. Blumenthal & D. J. Kupler (Eds.), Suicide over the life-cycle, (pp. 469-498). Washington, DC: American Psychiatric Press.

William, C. L., Davidson, J. A., & Montgomery, I. (1980). Impulsive suicidal behavior. Journal of Clinical Psychology, 36, 90-94.

Chapter 3

POLICE USE OF DEADLY FORCE IN THE PACIFIC NORTHWEST VICTIM-PRECIPITATED HOMICIDE

Richard B. Parent

Police Use of Deadly Force: International Comparisons

For law enforcement personnel, the decision to utilize deadly force is of such significance that the appropriateness of the action will always be questioned. In contemporary society, police use of potentially lethal force can only occur in those rare situations in which no other reasonable option is available. The use of deadly force is dependent upon both the unique circumstances of the incident and the particular decision-making strategies of the individual officer.

When police officers in North America use firearms against individuals, it may be assumed that they are using lethal force. Generally, officers who discharge a firearm or utilize other forms of potentially deadly force are attempting to immediately incapacitate a perceived lethal threat to themselves or another individual. This decision-making process will usually transpire at a time when the individual officer is under considerable stress, leaving him or her open to the influence of a variety of physiological and psychological factors.

In the United States there are approximately 282,000 million people and over 665,000 full-time sworn police officers in state and local government (U.S. Census Bureau, 2000). It is within this setting that roughly 300 individuals are shot and killed by U.S. law enforcement personnel each year (Uniform Crime Reports for the United States (UCR), 2001). In the neighboring nation of Canada with a population and police service that is approximately one-tenth of the U.S., roughly 10 individuals are shot and killed each year by police.

In comparison, approximately five individuals die each year in Australia due to gunshot wounds inflicted by police personnel (Australian Institute of Criminology (AIC), 1998). With a population of roughly 20 million people, the Australian justifiable homicide rate is lower than both the US and Canadian rate. Noteworthy is that in neighboring New Zealand with a population of 4 million people; there have been only approximately 20 fatal police shootings in the past 60 years! The vast majority of these shootings have occurred since the mid 1970's. (New Zealand Police, 2002)

In Europe, the U.K. with a population of approximately 50 million people recorded a total of 23 incidents involving the discharge of a firearm by police in England and Wales during the three-year period from 1991 to 1993. In seven of these incidents an individual was shot and killed by police reflecting a justifiable homicide rate of roughly two persons per year (Police Scientific Development Branch (PSDB), 1996).

The Netherlands with a population of 16 million people recorded a total of 67 fatal police shootings from 1978 through 1999. During this same time period, a total of 288 individuals were wounded by police as a result of shooting incidents (Timmer, 2002).

Noteworthy, in New Zealand, England and Wales, the police do not typically carry firearms; however, specially trained police personnel may be authorized to carry a firearm locked in a weapon's box inside their police vehicle. In addition, firearms are available for issue from all police stations.

When an unarmed officer confronts an "armed offender," the suggested police tactic is that of "contain and appeal." This will usually result in officers withdrawing from the immediate area and acting in an observation role until specially trained and equipped police personnel (The Armed Offenders Squad) arrive on the scene of the incident.

In North America, the eastern Canadian province of Newfoundland remained to be the last bastion of "unarmed policing" until as recently as 1999. Prior to June 1999, the "Royal Newfoundland Constabulary (RNC)" continued to be the only policing jurisdiction within Canada and the United States where day-to-day street level policing was conducted *without police having immediate access to firearms*. From 1979 through1999, the RNC had been involved in only one shooting incident, and it was non-fatal.

However, due to a changing society and the influx of visitors from the United States and the rest of Canada, members of the Royal Newfoundland Constabulary lobbied to have immediate access to firearms like their Canadian and American counterparts. In June 1999, the RNC was granted its request, *but not without incident*. Shortly after being equipped with firearms the RNC became involved in two shooting incidents. *Interestingly, one of these shootings would be classified as a fatal "suicide by cop" incident.*

Finally, it is also significant to note that in the United States, private citizens (non-police) "justifiably" kill roughly 200 individuals each year.

The vast majority of these individuals are shot and killed with a hand-gun. Justifiable homicide in the U.S.A. is defined as, and limited to, the killing of a felon by a law enforcement officer in the line of duty, or the killing of a felon by a private citizen during the commission of a felony (UCR, 2001).

The Risk to Police Personnel

Added to these figures are also numerous documented incidents where law enforcement personnel in the United States and Canada have faced potentially lethal threat, but the death of a felon *did not* occur. This includes those incidents in which a police officer utilized potentially deadly force by discharging his/her firearm, but death did not result. In these instances, the felon either survived his/her wounds or, in other instances, the police missed, so the felon was not shot.

Finally, it must be emphasized that there are also countless incidents of lethal threats to law enforcement personnel that are resolved each year, *without the discharge of a firearm.* During these instances, the officers utilized alternate tactics or less-lethal compliance tools such as pepper spray or taser guns to subdue the individual who was posing a lethal threat. Often, this method of resolution has occurred with an increased risk to the police officer.

This increased risk to police officers has at times resulted in their death. Due to the very nature of their day-to-day duties, operational police personnel routinely face the real possibility of being assaulted or murdered. On average, approximately 70 police officers are feloniously killed in the line of duty each year within the United States. In addition, approximately 60 police officers will accidentally be killed each year in the United States due to mishaps such as automobile and aircraft accidents (Bureau of Justice Statistics (BJS), 2001).

It is within this complex framework that researchers have attempted to understand and explain the underlying causes of lethal threats against police personnel. In their attempts, researchers have derived a number of theoretical perspectives, each providing a viewpoint that must be considered within the unique circumstances of the individual lethal-threat incident. In particular, the field of victimology and its focus upon the role of victim has lead to a series of unresolved questions.

What role does the so-called "victim" play during a lethal or perceived lethal encounter with the police? How does the victim's behavior factor into a police shooting incident? Are there implications for police training in relation to victimology? Can the police use of deadly force be linked to a broader social policy?

Victim-Precipitated Homicide

The term victim-precipitated homicide refers to those killings in which the victim is a direct, positive precipitator of the incident. Foote (1995) adds that victim-precipitated homicide is really made up of several dimensions that include risk-taking, aggressiveness and intentionality. It is within this framework that the concept of "suicide by cop" emerges. During victim-precipitated incidents, these factors culminate with a risk-taking person aggressively and intentionally engaging in *perceived life-threatening behavior*, typically resulting in a police officer or another individual taking his/her life.

The characteristics associated with an individual predisposed to subject-precipitated homicide are generally defined within the category of suicidal behavior. Schneidman (1981) identifies the main elements of *high lethality suicide* as being the desire to die, a direct and conscious role in bringing about one's own death, and the fact that death results primarily due to the deceased's actions. Specific psychological characteristics associated with suicide include a general sense of depression, hopelessness and low self-esteem on the part of the decedent. Often, these characteristics are overtly displayed by actions such as self-inflicted wounds, statements of suicide or the desire to die. During victim-precipitated incidents, these factors result in the suicidal person confronting an assailant, with a real or perceived lethal weapon, forcing the assailant to respond with deadly force.

In some instances, the individual act of suicide is pre-planned with the individual engaging in a *calculated intentional act* of life-threatening behavior ultimately resulting in a victim-precipitated homicide. In other instances the individual act of suicide is *impulsive* with suicidal motivation occurring *only after* police involvement in a given situation (Foote, 1995). For example, at the conclusion of a police pursuit, an individual may suddenly decide that it is better to die at the hands of the police than to face a public trial with the possibility of a lengthy prison term.

Geller & Scott's (1992) analysis of this phenomenon revealed that usually these cases are difficult to document, as there is little or no record of the victim's intent. Unfortunately, the actions of the victim have led to his/her demise without the benefit of a post-shooting explanation for his/her behavior. Investigations have equally confounded this situation by failing to examine, in detail, the *root causes* of the victim's behavior.

All too often the police shooting has been explained as a "crazy person who came at the officer with a knife or a gun." It is only within the last 10 years that police and conflict-management trainers within the United States have begun to examine and make reference to the phenomenon of victim-precipitated homicide as a cause of police shootings (Geller & Scott, 1992).

This phenomenon has also been cited in international studies of police shootings in nations, including England, Wales and Australia (PSDB, 1996; AIC, 1998), as well as being the topic of several academic papers that have been presented at various academic annual meetings (Keram, Perrou, and Parent, 2000; Lord, 1998). In addition, several empirical studies of the phenomenon colloquially known as "suicide by cop (SbC)" recently have been published in academic journals (Homant & Kennedy, 2000; Hutson, Anglin, Yarbrough, Hardaway, Russell, Strote, Canter, and Blum, 1998; Parent & Verdun-Jones, 1998; Wilson, Davis, Bloom, Batten, and Kamara, 1998).

The Pacific Northwest

The Pacific Northwest consists of Washington, Oregon, and British Columbia. Washington serves as a center-point located in the northwest corner of the contiguous forty-eight United States between 49 and 46 North Latitude. Washington State is bounded on the north by the Canadian province of British Columbia, to the south by the state of Oregon, to the west by the Pacific Ocean, and to the east by the state of Idaho.

Within these three western pacific regions, Washington, Oregon and British Columbia, there is a combined population of roughly 14 million people, policed by roughly 22,000 full-time sworn, police officers. The major urban areas within the Pacific Northwest include Seattle (2.3 million residents), Portland (1.8 million residents) and Vancouver, British Columbia (2 million residents).

One of the findings of a current study (Parent 2002) concerns the frequency and degree of victim-precipitated acts that have constituted lethal-threats to police personnel in the United States and Canada. Through the examination of official police investigations, coroner inquests, media reports, and interviews with police officers, the characteristics associated with victim-precipitated homicide appear to be a significant factor in police-shooting incidents that have occurred in these two nations within the Pacific Northwest.

During these police-shooting incidents, the victim caused or contributed to the lethal-threat of a police officer by intentionally provoking the officer to use deadly force. In several of these cases, the individual's statements and actions clearly reflect his/her intent to commit suicide at the hands of the police.

In addition to these cases, it is important to emphasize that there are numerous other instances of attempted "SbC" which *do not* result in death. In these cases, the suspect was wounded and survived, or alternative non-lethal means were used. Nonetheless, in all of these instances the subject posed a lethal or perceived lethal threat to police personnel. To what extent that this phenomenon occurs is unclear, but it is believed to extend well beyond the 10 percent figure attributed to the specific category of fatal police shootings (Parent, 1996).

The nature and scope of this phenomenon are delineated in the following description of a fatal police shooting, occurring in the Pacific Northwest.

Police officers were summoned to an apartment complex in response to a male vs. male domestic incident involving a knife. The first officer to arrive was met by the suspect's father. He advised the officer that his son, the suspect, was inside the residence holding an adult male (the suspect's cousin) at knife point.

The necessity of the situation required that the officer acts immediately, rather than waits for other units to arrive. As a result, the officer went to the doorway of the apartment and looked inside. When the officer glanced inside the apartment, a 22-year-old male was observed standing at the opposite end of the apartment, holding a knife.

Upon seeing the police officer the suspect said, "I'm glad you are here." The suspect then raised the knife above his head and began to advance at a fast pace towards the officer. In response, the officer began retreating with his gun drawn, ordering the suspect to drop his knife. As the officer repeated his commands several times, the suspect replied, "Shoot me. Shoot me."

When the officer was in immediate danger, he fired one shot, striking the suspect fatally in the chest. As the suspect lay dying on the floor, he looked up and smiled at the officer who had just shot him. He then stated, "Thank you, you did just what I wanted you to do. You killed me."

It was later discovered that from the time that the officer first made visual contact with the suspect until he fired the fatal shot, a total of five seconds had elapsed. It was also learned that the suspect had been drinking prior to the incident and was intoxicated. Family members later told the police that the suspect had talked of suicide on prior occasions. (Washington State)

Mental Illness, Substance Abuse & Irrational Behavior

At times, an individual's statements and actions *clearly* reflect his/her intent to commit "SbC," however; it is important to emphasize that each case is unique and that there are *varying means* of suicidal documentation. For example, in *many* of the cases examined, the individual did not make a clear suicidal statement at the time of his/her death, nor was an explicit "police-assisted suicide" note left behind.

In these cases, the conclusion is drawn that the individual was suicidal, on the basis of analyzing a wide range of his or her actions and bizarre behaviors, actions and behaviors consistent with the behaviors and characteristics most frequently associated with suicide.

In several of the cases examined, the perpetrator of the lethal threat had a documented history of mental disorder and/or suicidal tendencies. In addition, documentation in several of the cases indicated that the victim had a high blood-alcohol reading at the time of his or her death. In some instances, alcohol, substance abuse, mental disorder and suicidal tendencies were added to the complex picture of irrational behavior. This is illustrated in the following two cases.

Two police officers were dispatched to a 'man with a knife' complaint after a woman reported that a male brandishing a large knife had chased her down the street. Upon police arrival, witnesses indicated that suspect was inside his apartment, located within a large rooming house.

Upon entering the common hallway of the rooming house, the officers were suddenly confronted by a male with a blood stained eight-inch butcher knife in his left hand. The two officers immediately commanded the subject to drop his knife, because he was only a few feet away from them.

In response, the subject stepped back into the doorway of his apartment for a few seconds and then suddenly re-appeared in the doorway, clutching his bloodied knife in a downward position. Upon reappearing, the subject looked at the two police officers and stated, "Go ahead, shoot me, shoot me, shoot me."

Upon stating these words, the subject then turned his knife upwards into the air in a striking motion and pointed it towards the officers. In response, the officers once again ordered the individual to drop his knife, but to no avail. Fearing for their lives, one officer discharged his handgun killing the suspect.

The entire incident had occurred in less than one minute, from the time of the police arrival until the discharge of the police firearm. Upon checking the suspect's residence, the officers found a dead body. A subsequent police investigation revealed that just prior to confronting the two police officers, the suspect had fatally stabbed another individual inside his bedroom.

During the Coroner's Inquest it also was learned that the suspect was suffering from some unknown form of mental illness, which caused him to be violent at times. Two days prior to the police shooting, the suspect had been admitted to a nearby hospital due to his violent behavior. On the day before the shooting, the suspect had left the hospital against medical advice.

Also during the Coroner's Inquest, expert witnesses testified that within a 30-foot radius, a police officer is in imminent danger from a person in possession of a knife. Within this radius, an individual in possession of a knife can seriously wound or kill. The Coroner stated that as the police officers were only three feet away from the suspect (when he initially confronted them with his knife) they were in "grave danger from the outset" of being approached by the assailant. (British Columbia)

In a case from eastern Washington, police officers were summoned to deal with a 38 year-old suicidal male who was attempting to kill himself. The subject was a diagnosed paranoid schizophrenic, who had spent years in a state hospital and had a history of drug and alcohol abuse. Psychologists had stated that the individual was given to hallucinations, hostility and belligerent behavior.

During this instance, the subject had locked himself in the bathroom of his mother's residence where he began smashing things. The subject's mother called the police, as she feared that her son would kill himself or hurt her.

After arriving, the police spent a half-hour negotiating with the subject through the bathroom door, but to no avail. The subject would not come out of the bathroom. The police then heard glass breaking from inside. As a result, the officers deployed pepper spray under the door in an attempt to force the subject out of the bathroom.

Unfortunately, the pepper spray had no effect as the subject could be heard breaking more glass from within the locked bathroom. Fearing that the subject would commit suicide if the police did not intervene, a decision was made to kick-in the bathroom door in an attempt to apprehend the distraught male.

Upon kicking the bathroom door open the police officers once again sprayed the chemical, this time directly into the subject's face. The subject did not react to the sprayed substance and instead lunged at the officers with a jagged 9-inch piece of mirror.

As the officers were confined to a short, narrow hallway, there was no possibility of retreat. When the subject continued to approach the officers in his threatening manner, he was shot and killed at a distance of roughly eight feet. An autopsy later revealed that the subject had ingested razor blades and had sliced his wrists while in the bathroom. (Washington State)

The Perception of A Lethal Threat

For law enforcement personnel intervening in a domestic dispute, or proceeding in the apprehension of an alleged criminal, the circumstances may seem somewhat routine on the surface. However, the situation may quickly deteriorate with the individual suddenly posing a perceived lethal threat to the police officer for no apparent reason or motive.

A significant finding of this study is that indicators associated with "SbC" are not readily detected in all fatal police shootings. At times, a holistic investigative approach must be taken in order to make some sense of the perceived lethal threat faced by the police officer.

In these instances, it is unclear why the decedents confronted the police officer with a perceived lethal threat and why they continue in their behavior, ignoring police commands for compliance. During these cases, they are clearly confrontational their behavior, acting in a reckless and suicidal manner. For what purpose or means remains unclear. This is illustrated in the following two cases.

Shortly after one Christmas, police were alerted to a despondent male who drove to a parking lot of a police sub-station, requesting to speak to a police officer as he was "going to kill somebody." Attending police units quickly located the 6-foot-8, 300 pound, 25 year-old former football player who had returned to his vehicle and was inside his truck, "crying."

Two officers attempted to communicate with the despondent individual who stated that he was armed with a handgun, and that he was "going to shoot someone." The two officers, with their handguns now drawn, took a defensive position requesting backup from neighboring police agencies.

As the situation developed, a 95-minute "stand off" occurred in the parking lot of the police sub-station. Several police officers were in attendance with additional support from crisis negotiators and mental health professionals. Police personnel also deployed spike strips and less lethal weaponry in an attempt to safely resolve the situation.

After roughly 90 minutes from the onset, a decision was made to utilize a "flash-bang" device by throwing it into the bed of the truck. As this diversionary device explodes, police personnel rushed the driver's door attempting to extract the subject.

Unfortunately, the subject resisted the tactic and accelerated his vehicle, managing to hit several police cars before coming to a stop. The subject then quickly exited his truck, approaching the surrounding police officers while screaming that he was going to kill them.

Police personnel responded by authorizing beanbag rounds to be fired. As this is occurring, the subject reaches into his coat and pulled out an unidentified object. Fearing that the subject was about to produce a gun several officers discharge their firearms, killed the approaching subject. It is later learned that the subject was holding an empty razor case and that he was in fact unarmed. (Oregon State)

A motel clerk who had just been assaulted by a violent patron flagged down a marked police vehicle patrolling in the area. The lone officer was advised of the altercation, as well as a description of the suspect.

Within minutes the officer had located the fleeing suspect, running down the street. Now joined by a second officer, the *police officers pursued the suspect on foot until he was cornered in a parking lot. Upon being cornered the suspect suddenly stopped and turned towards one of the officers. He then reached into the front of his pants and pulled out a black object. The suspect then adopted a combat-shooting stance.*

The pursuing officer responded to the actions of the suspect by ordering him to "freeze" and "drop it." These commands were stated several times. The suspect did not comply. Instead he appeared to be angry and agitated, repeatedly stating "F**k you! F**k-you!" to the officers.

The suspect then suddenly swung around and pointed the black object at one of the officers. The officers responded to the perceived threat by firing their weapons and killing the suspect.

It was later learned that the suspect was unarmed. The black object in the suspect's hand was in fact a black portable radio. A subsequent autopsy revealed that at the time of his death, the suspect had a blood-alcohol reading of .240 milligrams. (British Columbia)

Why Death At The Hands Of The Police?

Durkheim (1897/1951:44) defined suicide as "death resulting directly or indirectly from a positive or negative act of the victim himself, which he knows will produce this result." Thus, by virtue of this definition, suicide becomes an intentional act and not an illness. Often, suicide is the end result of a complex interaction of a number of neurobiological, psychological, cultural and social factors that have had an impact on a person (Suicide, 1994:xii).

Committing suicide by "traditional methods" such as a self-inflicted wound requires a decision and commitment on the part of the victim. Psychological, emotional or physiological influences may override self-despair making it difficult for them to take their own life.

Van Zandt (1993) adds that suicidal individuals specifically single out the police as the only community agency equipped with firearms and the training to react to potentially life-threatening situations with accurate and deadly force. This has been reinforced by the entertainment industry that often portrays the law enforcement profession as one equated with violence and death.

In other instances, the individual's death plan may include self-destruction in a "blaze of glory." A high profile, self-induced death, may also serve to mitigate the actions of the irrational individual while placing the police officer's decision to use deadly force under scrutiny and, possibly, public contempt.

In many instances, it is not clear why the subjects confronted the police. Was it mental illness and suffering from delusions of paranoia? Did they actually believe that they were confronting the police, or did they perceive that they were simply protecting themselves from a *distorted* threat?

In other cases, alcohol or drugs appear to have influenced and shaped the suicidal behavior leading to a confrontation with the police. Did alcohol and drugs to an extent impair the ability to think grossly that they failed to recognize the identity of a police officer or that they failed to readily obey the police officers' commands?

Finally, in other documented instances, the individual adopted a confrontational and macho position that posed a lethal threat to the police officer. In these cases, the behavior by the decedent was clearly reckless and self-destructive. His/her motivation for this behavior remains unclear. Did the individual challenge the police officer so that he or she could simply "get a reaction"? Was the "flash" of a toy or simulated weapon only meant as a hoax that went terribly wrong? These complex questions remain unanswered.

Firearm Suicides: During Police Intervention

Another method of police-associated deaths that is only recently coming to light is those instances of suicide that occur during police intervention. Typically, these are incidents in which on-duty police officers are pursuing, confronting or apprehending an individual who suddenly produces a firearm and takes his or her own life. While firearm suicides during police pursuits are infrequent, they are believed to occur at a rate that is roughly half the rate of police related shootings (Harruff et al, 1993:409).

Harruff states that often the involved individual is emotionally distraught but not necessarily suicidal; however, the sudden presence of the police is believed to be a factor that precipitates the resulting suicide. Why this occurs is not clear. The emotionally disturbed and unpredictable individual may perceive that the option of suicide is less painful then the possibility of incarceration or medical treatment. The individual may also be contemplating events that will lead to a "SbC" shooting, but at the last moment, for reasons unknown, decides to take his or her own life.

Typically, the suicidal individual is a white male aged 19 to 50 years who, in most cases, uses a hand gun to fire a fatal wound to the head while being pursued or confronted by police officers. Often, the suicidal individual is involved in an emotional domestic dispute with a significant other resulting in the police being summoned. In other instances the individual has committed a crime that has led the police to his or her location with the resulting confrontation.

For the police officers intervening in the domestic dispute, or proceeding in the apprehension of the alleged criminal, the circumstances may seem somewhat routine on the surface. However, the situation quickly deteriorates with the individual suddenly killing him or herself for no apparent reason or motive.

The following two cases are typical examples of how routine police calls can suddenly erupt into firearm suicides.

A 34 year-old white male, with a history of drug problems, was arguing with his ex-wife in the parking lot when police were called to the scene. Officers arrived as he was leaving his pickup truck. They ordered him to show his hands, but the individual refused and then produced a .380 caliber semiautomatic pistol to the right side of his head and fired it. The individual died as a result of his self-inflicted wound. An autopsy later revealed that at the time of his death the individual had a blood-alcohol level of .142 mg. (Harruff et al, 1993:408)

Two 19 year-old male suspects were observed loading a pick-up truck with computer equipment and other belongings from a home that they were burglarizing. The homeowner had arrived home for lunch and unexpectedly confronted the two individuals during their crime. In response, one suspect produced a handgun and pointed it at the homeowner's head, ordering him back into his vehicle. The homeowner then drove off and alerted the police to the incident, providing a detailed description of the suspects and their vehicle.

Police responded and eventually spotted the suspect's vehicle and occupants traveling on the interstate highway towards Seattle. Several police units became involved, and the suspect vehicle was followed for a lengthy time, without a chase occurring. It was eventually stopped as a "high risk" takedown on the interstate highway. Police weapons were drawn and the suspects were ordered out of their vehicle with instructions to place their hands up and to lie face down on the ground.

The 19 year-old passenger complied with the police commands and exited the vehicle as instructed. However, the 19 year-old driver responded to the police commands by producing a handgun as he sat in the driver seat. The driver then placed the gun against his head and pulled the trigger, killing himself. There was no explanation or reason for the driver's actions.
(Washington State)

Firearm suicides during police confrontations create particular challenges for police agencies, as the media, family members and the public may be skeptical as to how the individual actually died. Did police attendance to the call serve as the catalyst, forcing the individual to commit suicide? What did the attending police officer(s) say or do that may have influenced the individual to take his/her own life? Was the incident in fact a suicide or were the police somehow responsible for the individual's death?

For police investigators and training personnel there are additional concerns surrounding firearm suicides. What, if anything, could have been done by attending police personnel to prevent the suicidal behavior? Would the incident have evolved into a SbC (SbC) shooting had the sequence of events occurred differently?

Suicide during A Motor Vehicle Pursuit

This phenomenon can become even more complex with the added dimension of a motor-vehicle pursuit. In these instances, the hazards associated with a moving motor vehicle can serve to disguise the suicidal intent of the driver (Murphy, 1989). For example, an individual's death can be initially declared to be the result of severe trauma caused by a motor vehicle accident; however, subsequent autopsy results may reveal that the individual died as a result of a gunshot wound to the head. Due to the proximity of placing the handgun directly against the head, the fatal bullet may exit the body, never being located. If the individual is involved in a police pursuit, the evolving circumstances can place police agencies in a precarious situation.

The following case illustrates how police officers run the risk of being criticized for bringing about the death of an individual during a motor-vehicle police pursuit.

A 50 year-old white male was wanted on outstanding warrants for forgery. Eventually police located the individual in his vehicle and a high-speed chase ensued on the highway. With the police in pursuit, the subject's car suddenly swerved off the roadway. The vehicle crossed the median and opposing lanes and then went down an embankment, eventually striking a tree where it came to a rest. When the police officers approached the car, they found the individual dead. Due to the severity of the crash, the officers assumed that the driver had died as a result of the blunt force injuries sustained. The autopsy revealed that the individual had died of a single gunshot wound to the head. As a result of the discovery, the police re-attended the wrecked vehicle and conducted a thorough search. Inside the vehicle the police located a .25 caliber semiautomatic pistol, a holster and one spent cartridge. Although the fatal bullet was never located, the coroner was able to conclude that the muzzle imprint around the entrance wound and the bullet hole in the skull matched the type of wound that the gun found in the vehicle. (Harruff, 1993:407).

For police investigators, caution should be exercised in any incident involving a motor vehicle pursuit in which there is no reasonable explanation for the event. Firearm suicide may be an explanation for the event. In these cases a thorough search of the decedent's vehicle must be made upon conclusion of the pursuit in an attempt to locate relevant evidence such as firearms, spent casings or suicidal notes. This may prove physically difficult to investigators depending upon the severity of the crash and the resulting damage to the vehicle.

Nonetheless, failure to do so can result in the police agency being suspected of directly or indirectly causing the death of the suicidal individual due to the outcome of the pursuit. In addition, a routine pursuit resulting in death could later place the police officer(s) in suspicion if a subsequent autopsy revealed that the driver had died as a result of a gunshot wound and *not* as a result of the motor vehicle accident. The police agency would be placed in the difficult position of attempting to locate evidence that may long be gone, in order to support evidence of death resulting from a self-inflicted gunshot wound.

The police agency could also be placed in the defensive, having to prove that the officers involved in the pursuit did not discharge their firearms, resulting in the fatal wound of the driver. Location of evidence absolving the police officers may be problematic if suicidal evidence was not obtained at the time of the vehicle crash or if bullet that resulted in the death is not located.

Suicide during Police Intervention and SbC

It is unknown exactly how firearm suicides during police intervention are linked to SbC shootings; however, the linkage between these two phenomena is illustrated in the following cases from Idaho, Washington State, and Oregon.

> *During June, an Idaho police officer observed a vehicle being driven erratically. When the police officer attempted to stop the vehicle, the driver refused to pull over and continued driving on the highway. Suddenly, it went off the road and crashed into a steel fence post and exploded. A subsequent autopsy determined that the 25 year-old female driver had in fact shot herself in the chest while being followed by the police. The female driver's death was ruled a suicide.* (Idaho State)

Noteworthy is that the decedent had a twin sister. The surviving sister was reported to be despondent about her twin sister's suicidal motor vehicle pursuit death. The depression appeared to be intensified on the anniversary of her sister's death and on their birthday, which was during the month of November. In addition, it was reported that the surviving sister had stated that "she wanted to go out like her sister. She wanted to die with the police chasing her."

Interestingly, some two years later and within days of their birthday, the surviving twin sister became involved in a police chase in western Washington. The police chase would result in the surviving twin being shot and killed by police in an apparent SbC incident.

> *On a November afternoon, a police officer noted a woman sitting in a parked vehicle at a neighborhood park. The vehicle did not have a license plate so the officer decided to check the vehicle and the occupant. The 27 year-old female provided ID and upon running the female's name, the officer discovered that she had been reported missing by a relative in California. When the officer went back to talk to the female, she suddenly sped off in her vehicle causing the officer to be struck in the leg as he attempted to jump out of the way.*

Police units then pursued the female at high speeds through heavy afternoon traffic. The vehicle eventually became stuck in traffic, and the driver pulled over to the shoulder of the road. Police then ordered the female driver out of the car at gunpoint. When the female exited the vehicle she was brandishing a handgun. She then began to point the handgun at the officers and motorists in nearby vehicles.

In response, police officers ordered the female to put the gun down. When she refused, the officers shot and killed her. It was later learned that the female was in possession of a non-lethal "BB pellet" gun. (Washington State)

A 21-year old male entered a small town police station with a loaded handgun. Upon entering the station, the male alternately pointed the loaded handgun at his head and then at the solitary police officer inside the police station, threatening to kill himself and the officer. The individual then fired two rounds in the office and warned officers who were positioned outside not to enter. The individual then opened the office door and fired at one officer that was outside, but missed. In response, two officers discharged their weapons and killed the individual.

It was later learned that the subject had a blood alcohol level of 0.22% with traces of methamphetamine and amphetamine in his system. He also had a history of major depression with previous suicide attempts. (Oregon State – Wilson, 1998).

As these cases and discussion illustrate, "police assisted suicides" go beyond the boundaries that are typically associated with "SbC" encounters. It is unclear as to how these suicidal phenomena relate and interact with police intervention. Nonetheless it remains to be a significant issue for police personnel who may unknowingly serve as a catalyst in an individual's sudden suicidal death. An individual act of suicide at times will result in a lethal threat to police personnel and innocent members of the public.

Critical Incident Stress – The Personal Impact

As this chapter has illustrated, there is a need for police to be aware of the dynamics associated with a police shooting and the tragic consequences that occur to both the decedent and the surviving officer. Often, the police officer and his/her family are left alone to understand and come to terms with the controversial death that has resulted.

Interviews with police officers who had been involved in a fatal shooting have revealed the personal impact that the event has had on their lives and their families. Without exception, all of the officers involved in a fatal shooting indicated that they had, to some degree, been subject to the physiological, psychological, physical and emotional factors associated with critical incident stress.

The most commonly cited physiological factors experienced by these officers included perception of time, visual and auditory distortions. As the incident unfolded, individual officers noted that their deadly-force encounter appeared to occur in slow motion. Often their vision was focused upon the perceived threat with minimal awareness of the events taking place around them. Finally, when shots were fired, they were generally heard as muffled sounds, even though the officers were not wearing ear protection devices.

> *"We stopped the car and got out. A couple of seconds later a shot rang out. My focus was on the threat. I fired three rounds off at the silhouette and hit the target, one fatal at the head. It was like a scene in a bad movie. It all happened in slow motion. I just knew I got him...it all happened in less than ten seconds. 'X' was lucky not to be killed."*

In addition to perception distortions, the majority of these police officers stated that they experienced a loss of fine motor co-ordination upon conclusion of their deadly encounter. Typically their hands would begin to shake or their legs would go into uncontrollable spasms. After the fatal-shooting incident concluded, the majority of officers interviewed stated that they faced a wide variety of psychological and physical effects associated with critical incident stress. The physical effects included a loss in appetite, sleeping pattern changes and a marked decrease in their sex drive resulting in an absence of sexual relations with their spouse or partner. One officer stated

> *"Your mind says 'You can't cope with this.' Sleep? I'd wake up every night for several months. I would never re-live the incident but my mind would focus on the incident."*

The psychological effects reported included depression, guilt, nightmares, flashbacks, and a heightened sense of danger and fear. One of the officers related the flashbacks as a "video going on in your head that you can't control; it just keeps playing the video over and over and over again and you've got no control to turn it off." Another officer reported an overwhelming and uncontrollable emotional state that caused him to suddenly weep and cry for days on end.

In some instances, the factors associated with critical incident stress are further intensified when the shooting incident is SbC. In these particular cases the officer is faced with the additional impact of killing an individual who is, in essence, seeking help from the police in doing something that he or she could not do – the taking of his/her own life. For some officers, this situation results in the additional impact of feelings that include anger and confusion for "being set up," manipulated, and tricked into using deadly force.

> *"I was angry, there was no reason for him to kill me. He was gonna shoot me, he would have killed me. If anything, I waited too long (before I shot and killed him). I was lucky."*

In other instances, the officer felt responsible for the surviving members of the deceased as the officer had taken away the life of their loved one. In this regard, one officer stated:

> *"No matter what I think about this guy and what he did, I can't help but feel responsible to his mother and father. I know that every Christmas, for the rest of their lives, it will never be the same for them because of me. I took away their son's life, and they will never have Christmas with him again. It will never be the same for them. No matter what you think, he is still a person."*

Another officer who was involved in a SbC shooting incident added:

> *"From the decent people, I got a lot of support. Generally supportive and understanding. However...some, the shit heads, they're critical. Sure he was a shithead, a 99 percent shit head and I shouldn't feel sorry (re: shooting him) but.. it's that one percent of him...it's tough for me to not think of him as a person."*

The media frequently intensified this situation and was cited by most of the police officers as one of the greatest sources of stress immediately after their fatal shooting incidents. This was a consequence of the continual coverage that surrounds many of the fatal shooting incidents. Particularly painful was the speculation and supposition taken by many journalists who were impatient regarding the release of the official police investigation.

These journalists often produce media articles that are written in a negative or distorted manner towards the actions of the shooting officer or the police agency. Issues such as racism, inadequate training or improper police procedure were often cited as explanations for the shooting incident, particularly during SbC incidents where the deceased was later found to have an inoperable or imaginary weapon.

These officers stated that the negative slant portrayed in many of the media articles served to further intensify their emotional and psychological state in regards to the fatal shooting incident.

> *"The media; I've never had a problem with what we did. We're the good guys and out here to help the public and did a good thing; what we're suppose to do; and now we're getting f**ked. I couldn't watch the television or read the papers; [they were] obvious examples of distortion."*

One of the police officers related to the event as to the "death of a child," an event in his life that he described as painful and sad, something that he wished had never happened, something that he has obviously tried to put behind him. When the officer was interviewed he produced a file containing more than 50 separate newsprint articles surrounding his fatal SbC-shooting incident.

The police officer's mother had followed the shooting incident through the local print media. She had clipped and saved all of the print articles that were related to her son's fatal-shooting incident. In conjunction with the 50 plus newsprint articles, the officer kept a "scrap book" regarding the legal, union and departmental correspondence that were related specifically to his shooting incident. The officer stated that he has never been able to bring himself to read most of the print articles within the file.

Many of the articles that were first published, initially after the shooting, indicate inappropriate action by the officer. Some of these headlines are as follows:

"Relatives Want Police Charged In Shooting," "Were Four Bullets The Only Answer?" "Police Procedures Deficient," "Mayor Queries Police Policy," "Police Training Called Flawed," "Slain Man's Mother Asks For Probe," "Police Stay Silent Until Inquiry Done."

However, months later when a public inquest into the shooting was held and independent evidence presented, the police were exonerated for their actions. During the public Inquest, the media coverage was less frequent and inflammatory but continued to be sensational in nature. Some of these newsprint headlines include:

"Said 'Stay Back,' Then He Died." "I Would Have Shot Him Too," "Cops Off Hook In Fatal Shooting," "Officer Sorry, But Says Forced To Shoot."

Only upon the conclusion of this public disclosure of evidence were many of the officers able to get on with life and leave the tragedy of the shooting incident behind them. Even years after the fatal-shooting incident had taken place, all of the officers reported that they considered it a significant event in their life, one that they will never forget. In this regard, one police officer stated:

"This guy is not gonna f**k-up my life forever. It's completely up to me whether I cope with this and get on with life. I'm sure I drank too much several times. I think about it every day."

Post-Shooting Effects and Deadly Force

In the months and years since their fatal-shooting incidents occurred, many of the police officers interviewed reported a variety of personal life changes, attributing these changes to their fatal shooting

Several of the police officers that were involved in a fatal shooting reported marital or relationship breakdowns shortly after the incident. Often these individuals stated that their relationship with their significant other was "o.k." prior to the shooting. However, when faced with the pressures and stresses that accompanied a fatal shooting, the relationship often crumbled. One officer stated "I went through two marriages after the shooting incident." Another officer reported, "My marriage ended within a year or two after the shooting. I became distant from my wife and I didn't talk about the shooting incident with her."

However there was an equal number of police officers who spoke highly of their spouses or significant others, intimate relationships that served to support the police officer during a time of personal crisis. Often these established relationships were strengthened as a result of the shooting incident. One officer in a smaller agency stated:

> "The Chief said to me – You should leave town because I'm gonna release your name. So the wife & I took off in a car and drove four hours away to a cabin and stayed there. We were there for a week. It gave me time to be with my wife, as a sounding board, with what happened. It took about a year for all of it to blow over."

Unfortunately, several of the officers stated that their spouses, significant others or their children suffered as a result of their shooting incident. The police officer's fatal shooting frequently became a "family crisis." One officer stated: "My wife needed help [psychological] after what happened to me."

Finally, in a small number of instances, individual officers had suffered post-traumatic stress to such a degree that they required extensive counseling and a lengthy time away from the work site. For these individuals, their personal goal was to come to terms with an incident that has had a profound impact upon their lives, an incident that they will never forget. One officer described the impact of the SbC shooting by stating:

> "I really look forward to retiring. I've got nine years to go. My wife has noted a change in me. I've noted a change in me. If I had known the shooting incident was gonna happen, I would have taken a sick day. I wish it would never had happened."

Conclusion

As this chapter has illustrated, it remains unclear why some individuals confront police with a lethal or perceived lethal threat. However, the findings of this study indicate that the phenomenon of "SbC" remains to be a *significant* factor in the lethal threats that law enforcement personnel within the United States and Canada face. Individuals predisposed to suicide, have in many instances, confronted armed police in an attempt to escalate the situation in which they have placed themselves.

In other instances, this study has noted that alcohol, substance abuse, mental disorder and *suicidal tendencies* were added to a complex picture of irrational behavior. Individuals acting in a bizarre or irrational manner have confronted armed police with either inferior or imaginary weaponry resulting in their death.

Regardless of the subject's motivation or mind-set, it remains that these individuals chose to pose a perceived lethal threat to law enforcement personnel. In this regard, the so-called *victims* must share some of the responsibility during a police shooting, as it is *their actions* that often precipitate the final outcome. An outcome that tragically has resulted in a "lose–lose situation," often having negative consequences for the victims, their family, the police agency and, the police officer involved.

These findings also illustrate the complexities that surround lethal threats to police personnel and how individual officers are often given seconds to decide how to resolve a potentially lethal conflict. In many instances, police officers have no other option, but to use deadly force.

References

Australian Institute of Criminology (1998) <u>Police Shootings 1990-9</u>. No. 89 Trends & Issues In Crime and Criminal Justice. Canberra.

Bureau of Justice Statistics (2000) <u>Sourcebook of Criminal Justice Statistics – 2000</u>. U.S. Department of Justice. Washington DC

Block, Carolyn Rebecca and Richard Block (1992) "Beyond Wolfgang: An Agenda For Homicide Research In The 1990's" <u>The Journal of Criminal Justice</u>, 14, 31-70.

Durkheim, E. (1951). <u>Suicide: A Study In Sociology</u>. (Translated by J.A. Spaulding and G. Simpson). New York: Free Press,. (Originally published, 1897.)

Foote, W. (1995) Victim-precipitated homicide. Chapter 6, pp. 175-201, in H.V. Hall (Ed.), Lethal Violence 2000: A sourcebook on domestic, acquaintance, and stranger aggression. Pacific Institution of Conflict.

Geller, William A. and Scott, Michael S. (1992). <u>Deadly Force: What We Know - A Practitioners Desk Reference on Police-Involved Shootings</u>. Washington, DC, Police Executive Research Forum.

Harruff, Richard C. and Llewellyn, Amy L. and Clark, Michael A. and Hawley, Dean A. and Pless, John E. (1993) "Firearm Suicides During Confrontations With Police." <u>Journal Of Forensic Sciences</u>. (July) 402-411.

Homant, Robert J, and Kennedy, Daniel B. (2000) "Suicide by police: a proposed typology of law enforcement officer assisted suicide," <u>Policing: An International Journal of Police Strategies & Management</u>, 23, 339-55.

Hudson, H.R., Anglin, D., Yarbrough, J., Hardaway, K., Russell, M. Strote, J., Canter, M. and Blum, B. (1998), "Suicide by cop," <u>Annals of Emergency Medicine</u>, 32, 665-669.

Keram, E., Farrell, B., Perrou, B. and Parent, R. (2000) "Suicide by cop: incident management and litigation in Canada and the United States" Paper presented at Annual Meeting of American Academy of Psychiatry and The Law.

Lord, V. B. (1998), "One form of victim-precipitated homicide: the use of law enforcement officers to commit suicide" paper presented at Annual Meeting of Academy of Criminal Justice Sciences.

Luckenbill, David F. (1977) "Criminal Homicide as a Situated Transaction" Social Problems 25, 176-186.

Murphy, Gordon K. (1989) "Suicide By Gunshot While Driving An Automobile." The American Journal of Forensic Medicine and Pathology. Vol. 10, No. 4. 285-288.

National Institute of Justice (1993) Questions And Answers In Lethal And Non-Lethal Violence. Quantico: FBI Academy (June) 13-17.

New Zealand Police (2002) Fatal Police Shooting Incidents 1941 – 2001. New Zealand Police National Headquarters Document. Wellington.

Parent, Richard B. (1996) Aspects Of Police Use Of Deadly Force In British Columbia: The Phenomenon Of Victim-Precipitated Homicide. Masters Thesis. Simon Fraser University.

Parent, R. B. and Verdun-Jones, Simon (1998), "Victim-precipitated homicide: police use of deadly force in British Columbia," Policing: An International Journal of Police Strategies & Management, 21, 432-48.

Parent, Richard B. (2002) The Phenomena of Suicide By Cop: Police Use of Deadly Force In North America. Doctoral Thesis. Simon Fraser University.

Police Scientific Development Branch (1996) A Review of The Discharge of Firearms By Police In England and Wales 1991-

1993. Joint Standing Committee On The Police Use of Firearms. St. Albans.

Schneidman, Edwin S. (1981) The Psychological Autopsy. *Suicide and Life Threatening Behavior. The American Association of Suicidology.* V 11, No. 4, 325-340.

Skolnick, Jerome (1966) Justice Without Trial: Law Enforcement in a Democratic Society. New York: Wiley & Sons, Inc.

Suicide In Canada: Update of the Report of the Task Force on Suicide in Canada. (1994) Health   and Welfare Canada.

Timmer, Jaap (2002) Police Work In Dangerous Situations. Vrije Universiteit Centre for Police Studies. Amersterdam, The Netherlands.

Uniform Crime Reports for the United States. (2001) Federal Bureau of Investigation. U. S. Department of Justice. Washington D.C.

Van Zandt, Clinton R. (1993) "Suicide By Cop." The Police Chief, (July) 24-30.

Wilson, E.F., Davis, J.H., Bloom, J.D., Batten, P.J. and Kamara, S.G. (1998), "Homicide or suicide? The killing of suicidal persons by law enforcement officers," Journal of Forensic Sciences, 43, 46-52.

Wolfgang, Marvin E. (1958). Patterns in Criminal Homicide. Philadelphia University of Pennsylvania Press.

PART THREE

LEGAL ISSUES SURROUNDING SBC

Chapter 4

"SUICIDE BY POLICE" IN SECTION 1983 SUITS: COURT SCRUTINY OF POLICE TACTICS

Robert J. Homant

On March 2, 1993 a distraught Christopher Davies called a mental health facility in Lafayette, Indiana trying to reach his counselor. When told that the counselor was not there, Davies declared that he had drunk a whole bottle of whiskey, he had a gun and a bullet, and he was going to kill himself within the hour. The mental health worker called the police, who dispatched officers to try to find Davies to prevent a suicide.

Officer Charles Wallace and Lieutenant Steven Hartman arrived at the apartment complex and attempted to find Davies' unit. All of the apartment buildings were three levels, and it appeared to the officers that Davies' apartment number would put him on an upper level. However, as the officers entered the building they realized that Davies' apartment was in fact a basement level, and that they had just passed it. The implication here is that this "mistake" caused the officers to walk past the ground level windows, perhaps alerting Davies that police were coming for him.

Holding his gun behind him, Lieutenant Hartman proceeded slowly down the stairwell toward Davies' door. Officer Wallace remained at the top of the stairs. Hartman listened for sounds from the apartment, but heard nothing. He then twisted the knob. Finding the door unlocked, Hartman turned to signal to his partner, Wallace. As he turned, "the door opened. The barrel of a shotgun appeared, and Davies walked straight out with the gun in an angled or port arms position. Davies looked at Hartman and started turning, lowering the angle of the shotgun. Hartman fired one shot and fatally wounded Davies." (*Wallace v. Davies*, 1997 at 425)

Davies' widow brought suit, both under Section 1983 and under Indiana common law. The police officers made a motion for summary judgment, but this was denied. At trial the plaintiff presented expert testimony to the effect that it was ridiculous and unreasonable for the officers to have gone down the stairway and tested the doorknob. According to the expert, the officers should have remained in a position of cover. The jury evidently agreed, and awarded Mrs. Davies $1.4 million.

The defendants appealed on the grounds that the evidence did not support the jury's verdict. The Indiana Appeals Court upheld the trial court. Whether or not Christopher Davies attempted "suicide by cop" as a way out of his own ambivalent suicide attempt is debatable, though such a scenario is one common way for suicide by cop to develop (Homant & Kennedy, 2000b). The purpose of this chapter is to examine how the courts have looked at police behavior in suicide by police (SbC) situations, as well as those related situations that have the potential to develop into SbC. (See also Flynn & Homant [2000] for a law review coverage of this area.)

Although *Wallace v. Davies* appears to place a heavy burden on police to be "tactically correct" in handling a suicidal person, two features of the decision make it a poor case for establishing any sort of precedent about police liability. First, the Appeals Court was careful to point out that the defendant-appellants were appealing the insufficiency of the evidence supporting the jury's verdict, rather than the trial court's original denial of summary judgment. (The Appeals Court, however, goes on to state that the denial of summary judgment based on the claim of qualified immunity was correct.) Secondly, as we shall see below, there is a real issue concerning the extent to which allegedly improper police tactics can be subjected to jury scrutiny. Because the defendants in *Wallace* did not challenge the trial court's admission of evidence, the Appeals Court did not rule on whether the expert's criticisms should have been admitted.

Before looking at specific cases that have been dealt with by the courts, it is important to clarify the nature of the data. In most cases, our knowledge of what happened in the incident comes from an appellate court's summary of the most legally relevant evidence. Most of these cases, in turn, involve appeals of a trial court's decision to grant qualified immunity, which would end the lawsuit. In such a decision, however, the key is whether the plaintiff has enough evidence to support a claim that an officer committed a constitutional violation. As long as there is sufficient evidence to support such a claim, the officers' version of events is largely irrelevant to the summary judgment decision. Thus, most of the scenarios that we will look at below are based primarily on the plaintiffs' versions of events. All courts agree that plaintiffs cannot simply assert a version favorable to themselves (except insofar as they were a conscious, alert witness to what happened); they must offer competent evidence to support their allegations. Various appellate court judges, however, seem to have widely differing standards as to what the minimal necessary evidence is.

Wallace provides an illustration: although the only version of what happened in the encounter was the testimony of the two officers, there was apparently some ambiguity as to how far Davies lowered his shotgun after opening the door. The Appellate Court opinion simply asserted that the jury could have believed that the gun was not lowered enough to pose a threat to Lieutenant Hartman. (Compare *Nowell v. Acadian Ambulance*, 2001 for a case in which the plaintiff's testimony was largely discounted.)

In any event, the incident summaries presented throughout this chapter should not be taken as necessarily describing "what really happened." Rather, they are summaries of what the plaintiff asserted to have happened, limited to some extent by the requirements that there be competent evidence at least offering some support.

Police Use of Force

Two United States Supreme Court cases establish the basic legal principles for evaluating the constitutionality of police use of force. In *Tennessee v. Garner* (1985) a Memphis police officer shot and killed a young, unarmed burglary suspect to prevent his escape. The Supreme Court nullified the common law, fleeing-felon rule. The new standard is that in order to use deadly force in apprehending someone, the officer must have probable cause to believe that the suspect poses an immediate threat of serious physical harm to the officer or others. The *Garner* court gave the example of preventing the escape of an offender who has committed a crime involving the threatened infliction of serious physical harm as a situation in which deadly force may be used. Nevertheless, courts are often inclined to impose a more restrictive definition of "immediate danger" (see Smith, 1996). It should also be pointed out that the various states, either through their legislatures or by their court decisions interpreting the state constitution and law, are free to impose more restrictive rules concerning police use of force, deadly or otherwise. Likewise, exactly how deadly force is defined and what constitutes it often differs among jurisdictions (cf. *Omdahl v. Lindholm*, 1999).

The implications of *Tennessee v. Garner* were further clarified in *Graham v. Connor* (1989). In this case, plaintiff Graham suffered multiple injures as the result of an investigatory stop by Connor, a police officer. The U. S. Supreme Court ultimately ruled that the test for whether a police officer uses excessive force is to be an objective one, namely whether in the totality of circumstances a reasonable officer on the scene would find the use of force reasonable. The *Graham* court stressed one other point: that in assessing what a reasonable officer would do, one must make allowances for the fact that decisions are typically made in emergency, heat of the moment situations, with little time to reflect. As long as some hypothetical reasonable officer might have used the level of force that occurred, then the force was not excessive. Furthermore, the "totality of circumstances" does not refer to the actual situation as determined after the fact, but to how the situation would reasonably appear to be, given the information available at the time to the officers involved.

The *Graham* formula may sound more subjective than objective. How can one ever determine how a situation might appear to someone, let alone what that hypothetical reasonable officer might do? The test is referred to as "objective reasonableness" in that the actual officer's beliefs and intentions are not directly relevant. Regardless of why the officer used a given level of force (a "subjective" question), the issue is whether a reasonable officer might have used such force.

It may seem paradoxical that police use of force in dealing with disturbed persons is universally treated as a "seizure" to be analyzed by the fourth amendment standards developed under *Garner* and *Graham*. From the officer's point of view, dealing with a disturbed person is not much like trying to effect the arrest of a fleeing felon, and "self defense" might seem more relevant. However, self defense normally carries an obligation to retreat, if possible. When officers use force to restrain or kill a disturbed person, the situation normally arises out of the officer's peace-keeping functions. While treating such cases as self defense might require a different set of legal citations, it seems doubtful that the underlying principles would be changed.

In contrast, excessive force claims outside of a seizure situation are evaluated by 14th amendment substantive due process principles. Thus, in a jail situation, the subjective intent of the officer to maliciously inflict harm would be relevant (cf. *Garcia v. Boston*, 2000).

The 1983 Suit

The normal vehicle for a plaintiff to seek redress for an unjustified police use-of-force is a "1983 suit," referring to a civil action brought under Section 1983 of U.S.C. 42, an 1871 civil-rights law that prohibits violations of citizens' constitutional rights by agents of state government, including police officers. According to Chiabi (1996), the 1983 suit is "the most utilized and lucrative form of liability litigation against law enforcement officers." (p.85) A U.S. Supreme Court decision, *Bivens v. Six Unknown Named Agents of the Federal Bureau of Narcotics* (1971), created a parallel means of litigation against federal law enforcement agents.

Section 1983 does not create civil rights, but provides a vehicle for redress should one's established rights be violated. As indicated above, with police use-of-force cases, the person involved (or typically his estate, in deadly-force cases) must allege a constitutional violation of his fourth amendment right against unreasonable arrest or seizure (the unreasonable force makes the seizure unreasonable).

The 1983 suit is not the only vehicle for redress. One can also sue the police for wrongful death or assault and battery under a state tort law claim. State standards for police use-of-force are often more restrictive than the federal constitutional standards, and it would seem that plaintiffs' would often be better served by pursuing the state law claim.

A case in point here is *Quezada v. County of Bernalillo* (1991). In this case, a suicidal woman was shot and killed by a police officer after she pointed her gun at him when he tried to force her to exit her car. The federal appeals court ruled that the plaintiff may not have met the burden of *Graham's* objective reasonable test–a reasonable officer may well have used deadly force when a gun was leveled at him. (Further review of the evidence by the trial court was ordered.) However, under New Mexico tort law the concept of ordinary negligence applied, and it was therefore valid to take into account the officer's tactics that put himself in a position of danger.

The obvious solution for the plaintiff, then, would appear to be suing simultaneously under Section 1983 and state law, and this is indeed often done. Attorneys, however, would rather proceed under Section 1983 because of the rule that all attorneys' fees and expenses–which can be quite large when suing a city–are paid independently of any damages awarded (rather than having to take them out of the contingency fee). Because the person bringing the suit is often a criminal offender or suicidal person, damage awards are often low, should the plaintiff prevail. Thus, the preferred method for challenging police use of force remains the Section 1983 suit (cf. Chiabi, 1996).

It should also be mentioned that the 1983 suit, with or without state tort claims, can be filed in either state or federal court. (If the 1983 claims are dismissed, the federal court will typically decline to rule on the state claims; otherwise it applies state law to those claims.) While hard data are lacking, it seems that plaintiffs' attorneys prefer to file their 1983 claims in the federal courts, perhaps feeling that state judges may be more sympathetic to local police.

A final point should be mentioned. In addition to suing the individual officers who used the allegedly excessive force, plaintiffs typically sue the department chief for failure to train, as well as other local government entities. A host of legal issues are raised by this additional aspect of the lawsuit, and these are beyond the scope of this chapter. In general, the plaintiff must first prevail against the officers who used the force before the issue of liability for the officers' superiors can be reached.

Qualified Immunity and Summary Judgment

When an officer is notified of a 1983 suit, the first response is normally to assert qualified immunity. *Harlow v. Fitzgerald* (1982) and *Anderson v. Creighton* (1987) are the United States Supreme Court cases generally cited for clarifying qualified immunity standards. Basically, law enforcement officers are immune to suit under Section 1983 unless they violate clearly established law. In the case of an excessive force claim, this means that the law governing unreasonable force must have been clearly established so that a reasonable officer would be aware that what he or she was doing was excessive.

An illustrative SbC case occurred on August 13, 1991. Michael Roy was involved in an episode of domestic violence. He was armed with two knives, and reportedly told his wife that he would use them against any police who approached him. Three police officers found Roy lying on the ground behind his house. Roy then went into the house, and returned with a knife in each hand. The officers drew their weapons and ordered him to put down the knives. Roy advanced on the officers as they retreated toward a sharp incline. Finally, when he lunged at two of the officers, one of them shot twice, badly injuring Roy. Roy sued for unreasonable use of deadly force. Although Roy did not seriously challenge the police version of events, he presented an expert affidavit asserting that the officers could easily have arrested Roy without using firearms. The expert specifically stated that the officers should have had pepper spray available.

The defendant police officers asserted qualified immunity and the trial judge agreed, granting summary judgment. In reviewing the decision, the federal Appeals Court agreed, stating: "In close cases a jury does not automatically get to second-guess these life and death decisions, even though the plaintiff has an expert and a plausible claim that the situation could have been handled differently" (*Roy v. Inhabitants of City of Lewiston*, 1994, p. 695). Thus, although "reasonableness" is normally a matter of law for a jury to determine, in cases where qualified immunity is at stake the judge's task is to determine whether a reasonable jury could find that **no** reasonable police officer would have acted in the manner in question.

Qualified immunity is meant to be a protection against the legal entanglements of a law suit, not merely a defense to be asserted during trial. Thus, the Supreme Court has stated that trial judges should rule on qualified immunity as early as possible in the proceedings. Generally this means that as soon as an officer receives notice of a lawsuit, the officer asserts the immunity. The plaintiff then has the burden of offering proof that the officer committed a constitutional violation and is therefore not entitled to immunity. At the pre-trial stage this proof is generally in the form of sworn depositions and affidavits, along with medical records, videotapes of the incident, etc.

A problem that arises in excessive force cases, however, is that the ultimate issue is whether the officer's behavior was reasonable. As the *Quezada v. County of Bernalillo* (1991) court put it: "[T]he qualified immunity defense in excessive force cases is of limited value... [T]he substantive inquiry that decides whether the force exerted by police was so excessive that it violated the Fourth Amendment is the same inquiry that decides whether the qualified immunity defense is available to the government actor" (p. 718). In other words, the officer is accused of the very thing that would cancel the immunity.

There is widespread disparity in how judges deal with this issue of qualified immunity. Some judges are quite ready to use their discretion to rule that no reasonable jury could find the officer's conduct unreasonable, and therefore summary judgment was granted (e.g, *Bell v. Irwin*, 2002). Other judges are more inclined to assert that since "reasonableness" is a matter of fact rather than law, it is for the jury to say what is reasonable (e.g., *Bennett v. Murphy*, 2000). Complicating matters still further, the trial judge's decision on granting summary judgment (typically at federal district court) is immediately appealable to the federal circuit court. But circuit courts differ in their willingness to second guess trial court decisions. Some opinions assert that only if the trial judge made a clear error of law (e.g., applying the wrong legal test) can the circuit court overturn the ruling (e.g., *Medina v. Cram*, 2001); other circuit courts are quite ready to impose their own standards of objective reasonableness (e.g., *Pace v. Capobianco*, 2002). Although some of the circuit court differences are accounted for by precedents within the circuit for reviewing trial-court decisions, in many cases it seems to be more a matter of a particular judge's sympathy for excessive force cases.

The U.S. Supreme Court recently attempted to resolve this issue in *Saucier v. Katz* (2001). In the fall of 1994, Elliot Katz had smuggled a banner onto a military base where Vice-President Gore was speaking. When he unfurled the banner (protesting animal torture), two military police (Saucier and Parker) hustled him away from the area, eventually shoving him inside a military van. Katz then sued the military police in a *Bivens* action. Although there was no significant disagreement between the parties as to what occurred, both the federal district and appeals courts ruled that there was a genuine issue of fact involved, namely whether the force used was objectively reasonable, and therefore they refused to grant summary judgment based on qualified immunity.

The Supreme Court in *Saucier* resolved the problem by establishing a distinct, two-part test for determining qualified immunity. The court first must decide if based on the facts alleged a constitutional violation occurred. It is clear that the trial (and eventually the appellate) court is expected to apply the objective reasonableness standard as a matter of law (apparently being guided by what a reasonable jury might find to be reasonable). More importantly, even if the court determines that the officers' behavior did constitute excessive force, it must then determine whether the right had been clearly established.

Appellate courts had, of course, been aware of the "clearly established" requirement. But since *Graham* had "clearly established" that objectively unreasonable force was unconstitutional, the second prong was typically not thought to be relevant. The Supreme Court in *Saucier* prescribed a delicate balancing act on this point. On the one hand, every factual situation is different, so "clearly established" cannot mean that an extremely close parallel must exist in some applicable court decision. On the other hand, a gratuitous shove to a demonstrator while maintaining security for the vice president seemed quite different from previous excessive force cases. Without ruling on whether or not the handling of Katz used excessive force, the Court ruled that even if it was excessive, it had not been clearly established, and thus reasonable officers might reasonably make the mistake of thinking that they were within their rights.

In a concurring opinion, a minority of the court found this reasoning unnecessarily convoluted. If a reasonable officer could believe that the use of force was justified, then–by definition–the force was not constitutionally excessive. But the majority opinion does have two consequences: it allows the courts to clarify the concept of reasonable force without having to penalize individual officers (and cities) as standards change, and it provides appellate courts with a legal rationale for reviewing summary judgment decisions.

A good example of this occurred in *Robinson v. Solano* (2002). Police pointed a gun at Robinson in holding him on suspicion of shooting a neighbor's dogs that had been going after his chickens. Robinson filed a 1983 suit on the grounds that pointing a gun at him was excessive force, given that there was no objective reason to think he was dangerous. From the police point of view, the use of a gun in effecting the arrest was an attempt to avoid using force, not a use of force per se. The Appeals Court agreed with Robinson, and at least in the ninth circuit it is now established law that police may not point a gun in making an arrest unless they can justify it as needed. Since the law was not sufficiently established, however, immunity was granted in this particular case, as required by *Saucier.*

An Application of Saucier

On September 9, 1996 police responded to a call from the wife of Richard Deorle. Deorle was upset, drunk, banging on the walls, and apparently suicidal. As wife and children left the house, some 13 or more officers arrived, cordoned off the house, and awaited a "Special Incident Response Team," or SIRT, which would include a trained negotiator. At one point Deorle came out of the house, brandished a hatchet at police, and shouted, "Kill me" (*Deorle v. Rutherford*, 2001, p. 1276). Deorle repeatedly asked officers to shoot him. Eventually Officer Greg Rutherford arrived, a member of the SIRT though not a negotiator. Rutherford was armed with a shotgun loaded with beanbag rounds. Deorle advanced on Rutherford, said that he would "kick (Rutherford's) ass," (p. 1277) and brandished an "unloaded plastic crossbow" (p. 1277) and a can or bottle of lighter fluid. Deorle dropped the crossbow in response to Rutherford's shouted order, but continued to walk steadily toward him, with Rutherford aiming the shotgun at him. At about 30 feet, Rutherford fired a beanbag round, aiming, he said, at Deorle's lower right rib area. Unfortunately, Rutherford missed his target area. Deorle was struck in the face, suffering multiple fractures to the cranium, loss of his left eye, and lead shot embedded in his skull.

The District Court found that Rutherford's behavior was objectively reasonable, and granted summary judgment based on qualified immunity. Deorle appealed to circuit court. Applying the two-pronged test prescribed by *Saucier*, the court majority found a number of things to criticize in Rutherford's decision to shoot. The key logic was that there was not sufficient government interest in quickly resolving the situation to justify this extreme a level of force. Deorle had complied with a number of police requests, such as letting his family leave, dropping his hatchet, discarding the crossbow, etc. Rutherford could easily have retreated; there was little danger of Deorle leaving the area, and even if he did, there was no basis for believing he was a danger to anyone. Thus, "the shooting violated Deorle's right to be free from unreasonable seizures" (p. 1285). Since the shooting was unreasonable, the court then applied the second *Saucier* test, whether Rutherford should have known it was unreasonable (i.e., was the right clearly established). In examining this point, the court basically argued that since the error in judgment in shooting Deorle was so obviously unreasonable, Rutherford should have known this.

A strong dissent looked at the case differently. Deorle is described in more threatening than comic/pathetic terms; the crossbow, example, was for target practice, looked real, and shot a real arrow. When Deorle dropped the crossbow he advanced on Rutherford, saying, "I'm going to kick your ass, motherf**ker" (p. 1287). Rutherford was trained in the use of beanbag rounds, which are designed to incapacitate a person without causing serious injury. "The evidence is uncontradicted that the beanbag round was fired at Deorle's lower right abdomen but that it suddenly 'flew' up and unexpectedly and unintendedly hit Deorle in the face." (p. 1287) Failure to shoot when he did would have meant that Deorle would have gotten too close to use the beanbag round safely, and any of a number of things could have happened: hand to hand fighting, Deorle dousing Rutherford or himself with lighter fluid, etc. Even if use of a beanbag round under these circumstances is determined to be too dangerous, thus excessive force, there's no clearly established law (court decisions) such as *Saucier* requires. The dissent, therefore, would have upheld the district court's grant of summary judgment.

This is no doubt a case on which reasonable people can disagree. Some will applaud the Circuit Court majority for boldly stepping in and over-ruling the district court; perhaps beanbags should only be used in deadly force situations. (This is the effect that the majority ruling may have in the Ninth Circuit, especially should plaintiffs win at trial.) But it is difficult to reconcile the majority opinion with the law established by *Saucier*. Rutherford was part of a special response team trained to handle situations without them escalating into deadly force. He acted in accord with his training. Both the circuit court judge and the dissenting district court judge felt that Rutherford's behavior was objectively reasonable. As framed by the dissent, it even sounds like prudent behavior. Thus, how could one argue that **no** reasonable officer would have acted as Rutherford, let alone that the officer should have known this was constitutionally unacceptable?

A more consistent application of *Saucier* is illustrated in *Cruz v. Laramie* (2001), which involved a naked, out-of-control cocaine user who was subdued and hogtied (or possibly just hobbled). Here the Appellate Court found that the use of force, if it was as the plaintiff described, was unconstitutional, but the circumstances were novel enough that the right was not clearly established.

Legal Relevance of SbC

Because the relevant facts for determining whether the use of force is objectively reasonable include only those facts known to the officer at the time of the shooting, the intentions or motives of the person shot or otherwise seized are not directly relevant. Thus, whether a person was attempting SbC when he came at officers with a knife is not relevant; what matters is the degree of danger that a reasonable officer would perceive him or herself to be in, given what the shooting officer was aware of at the time. This principle was clearly articulated in an Illinois case, *Palmquist v. Selvik* (1997).

Palmquist stemmed from an incident that occurred in Bensenville, Illinois in 1990. The Bensenville police responded to an early morning call concerning Paul Palmquist, who had been screaming obscenities and incoherent statements, had broken his neighbor's windows, and had threatened to kill the newspaper delivery person. The police encountered Palmquist brandishing a long, rusty muffler pipe and a fan blade. When the officers attempted to arrest Palmquist, he refused to cooperate. He spread his arms wide, exposing his chest, and invited offices to kill him. After several more exchanges, during which Palmquist repeatedly challenged police to kill him, Palmquist eventually swung his pipe at Officer Selvik, who had slipped and fallen. At this point Officer Selvik shot Palmquist two or three times in the leg. Palmquist fell, but got back up and said to Selvik, "You only winged me—you'll have to kill me" (p. 336). He then swung the pipe in the direction of Selvik. Shots directed at Palmquist's pipe-wielding arm failed to stop him, and Selvik eventually fired a total of 17 times, hitting Palmquist 11 times and killing him.

Palmquist's mother brought a 1983 suit claiming excessive force in the seizure of Palmquist, as well as inadequate training by the Village of Bensenville. A jury awarded Mrs. Palmquist $165,000. The defendants appealed on several grounds, the relevant one here being Selvik's claim that the trial court improperly excluded evidence of Palmquist's death wish, which amounted to SbC.

The excluded testimony included, among other things, the fact that Palmquist had told a friend just the previous day that he intended to provoke the police to kill him. According to another friend, Palmquist had lost his job about a month earlier, his drinking problem had worsened, he was depressed, and he wanted to die. A neighbor who lived in the apartment below Palmquist also stated that Palmquist had told him about one month before the incident that he wanted to be killed by the police. However, because Officer Selvik was unaware of Palmquist's death wish, the trial judge ruled such testimony inadmissable.

The Appeals Court essentially agreed with the logic of the trial court's ruling and upheld the award insofar as it pertained to the excessive force claim. The Appeals Court took care to note, however, that much testimony about SbC had in fact been admitted. All of the testimony about Palmquist asking the officers to shoot him had been admitted as known to Selvik. Furthermore, both sides' experts, in commenting on the appropriateness of the police response, described the case as being about SbC. The Appeals Court then buttressed its support of the trial court's exclusion of the additional testimony by arguing that such testimony would have been cumulative and prejudicial. The basic principle seems to be that such evidence would be admissible if it serves to help resolve a significant factual dispute.

In sum, then, according to *Palmquist*, either side may introduce testimony about SbC if it was (or should have been) known to the police that this is what the subject was attempting (and presumably this knowledge should have had some bearing on police tactics), or if information about the subject's motivation had sufficient probative value to help resolve a dispute as to the relevant facts (e.g., whether a subject may or may not have appeared to be reaching for a weapon even though there was none).

Parenthetically, the *Palmquist* court also pointed out that evidence of a subject's suicidal motivation could be relevant for determining damages. If this is its only relevance, however, then the damages aspect of the trial will typically be separated from the liability phase.

Scrutiny of Police Tactics

It is not clear from *Palmquist* whether the jury based its decision solely on the degree of danger faced by Selvik at the time he shot Palmquist, or whether they felt that better police tactics in handling a disturbed person would have obviated any need to shoot.

Police tactics, however, were clearly implicated in *Rowland v. Perry* (1994). Although not a SbC situation, the logic used by the Appeals Court has direct implications for the issue of how police handle such situations. Police officer Perry attempted to intervene in a dispute over a $5 bill. A possible misunderstanding and an escalating use of force resulted in a mildly retarded Rowland suffering a disabling injury. Perry was sued for excessive force and moved for summary judgment based on qualified immunity. The trial court denied summary judgment and the Federal Appeals Court upheld this denial. In explaining its ruling, the Appeals Court stressed that it was applying a totality of circumstances test to the entire episode, specifically rejecting a segmented, step-by-step view according to which each of Perry's actions became reasonable. (For a similar approach see also *Abraham v. Raso*, 1999.)

This "totality of circumstances" approach is prescribed by both *Garner* and *Graham*. The usual way of applying this concept, however, is to take it as meaning all of those circumstances known to the officer at the time that force is used in effecting a seizure. Thus, with deadly force, the issue is whether the officer reasonably believed him or herself, or others, to be in immanent danger of death or serious injury, at the time of shooting. All of the circumstances affecting the officer's judgment are to be looked at together. This does not normally mean that because a small dispute escalated, the situation should have been avoided. Thus, *Rowland* seems to represent the sort of second guessing cautioned against in *Graham*.

In contrast to both *Palmquist* and *Rowland*, *Plakas v. Drinski* (1994) represents the more common approach for analyzing police tactics. Plakas was involved in a single-car accident that eventually led to his arrest for drunk driving. He escaped custody, ran to some friends' house where he maneuvered his handcuffs from back to front and picked up a poker. After a series of confrontations he was eventually cornered in a field by three police officers with guns drawn. For at least a quarter hour the police, especially Officer Drinski, attempted to talk Plakas into surrendering. Plakas responded that either he or Drinski was going to die there. He challenged the police to go ahead and shoot, because his life wasn't worth anything, and he often repeated these ideas. Eventually, with poker raised, he charged at Officer Drinski. Drinski was unable to retreat (which was not required, regardless) and fired once, killing Plakas.

Plakas' estate brought a 1983 suit. Plaintiff's attorney presented expert testimony that Plakas was attempting a SbC, and that therefore police should have used alternative means of subduing Plakas to avoid shooting. Specifically mentioned were the possibilities of a chemical spray, possessed by one of the officers, or use of a police dog, which had been offered some minutes earlier by the Indiana State Police. The trial court granted summary judgment to the defendant, and in rejecting the plaintiff's appeal the Federal Circuit Court concluded that there is no requirement that officers "use the least intrusive or even less intrusive alternatives in search and seizure cases" (p 1149); all that is required is that the officers acted reasonably.

The court then proceeded to offer a method for analyzing an officer's pre-shooting behavior by breaking the situation into segments. At each decision point in the police officers' interaction with Plakas (arresting, tracking, drawing weapons, etc.), the police behavior was objectively reasonable. Therefore, at the time of the shooting, only the reasonableness of the deadly force based on what Drinski knew at that time was relevant. Although the court did not spell out a test for what would make one of the preliminary tactics unreasonable, the clear implication is that the tactic would have to amount to a constitutional violation of Plakas' rights, e.g., would in itself have to constitute the use of excessive force. Even more problematic, it is not clear what the implication would be if the use of a chemical spray at the time of the shooting would have had some particular probability of controlling Plakas. (The legal implications of less lethal weaponry are further explored in Chapter 8.)

Another SbC incident that raised the issue of police tactics occurred in *Rhodes v. McDannel* (1991). Police received a call that James West was chasing Shari Heffington inside the house with a machete. Several police arrived, and Heffington escorted two of them into the house. West appeared and advanced on the officers with the machete, despite their drawn guns. He ignored several repeated orders to drop his knife. Finally, when West had advanced within four to six feet, Officer McDannel shot and killed him. Tonya Rhodes, representing West's estate, brought a 1983 suit against McDannel for gross negligence (with respect to his tactics) and use of unreasonable deadly force. The trial court granted summary judgment to the defendant and the Federal Appeals Court upheld the ruling.

In explaining its decision in *Rhodes*, the Court held that to be grossly negligent the officer would have to have intentionally (i.e., not accidental behavior) done something unreasonable with disregard to a known risk, or at least with a high probability that harm would follow. The implication here is that grossly negligent behavior preceding a shooting could ultimately make an otherwise justified shooting actionable. (Had this standard been applied in *Wallace v. Davies*, discussed at the opening of this chapter, it seems doubtful that the jury's decision could have been sustained.)

Another case in which the court took a strong "pro-police" case is *Martinez v. County of Los Angeles* (1996). Two sheriff's deputies were confronted by Luis Martinez. Wielding a knife and urging the deputies to shoot him, Martinez advanced slowly on the officers. The officers retreated, telling Martinez to drop the knife some 14 times. When Martinez was within 10 to 15 feet, both officers fired several times, killing him.

In the 1983 suit that followed, the plaintiff presented expert testimony to the effect that the shooting had been totally premature. There should have been more officers at the scene, and they should have used such equipment as Tasers, containment nets, and mace. In upholding the trial court's granting of summary judgment to the officers, based on qualified immunity, the California Appeals Court dismissed the expert's opinion as mere conclusory speculation. Furthermore, the court added (citing *Plakas*), "There is no constitutional duty to use non-deadly alternatives first." (p. 348). All that mattered was that the use of deadly force was otherwise justified (i.e., objectively reasonable). Even so, the court sidestepped the issue of whether such a shooting would be reasonable if those other alternatives had been available.

Several police tactics were at issue in *Medina v. Cram* (2001), where a criminal arrest situation evolved into a SbC attempt. On June 10, 1996, after Ernest Medina resisted an arrest attempt by a bail bondsman, several officers arrived at his Colorado Springs residence. Medina refused to exit the house. He began drinking rum and using cocaine. He called a friend, asking for a syringe to get high and a gun to make a break. He had suicidal thoughts and cut his left wrist. A phone conversation with Officer Bruning failed to persuade him to surrender. Medina threatened to use his gun (which he turned out not to have).

Finally, Medina came out with his right hand wrapped in a towel. Officers ordered him to stop, but he proceeded to the street. Beanbag rounds failed to stop him. Police then released an attack dog, trained to bite and release. After the first use of the dog, Officer Cram followed behind Medina, planning on rushing him. The dog was released a second time and Medina dropped to the ground exposing a staple gun. Cram believed the staple gun was a weapon pointed at the other officers; he shot three times, as did Officer Bruning.

Medina survived his injuries and filed a 1983 suit. The trial court rejected qualified immunity and the defendants appealed. Medina basically claimed that the officers' pre-seizure conduct had been unreasonable, and this had created the need to use force. He offered expert testimony to the effect that police did not follow accepted police guidelines. The Appeals Court articulated a standard that the conduct in question "must be immediately connected with the seizure and must rise to the level of recklessness, rather than negligence" (p. 1132). Failure to follow guidelines was specifically rejected as a basis for a recklessness claim. Likewise, Medina had no right to have police use alternative, less intrusive means. Therefore, the Appeals Court reversed the district court and granted the defendants summary judgment.

Once again, however, a dissenting opinion complicated matters. Despite citing *Saucier*, the dissent strongly argued that it should be for a jury to decide whether the officers' behavior was objectively reasonable. The dissent went on to severely criticize the police tactics, especially since Medina had repeatedly urged the police to shoot him. Ordering Medina out of the house, not keeping cover, use of an attack dog, and attempting to sneak up on Medina were all criticized as poor tactics. The dissent saw these poor tactics as part of the totality of circumstances that should be used to evaluate the reasonableness of the shooting. (See also *Headwaters v. Humboldt*, 2000; A. 2001, for a case in which the availability of less forceful means to compel compliance from protesters made the use of pepper spray to be potentially excessive force.)

Raising the SbC Issue

It is ironic that in *Medina* and other case cited above it is often the plaintiff who raises the issue of SbC. The first research that I was involved with in this area was an attempt to assess the frequency with which suicide by cop occurred (cf. Kennedy, Homant, & Hupp, 1998). Our first attempts at publication were rejected for a variety of reasons, but one candid reviewer acknowledged simply not liking the concept. It was felt that publishing research on "suicide by cop" would legitimize the concept and make it too easy for police to justify shootings. In a personal communication, a journal editor also expressed his belief that some journals were reluctant to publish in this area because it could be perceived as justifying police shootings.

Prior to 1998, in fact, I can find only sporadic and anecdotal references to suicide by cop in the academic literature. In 1998, however, five separate empirical studies of suicide by cop were published (see Homant, Kennedy, & Hupp, 2000, for a review of this area). At about this same time, many police departments began including suicide by cop as a specific issue in their training, and therefore some basis now exists for generalizing about ways to deal with these situations (see Chapter 10).

Dudley v. Eden (2001) represents a case in which the plaintiff argued that because he was attempting to commit SbC, he was no threat and should not have been shot. On April 5, 1996 Daniel Dudley walked into an Eastlake, Ohio bank and demanded money. He then drove a stolen car to a nearby lot and waited for police to arrive. "Dudley's plan was to commit suicide by way of police intervention." (p. 723) The bank reported the robbery, along with the fact that the robber had not shown a weapon. A few minutes later Officer Lewis spotted Dudley. Gun drawn, he approached and ordered Dudley out of his car. Dudley refused to exit, as two other officers arrived and surrounded the car. Lewis reached into the car attempting to unlock a door, and Dudley sped away. The officers shot at the fleeing car, hitting at least one tire. Officer Eden arrived in time to see Dudley accelerate out of the lot and to hear the shots. He saw Dudley swerve into on-coming traffic before returning to the correct lane. Officer Eden pursued. Dudley maintained that Eden cut him off, the cars came to a complete stop, and Eden fired, hitting him three times. Eden, however, said that Dudley rammed his driver's side door, and that he (Eden) "was afraid for the public because of the extreme emotion that Dudley had shown when he was trying to escape the officers' custody." (p. 724) The other officers arrived. They found the stolen money but no weapon. Dudley appeared to have been shot in the right arm. He was hospitalized, where it was also determined that his blood alcohol level was .30. In 1998 Dudley filed a 1983 suit against the officers, claiming excessive force was used along with a variety of state law claims.

Dudley's main argument was that he did not pose a threat to anyone. He was merely waiting for the police, "Hoping that they would help him commit suicide by killing him." (p. 726) Although he changed his mind and drove away, he claimed he did so at a low rate of speed. His venture into the oncoming traffic lane was explained as caused by a car he had to get around. He collided with Officer Eden's vehicle only after he had been cut off. Once he was cut off, he was in effect captured and there was no need to shoot. Therefore, a rational jury could find that Officer Eden acted unreasonably. In this case, then, the concept of "SbC" may be seen as helping to resolve the slight differences in the versions of what occurred, in favor of Dudley. (Furthermore, for summary judgment, the court is expected to assume Dudley's version.)

The Appellate Court, however, pointed out that only four minutes elapsed between the call from dispatch and the shooting. In the meantime, Officer Eden knew that a bank robbery had been committed, that Dudley had refused to comply with the orders of armed officers, and that he had evaded arrest and sped recklessly out of the parking lot. Also, the collision had not immobilized Dudley's car, and had Dudley been armed he would have had a clear shot at Eden. Therefore, "it was reasonable for Officer Eden to conclude that Dudley posed a serious threat to himself and others" (p. 727) and no reasonable jury could find his decision to shoot unreasonable.

Police and Suicide Intervention

The Dudley incident described above was somewhat unusual in that it actually began as a planned suicide by cop. This is just one of several types of scenarios that comprise SbC incidents (cf. Homant & Kennedy, 2000b). Interventions with disturbed, suicidal persons tend to make up the majority of suicides by police. They are also the type of SbC most likely to result in a law suit, since there tends to be more opportunity for the police to engage in negotiations and use special response teams. While almost all police departments have at least some training pertaining to suicide intervention, up until recently very few have dealt specifically with SbC scenarios.

An exception is California, where researchers have been studying the phenomenon for a number of years. In fact, the California Commission on Peace Officer Standards and Training (1999) has recently (July/ August, 1999) sponsored a two-part POST telecourse specific to suicide by cop. This telecourse and its accompanying manual contain extensive information and tactical advice for dealing with SbC scenarios. It is somewhat ironic, therefore, that a recent California State Appeals Court decision has given police officers extensive protection from negligence suits in state court.

Adams v. Freemont (1998) stemmed from an incident in which police had been summoned to help with the apparently suicidal Patrick Adams. Adams had a chronic drinking problem and had fired a gun in his house and refused to communicate with family members. The police eventually located him sitting under a bush in the back yard, half clothed and pointing a gun at himself. Due in part to their fear that Adams might attempt SbC, the police approached Adams very cautiously. At one point they used a trained police dog to get a response from Adams. Eventually a trained negotiator failed to establish any sort of rapport with him, although brief comments were exchanged. Adams expressed an indifference as to whether or not the police shot him, but both the police and Adams tried to make clear that they had no intention of hurting each other. Adams repeatedly asked the police to leave, but they responded that they had to do their job. Finally, Adams said that he knew how to make them leave, and a shot was heard. Several armed police officers who had their guns trained on Adams' position believed that they had been fired on and they returned fire, hitting Adams several times. The initial shot proved to have been Adams shooting himself. The self-inflicted wound would probably have been fatal, but the medical examiner was apparently unable to say whether Adams would have died had the police not fired and had medical attention been given immediately. (This was not literally a SbC incident, but rather one in which the concern over SbC affected police tactics.) Adams' spouse and stepdaughter sued under state law for negligence and wrongful death. After hearing widely differing expert testimony on whether the police had acted reasonably, a jury agreed with plaintiffs and awarded them more than $5 million. Defendants appealed.

The California Court of Appeals overturned the jury's verdict and ordered judgment for the defense. The Appeals Court determined that under California law the police have no duty to intervene in suicide situations. Because Adams was determined to have been already suicidal when the police arrived, the negligent intervention by the police could not be found to be the cause of the suicide. The court seemed to ignore one aspect of the plaintiffs' case here. Plaintiffs had not merely alleged that the police had failed to prevent the suicide; they had also offered expert testimony to the effect that Adams would probably not have committed suicide had the police just left. While such testimony seems speculative at best, the fact that the point was not addressed leaves the final ruling ambiguous. It would seem, however, that at least in those suicides by police that emerge from suicide interventions, police in California are fairly well protected from state-level claims that they intervened negligently (unless they themselves clearly shoot unreasonably). Plaintiff would appear to have the burden of proving that the death would not have happened had not the police intervened in a negligent fashion.

A somewhat similar ruling was made by a Federal District Court in a 1983 suit. *Lansdown v. Chadwick* (2000) presents a factual situation that defies summary, but essentially the court ruled that Officer Chadwick had no duty to prevent the suicide of Roger Lansdown, a mentally disturbed individual who died of smoke inhalation after setting fire to his house. Meanwhile, dicta in *Monday v. Oulette* (1997) raise the possibility that someone attempting suicide might be able to allege a right to commit suicide and thus raise an excessive force claim should police intervene. "Doing nothing" would seem to be the safest course for police in dealing with suicidal individuals–if avoiding litigation were the main consideration.

An Illustrative Case

Many of the legal issues in SbC cases were revisited in a Michigan case, *Crouch v. Breischaft* (1999). In *Crouch*, two officers confronted Pamela Crouch, who had been attempting to kidnap a store owner against whom she had a grudge. Armed with a loaded revolver, Crouch refused to comply with repeated commands yelled by Officer Breischaft. She frequently told the officers to go ahead and shoot her because she had nothing to live for anyway. Officer Breischaft cautioned her that she was threatening him and everyone in the area by waving around a loaded gun. A third officer, Chase, then arrived at the side of the building behind Crouch. As he was out of her field of vision, Chase attempted to sneak up on Crouch, using a slight incline for partial cover. She spotted him, however, and when he continued to advance on her she raised her gun in his direction and Chase fired. She recoiled and raised the gun again as Breischaft fired. She died within a few minutes. Her husband brought a 1983 suit in federal court, alleging excessive force.

Plaintiff offered expert testimony to the effect that the tactics of both Breischaft and Chase were negligent. Breischaft should have attempted to calm Crouch down and establish rapport, while Chase should not have left cover and escalated the situation. With more time, Crouch would surely have cooperated.

The defense was prepared to offer expert testimony to the effect that Crouch had committed SbC. Much information supported the conclusion that Crouch intended to die when she kidnapped the store owner. Whether or not she also intended to kill the store owner was less clear. Although this information was unknown by the officers on the scene and therefore probably not admissible, the plaintiff's expert had described the incident as a probable SbC, and it was the plaintiff's contention that other tactics would have worked to control Crouch. This contention made it necessary to analyze Crouch's motivation.

While plaintiff's expert was correct that most police trainers would recommend keeping cover in dealing with a disturbed person, there were other circumstances (e.g., arrival of children at a neighboring roller rink) that provided a reason for resolving the situation quickly. Furthermore, there is nothing in the research on SbC to suggest that stalling necessarily leads to a better outcome (cf. Homant & Kennedy, 2000a, and Chapter 10).

Before a "battle of the experts" could ensue, the defense moved for summary judgment on the grounds that at the time of the shooting Chase was in immediate danger and therefore the shooting was objectively reasonable. Plaintiff's expert had conceded as much, but plaintiff argued that the unreasonableness of the behavior leading up to the situation nullified the reasonableness of the shooting. Citing a controlling Sixth Circuit case, *Dickerson v. McClellan* (1996), the District Court agreed with the defendant and granted summary judgment. The District Court concluded that the inquiry into objective reasonableness was limited to the moments immediately preceding the shooting. Whether or not the tactics of Breischaft and Chase were ill advised, they did not justify Crouch raising a loaded weapon in Chase's direction, which even plaintiff's expert conceded was a shoot situation.

Obviously, from the cases reviewed above, other federal districts, as well as courts applying state negligence law, may be much more inclined to scrutinize the pre-shooting behavior of the officers. The Sixth Circuit decision in *Crouch* is silent as to what the circumstances would have to be in order for the pre-shooting behavior to be relevant. Perhaps this court would follow the lead of those circuits where gross negligence could be a basis for finding an otherwise objectively reasonable shooting to be a 1983 violation. Or, perhaps in a 1983 suit the pre-shooting tactics would have to amount to a constitutional violation in their own right, e.g., excessive force during the early phase of an arrest scenario might trigger a series of events leading to a shooting, (cf. *Alexander v. City and County of San Francisco*, 1994).

Conclusion

An Appendix at the end of this chapter summarizes the main cases that have been reviewed above. Published court cases, by their very nature, tend to deal with borderline or difficult factual and legal situations. Therefore, the preceding review of cases may tend to exaggerate the differences between judges and jurisdictions in their willingness to "second-guess the police," or "to hold police accountable" (pick your preferred phrase). Nevertheless, it seems that more thought must be given to setting a standard for scrutinizing tactics in police use of force cases in general and in SbC incidents in particular. A blanket refusal to scrutinize tactics would seem to invite reckless and irresponsible police behavior. On the other hand, holding police responsible for having someone aim a shotgun at them because they checked a doorknob (as in *Wallace*) would at best be likely to have a chilling effect on police intervention into any situation.

The dicta of one court (*Plakas*), to the effect that the tactical behavior must itself constitute excessive force, may serve as a useful guideline for 1983 suits, but states may wish to adopt a somewhat broader policy for state negligence suits. Whatever standard is adopted, however, certain tentative findings about SbC should be kept in mind.

First, most SbC situations present a high level of danger. Homant, Kennedy, and Hupp (2000) found that only 22% of such situations involved an empty gun or a prop of some sort; in most situations the subject confronted an officer or a bystander with actual lethal force. More importantly, police were generally unable to distinguish the non-dangerous situations, as evidenced by the somewhat higher lethality rate in these incidents.

Second, a study of police tactics found that relatively high risk tactics, such as attempting to tackle the subject, had the highest rate of successful outcomes (Homant & Kennedy, 2000a; see also Chapter 10). While no department would be likely to recommend such tactics out of safety concerns for the officers, it does not seem fair to legally penalize the officer who risks such an approach (and to thus reward the subject who was responsible for creating the original situation). Especially on the state level, it will take the combined wisdom of courts and the state legislatures to determine the level of scrutiny to which they wish to subject the police.

References

California Commission on Peace Officer Standards and Training (1999). "Suicide by Cop" Telecourse. For availability, contact Training Program Services Bureau, 1601 Alhambra Blvd., Sacramento, CA 95816-7083.

Chiabi, D. K. (1996). Police Civil Liability: An analysis of Section 1983 Actions in Eastern and Southern Districts of New York. American Journal of Criminal Justice, 21, 83-104.

Flynn, T. P., & Homant, R. J. (2000). "Suicide by Police" in Section 1983 suits: Relevance of Police Tactics. University of Detroit Mercy Law Review, 77, 555-578.

Homant, R. J., & Kennedy, D. B. (2000a). The effectiveness of less than lethal force in suicide by cop incidents. Police Quarterly, 3, 153-171.

Homant, R. J., & Kennedy, D. B. (2000b) Suicide by police: A proposed typology of law enforcement officer assisted suicide. Policing: An International Journal of Police Strategies and Management, 23, 339-355.

Homant, R. J., Kennedy, D. B., & Hupp, R. T. (2000). Real and perceived danger in police officer assisted suicide. Journal of Criminal Justice, 28, 43-52.

Kennedy, D. B., Homant, R. J., & Hupp, R. T. (1998). Suicide by cop. FBI Law Enforcement Bulletin, (August), 21-27.

Smith, M. R. (1996). Police use of deadly force: How courts and policy-makers have misplaced Tennessee v. Garner. Kansas Journal of Law and Public Policy, 7, 100-117.

Cases Cited

Abraham v. Raso, 183 F.3d 279 (1999).

Adams v. Freemont, 80 Cal. Rptr.2d 196 (Cal Ct.App. 1998).

Alexander v. City and County of San Francisco, 29 F.3d 1355 (9th Cir. 1994).

Anderson v. Creighton, 483 U.S. 635 (1987).

Bell v. Irwin, Case No. 00-CV-4078-JPG. U.S. District for the Southern District of Illinois, 2002).

Bennett v. Murphy, 127 F.Supp 2d 689. U.S. District for the Western District of Pennsylvania, 2000).

Bivens v. Six Unknown Fed. Narcotics Agents, 403 U.S.388 (1971).

Crouch v. Breischaft et al., U.S. District for the Western District of Michigan. Case No. 5:97-CV-220. (6th Cir.) Order for summary judgment for defendants granted June 2, 1999.

Cruz v. Laramie, 239 F.3d 1183 (10th Cir. 2001).

Deorle v. Rutherford, 272 F.3d 1272 (9th Cir. 2001).

Dickerson v. McClellan, 101 F.3d 1151 (6th Cir. 1996).

Dudley v. Eden, 260 F.3d 722 (6th Cir. 2001).

Garcia v. Boston, Civ.Action No 97-12047-MEL; 115 F.Supp. 2d 74; 2000 U.S.Dist. LEXIS 14032.

Graham v. Connor, 490 U.S. 386 (1989).

Harlow v. Fitzgerald, 457 U.S. 800 (1982).

Headwaters Forest v. Humboldt, 240 F.3d 1185 (9th Cir. 2000; Amended 2001).

Lansdown v. Chadwick, 152 F.Supp. 2d 1128 (U.S. District for the Western District of Arkansas, Harrison Div.); CV 99-3062 (2000).

Martinez v. County of Los Angeles, 47 Cal.App.4th 334 (Cal. Ct.App. 1996)

Medina v. Cram, 252 F.3d 1124 (10th Cir. 2001).

Monday v. Oulette, 118 F.3d 1099 (6th Cir. 1997).

Nowell v. Acadian Ambulance, 147 F.Supp. 2d 495 (U.S. District for the Western District of Louisiana, Lafayette-Opelousas Div. 2001).

Omdahl v. Lindholm, 170 F.3d 730 (7th Cir. 1999).

Pace v. Capobianco, 283 F.3d 1275 (11th Cir. 2002).

Palmquist v. Selvik, 11 F.3d 1332 (7th Cir. 1997).

Plakas v. Drinski, 19 F.3d 1143 (7th Cir. 1994).

Quezada v. County of Bernalillo, 944 F.2d 710 (10th Cir. 1991).

Rhodes v. McDannel, 945 F.2d 117 (6th Cir. 1991).

Robinson v. Solano, 278 F.3d 1007 (9th Cir. 2002).

Rowland v. Perry, 41 F.3d 167 (4th Cir. 1994).

Roy v. Inhabitants of the City of Lewiston, 42 F.3d 619 (1st Cir. 1994).

Saucier v. Katz, 121 S.Ct. 2151 (2001).

Tennessee v. Garner, 471 U.S. 1 (1985).

Wallace v. Davies, 676 N.E.2d 422 (Ind.Ct.App. 1997).

Appendix

Summary of Selected Court Decisions on Police Use of Force

Decision	Date	Court	Main Point
Adams v. Freemont	1998	State App	(In California) police have no duty to prevent suicide.
Crouch v. Breischaft	1999	Fed Dist	Only the moments immediately preceding a shooting are relevant for determining objective reasonableness.
Deorle v. Rutherford	2001	Fed Cir	Use of beanbag round to stop suicidal man advancing on officer held to violate a clearly established right.
Dudley v. Eden	2001	Fed Cir	Appellate court looks at totality of circumstances to grant defendant immunity.
Graham v. Connor	1989	USSC	To not be excessive, a "reasonable officer" must be able to see the force as reasonable.
Medina v. Cram	2001	Fed Cir	For pre-seizure conduct to be relevant to plaintiff's claim, it must be "immediately connected" to the use of force and be "reckless" rather than merely negligent.
Palmquist v. Selvik	1997	Fed Cir	Suicide by cop motivation by subject only relevant to extent officer was aware at time force was used (or to resolve factual dispute).
Plakas v. Drinski	1994	Fed Cir	(Implies that) pre-shooting tactics would have to be a constitutional violation in order to make use of force unreasonable
Quezada v. Bernalillo	1991	Fed Cir	State negligence law provides means for challenging police tactics.

Decision	Date	Court	Main Point
Rhodes v. McDannel	1991	Fed Cir	Gross negligence in pre-shooting behavior could make a shooting unjustified.
Robinson v. Solano	2002	Fed Cir	Pointing a gun at someone in making an arrest is itself a use of force that could be deemed excessive and must therefore be justified by the objective reasonableness standard.
Rowland v. Perry	1994	Fed Cir	"Totality of circumstances" used to critique officer's decisions leading to use of force.
Roy v. Lewiston	1994	Fed Cir	A "strong" statement of qualified immunity: judge should grant unless no reasonable officer would have used such force.
Saucier v. Katz	2001	USSC	A two-pronged test should be used to grant qualified immunity: objective reasonableness of officer's actions and clearly established right.
Tennessee v. Garner	1985	USSC	Use of deadly force requires "immediate threat."
Wallace v. Davies	1997	State App	Officers' questionable prior tactics can make a shooting unreasonable.

Note: the above summaries necessarily oversimplify the various holdings. More importantly, except for U.S. Supreme Court decisions, precedents may only apply to a particular state or federal circuit.

Chapter 5

LEGAL DEFENSE OF LAW ENFORCEMENT OFFICERS IN POLICE SHOOTING CASES

John J. Cloherty III, Esq.

> *The masculine pronoun is used herein only for ease of reading. It is important to realize that the female gender is assumed.*

Introduction

The legal defense of civil lawsuits arising from alleged police misconduct is a complex endeavor, requiring the successful attorney to marshal considerable legal knowledge, experience and skill to prevail. This chapter will assess the legal and factual issues confronting the defense attorney in civil cases arising from police shootings, and in particular, where the shooting involves a suspect believed to be attempting "suicide-by-cop (SbC)." Of course, litigation strategy varies considerably from case to case depending on the circumstances involved. Although addressed to defense counsel, this chapter is designed to provide law enforcement professionals, and perhaps to their legal counsel, insight into the typical procedures in defending police-shooting cases. There is a large body of law addressing civil rights and alleged police misconduct, as well as many treatises concerning trial practice. This chapter is merely an overview of legal procedure, defense counsel tactics, and decision points encountered in defending a police shooting case. A more detailed discussion of every legal aspect of such cases is beyond the scope of this chapter. Because the majority of lawsuits arising from police shootings are civil rights claims, which are brought in federal court or are subject to removal to federal court, this chapter focuses on federal civil procedure. The discussion that follows is structured according to the usual progress of a lawsuit from filing of the complaint through discovery, trial and post-trial events.

Legal Liability in Police Shootings

As is discussed in other chapters, a lawsuit arising from a police shooting usually involves claims that the police violated the constitutional rights of the suspect. In addition to claims of civil rights violations, a police shooting may also give rise to claims of state tort laws. To provide context to the ensuing discussion, it is helpful to set forth the framework under which such claims of liability are made. It is also important to note that the plaintiff is often the executor or administrator of the estate of the suspect, if the suspect was killed in the shooting. Thus, references to "plaintiff" throughout this chapter should be read to refer to the suspect or the executor or administrator.

The vehicle for a plaintiff to bring a legal action asserting violations of civil rights is the federal statute found in 42 U.S.C. § 1983. Section 1983 does not create any substantive rights, but rather provides a vehicle for the protection and vindication of rights secured by the United States Constitution or by federal law. *See Baker v. McCollan*, 443 U.S. 137, 146 n.3 (1979); *Boveri v. Town of Saugus*, 113 F.3d 4, 6 (1st Cir. 1997). The plaintiff in a civil rights action under § 1983 must plead and prove, by a preponderance of the evidence, that a person acting under color of state law deprived him of a constitutional or federally-protected right. *See* 42 U.S.C. § 1983; *see also Tatro v. Kervin*, 41 F.3d 9, 14 (1st Cir. 1994). In police shooting cases, the "color of state law" element is usually not an issue, as the vast majority of cases arise from the officer's use of his weapon while on duty during a confrontation with a suspect. *See, e.g. Deering v. Reich*, 183 F.3d 645 (7th Cir. 1999) (The Court's decision holds that the deputy county sheriff who shot a suspect in a Wisconsin county other than the county in which he was employed was nonetheless acting under color of law so as to be potentially liable under § 1983).

The courts have uniformly held that the use of excessive force by an arresting officer constitutes a denial of due process for which an action for damages lies under Section 1983. *See, e.g. Graham v. Connor*, 490 U.S. 386, 109 S.Ct. 1865 (1989) (The Court's decision holds claim that law enforcement officials having used excessive force, deadly or not, in course of arrest, investigatory stop or other "seizure" of a person are properly analyzed under the Fourth Amendment's "objective reasonableness" standard). Claims of excessive force against police officers are properly analyzed under the Fourth Amendment rather than under a substantive due process standard. The Fourth Amendment establishes the right of every person "to be secure in their persons, houses, papers, and effects, against unreasonable searches and seizures."

Thus, liability on the part of the officers turns on whether their use of force was "unreasonable" both as to the type of force applied – e.g., a flashlight, a kick using a shoe or boot, or a gun shot – as well as to the amount of such force. The test, as articulated by the United States Supreme Court, is one of "objective reasonableness." *Graham v. Connor*, 109 S. Ct. 1865 (1989).

> [T]he question is whether the officers' actions are "objectively reasonable" in light of the facts and circumstances confronting them, without regard to their underlying intent or motivation. An officer's evil intentions will not make a Fourth Amendment violation out of an objectively reasonable use of force; nor will an officer's good intentions make an objectively unreasonable use of force constitutional.

Id., 109 S. Ct. at 1872 (citations omitted).

In applying this test of "objective reasonableness," the Federal Courts have been careful to point out that the "inquiry must be undertaken from the perspective of 'a reasonable officer on the scene, rather than with the 20/20 vision of hindsight.'" *Alexis v. McDonald's Restaurants of Massachusetts, Inc.*, 67 F.3d 341, 352 (1st Cir. 1995) (quoting *Graham*, 109 S. Ct. at 1872). Hence, whether the force used to effect an arrest was reasonable under Fourth Amendment standards depends on (1) "the severity of the crime at issue;" (2) "whether the suspect poses an immediate threat to the safety of the officers or others;" and (3) "whether [the suspect] is actively resisting arrest or attempting to evade arrest by flight." *Graham*, 109 S. Ct. at 1872; *Gaudreault v. Salem*, 923 F.2d 203, 205 (1st Cir. 1990). These are the factors – the so-called "totality of the circumstances" – that must be critically examined in the circumstances of this case to assess the potential civil rights liability of an officer in a police-shooting case. Notably, under federal law, a municipality cannot be held vicariously liable for the unconstitutional acts of its officers or employees. *Monell v. Dept. of Social Services of the City of N.Y.*, 436 U.S. 658, 665 (1978). The municipal employer may only be held liable if there is evidence of an official custom, policy or practice that is affirmatively linked to the violation of the plaintiff's civil rights. *Id.; see also Oklahoma City v. Tuttle*, 471 U.S. 808 (1985).

There are other Federal statutes beside Section 1983 giving rise to civil rights claims, although these statutes are not as prevalent in police shooting cases. Section 1985 of Title 42 prohibits conspiracies to deprive civil rights; however, it is limited to conspiracies in which there is specific intent to deprive plaintiff of equal privileges and immunities. *See* 42 U.S.C. § 1985. In addition, under 42 U.S.C. § 1986, any person having prior knowledge of a conspiracy under § 1985, and who has the power to prevent or help prevent its consummation, is subject to liability for resulting injuries. Civil-rights claims may also be based on state laws protecting civil rights, or on rights guaranteed under state Constitutions. Many states have enacted local "Civil Rights Acts," often having elements different from, or in addition to, the Federal law. *See, e.g.* Mass. Gen. L. ch. 12 §§ 11H, 11I (The Massachusetts Civil Rights Act requires the plaintiff to establish that the defendants interfered, or attempted to interfere, with the plaintiff's rights by "threats, intimidation or coercion.") A plaintiff's right to recover under federal law cannot limit the plaintiff's right to also proceed under state law; however, there should not be double recovery for the same damages. *See General Tel. Co. of the Northwest, Inc. v. EEOC,* 446 U.S. 318, 333, 100 S.Ct. 1698, 64 L.Ed.2d 319 (1980) ("It also goes without saying that the courts can and should preclude double recovery by an individual.").

A police-shooting case also may expose a police officer to civil liability under state law for negligent or wrongful acts causing personal injury or death. Examples of frequent tort claims asserted are negligence, as well as intentional torts of assault, battery, false arrest or false imprisonment. Plaintiffs also often allege a claim for wrongful infliction of emotional distress, either negligently or intentionally inflicted. In a negligence claim, the familiar required elements are duty, breach, harm, and causation. Thus, to establish a cause of action for negligence, plaintiff must demonstrate the defendant's legal duty of care owed to the plaintiff, the defendant's breach of that duty of care, injury to the plaintiff as a result of the breach of that duty, injury proximately caused by the defendant's negligent conduct, and damage to the plaintiff. The legal question created in negligence cases is often whether a duty of care was owed, while the other elements of breach, causation and harm are typically questions of fact reserved for the fact-finder (either the jury, or the judge in jury-waived cases).

In many jurisdictions, assault and battery are considered separate acts, usually arising from the same transaction, each having independent significance. An "assault" is often defined as a physical act of a threatening nature, or an offer of corporal injury which puts an individual in reasonable fear of imminent bodily harm. While many jurisdictions define "battery" as an act that was intended to cause and did in fact cause an offensive contact with, or uncontested touching of, the body of another. The battery is thus the consummation of an assault. The torts of a false arrest and false imprisonment are often interpreted the same. To state a claim for false imprisonment and false arrest, in a typical jurisdiction, the plaintiff needs to state (1) the defendant intended to confine him; (2) the plaintiff was conscious of the confinement; (3) the plaintiff did not consent to the confinement; and (4) the confinement was not otherwise privileged. The element of privilege refers to the burden that the plaintiff must show that he was detained without legal justification. Thus, if probable cause exists at the time of the arrest, the plaintiff's claims for false imprisonment and false arrest must fail. There are many cases discussing the elements of claims for infliction of emotional distress. Typically, for the plaintiff to state a claim for intentional infliction of emotional distress:

1. The conduct must be intentional and reckless disregard of the probability of causing emotional distress;
2. The conduct must be extreme and outrageous;
3. There must be a causal connection between the lawful conduct and the emotional distress; and
4. The emotional distress in question must be severe.

In addition, many jurisdictions have required at least some proof of medically established physical symptomology for both intentional and negligent infliction of mental distress.

Pre-Lawsuit Legal Counsel

In the immediate aftermath of a police shooting, legal counsel is often consulted. The attorney's role and activities will depend on who the attorney has been retained to represent. Often attorneys are sought by the individual officers involved, the police officer's union (on behalf of the officers), the police department itself, or the municipality or county employer. For purposes of this discussion, we will address areas of concern for those attorneys representing the individual officers.

The first necessity, of course, is to meet with the client police officer. This meeting may be at the shooting scene, or at the station. Many police departments will seek to interview the officers involved immediately following the shooting to take a statement. Counsel would be wise to seek a "stall" period after a shooting incident to permit the client to calm down before any formal interviews. The stress, emotions and excitement created by the use of a firearm during an on-duty confrontation may make the officer a poor witness in communicating the events in their immediate aftermath. Counsel, of course, will always want to cooperate with investigators, but should not be reluctant to control **how** the cooperation takes place. In fact, many police union contracts provide for a stall period after a "critical incident" before permitting officers to submit to interviews.

Frequently a police shooting will result in the initiation of two or more contemporaneous investigations. For example, the internal affairs division of the police department may investigate to determine if the officers complied with departmental use-of-force policies, while the local prosecutor's office may commence a criminal investigation to determine whether the officers violated any state or federal law. It is important for an attorney to control the scheduling of interviews, to avoid multiple interviews on the same day or evening. This protects the client from the psychological stress of submitting to back-to-back interviews, as well as avoiding potential for fatigue-induced inconsistencies in the officers rendition of the events. The officer's attorney should also communicate with the officer's family or spouse. This provides emotional support during a stressful time, and family members may also act as gatekeepers for any attempts by investigators to conduct unscheduled interviews. For example, the concerned spouse should be advised to refer any inquires to counsel, rather than answering a late-night knock on the door from investigators seeking to interview the officer on the evening of the shooting. The officer's family may also provide insight into the officer's personality, advising counsel whether the officer's post-incident demeanor is out of character and providing further basis to request a "stall period" before any formal interviews.

During the "stall" period before interviews, it may be advisable for the officer to preserve his memory of incident in writing. Any such draft version of events should be prepared as correspondence to counsel as part of an attorney-client communication, thus arguably rendering the officer's notes privileged. There is nothing wrong, however, with the officer immediately preparing a formal incident report if that is the officer's standard practice. In addition to formal interviews, the officer involved in a shooting may be referred to the department's psychologist or stress counselor (or even to another department officer designated as a "Stress Liaison Officer"). These experts perform laudatory services for police involved in a shooting, but counsel should caution their clients that any discussions with these experts may not be privileged, depending on the professional qualifications of the stress counselor.

Pre-Lawsuit Claim Procedures

Typically prior to filing suit, plaintiff's counsel will seek to present a claim for settlement to potential defendants to avoid the time and expense of initiating legal proceedings. The claim letter presented by counsel will usually contain a detailed recitation of the facts (as alleged by plaintiff), a brief description of the theory of liability arising from those facts, and a demand for relief by way of monetary payment and/or injunctive relief (such as requesting a change in police tactics or further training). Often claims made under state law (such as tort claims of assault, battery, false imprisonment, etc.) first must be presented to the state or municipal governmental body for investigation and potential resolution prior to a lawsuit being commenced. Failure to make this pre-suit presentment of a tort claim may be a basis for dismissal under some state statutes. These presentment requirements, however, cannot abrogate rights under federal law and are thus not a prerequisite to a federal civil rights suit. *See Felder v. Casey*, 487 U.S. 131, 108 S.Ct. 2302 (1988) (The Court's decision holds that state statute requires notice of claim prior to suit against local governmental entity inapplicable to action under Section 1983).

The claim letter provides an opportunity to engage in settlement discussions before suit. Depending on the circumstances, the municipal or governmental employer of the officer may desire to bring the matter to a quick resolution, avoiding the expense and publicity of a lawsuit. The parties may agree to engage to services of a third-party mediator to assist in the valuation of a claim. Any discussions made in the course of settlement negotiations are prohibited from admission into evidence. *See* Fed. R. Evid. 408. (The law states that it is inadmissible to render evidence of compromise or offers to compromise.)

The Typical Lawsuit Arising from a Police Shooting

Most lawsuits arising from a police shooting will name the officers involved in the shooting, and also will include the municipality or county employer as a co-defendant. Often supervisory personnel, such as the chief of police, also will be named as defendants. Usually the suit will be filed in federal court and will allege the violation of civil rights under 42

U.S.C. § 1983 and under applicable provision of state law or state constitutions. As discussed above, most civil suits allege state law tort claims in addition to civil rights violations.

The format of a standard civil complaint is to first identify the parties, then set forth the grounds for the Court's jurisdiction and venue, followed by a detailed recitation of the alleged facts that support liability. The Complaint then proceeds to enumerate counts, which are discrete theories of relief under which plaintiff expects to recover. The Complaint typically has a demand for relief at the end of each count, where plaintiff claims an award of damages, as well as reimbursement for fees. Requests for injunctive relief are usually covered as separate counts of the Complaint, rather than included in the so called "ad damnun" clause at the end of each count.

When the complaint identifies the parties, the plaintiff usually will allege in what capacity the defendants are being sued, either in their official capacity or individual capacity. This is significant because a suit against a municipal official in his or her official capacity is tantamount to a suit against the municipality itself. *See Hafer v. Melo*, 502 U.S. 21, 25 (1991). Often plaintiff's attorneys name high-ranking public officials, such as the Mayor or Sheriff, as official-capacity defendants. This does no more than name the City or the County itself as defendant. When the jurisdiction and venue of the Court is alleged, defendants seldom contest these allegations. If the case is brought in federal court in the first instance, the plaintiff must make allegations of jurisdiction. Simply stated, federal jurisdiction may exist in one of two ways: 1) if there is a diversity of citizenship among the parties (i.e. the parties are citizens of different states), and the amount in controversy exceeds $75,000, or 2) if there is a federal question at stake. *See* 28 U.S.C. §§ 1331, 1332. The congressional grant of "federal question" jurisdiction, as it is known, provides: "The district courts shall have original jurisdiction of all civil actions arising under the Constitution, laws, or treaties of the United States." *See* 28 U.S.C. § 1331. Thus civil rights cases brought under 42 U.S.C. § 1983 provide federal question jurisdiction because the cases invoke a federal statute concerning civil rights.

In order to withstand a motion to dismiss, plaintiffs' attorneys drafting a civil rights complaint state the alleged facts concerning police actions in detail. Furthermore, the Complaint must set forth each element of the alleged civil rights claims or state law causes of action in order to avoid vulnerability to a motion to dismiss. In an action under 42 U.S.C. § 1983, the Complaint must allege (1) that the plaintiff has been denied of a right, privilege, or immunity secured by the Constitution or laws of the United States; (2) that the defendant subjected the plaintiff to such deprivation, or caused him to be so subjected, and (3) that the defendant acted under color of a statute, ordinance, regulation, custom, or usage of a state. Where the Complaint is also brought against the municipal or governmental employer of the police officer, further allegations must be made to properly plead liability, because municipalities cannot be held liable merely as *respondeat superior* for the officer.* *See Monell v. Department of Social Services*, 436 U.S. 658 (1978). Instead, municipal liability "attaches where – and only where – a deliberate choice to follow a course of action is made from among various alternatives by the official or officials responsible for establishing final policy with respect to the subject matter in question." *Pembaur v. Cincinnati*, 475 U.S. 469, 483 (1986). Thus most suits allege a "policy" on the part of the city to violate the rights of citizens, inadequate training of the police officers, inadequate supervision of police officers, and/or prior allegations of police misconduct, either on the part of the defendant police officer or other nonparty officers.

In the police misconduct cases, plaintiffs may seek compensatory damages as well as punitive damages. Compensatory damages generally are the damages recoverable in other tort actions for personal injury and include physical and emotional injury and expenses, costs, and impairment. These include, for instance, medical expenses, lost wages, lost earning capacity, emotional distress damages, and compensation for future physical limitations. If plaintiff has brought several counts in the complaint; however, this does not permit multiple recovery for the same harm. Significantly, even if a plaintiff suffered no actual damages (though not applicable to a police shooting case), the plaintiff may recover damages for the value of having one's constitutional rights denied. Even if these damages are nominal, they may have significance because a nominal award from a jury may permit plaintiff to be awarded attorney's fees under 42 U.S.C. § 1988.

Punitive damages are available in a civil rights action under § 1983 against individual police officers. *See Kentucky v. Graham*, 473 U.S. 159 (1985). In contrast, the municipal or governmental employer is immune from punitive damages under Section 1983. *See Newport v. Fact Con-*

---

* Respondeat Superior ("Let the master answer") is a legal doctrine under which the master is liable for the wrongful acts of his servant. Typically applied to employer-employee relationships, the doctrine is inapplicable where the servant is acting outside of the scope of his authority at the time the injury occurs.

certs, Inc., 453 U.S. 247 (1981). Punitive damages are those damages awarded as punishment or penalty, and thus unrelated to the actual harm suffered by plaintiff. Generally punitive damages are not recoverable under most state law claims, unless there is a specific statutory provision authorizing such an award. As stated by the U.S. Supreme Court, "a jury may be permitted to assess punitive damages in an action under § 1983 when the defendant's conduct is shown to be motivated by evil motive or intent, or when it involves reckless or callous indifference to the federally protected rights of others." *Smith v. Wade*, 461 U.S. 30, 56 (1983). This standard for awarding punitive damages is generally regarded as a high one. *Id.*

Defending the Lawsuit

Pre-Trial Practice

Preliminary Matters

   Service of process: In a Section 1983 lawsuit alleging police misconduct, plaintiffs frequently name as defendants the municipality, police department administrators and numerous individual officers. No responsive pleading is required unless the complaint has been served upon the defendant, or service of process has been waived. Answering the complaint may be deemed to waive any claims concerning defective service. Motions to dismiss may be made as to those defendants not served within 120 days of the filing of the complaint. *See* Fed. R. Civ. P. 4(j).
   In Federal Court, however, the rules create a duty on defendants to save costs of service by the waiver of service provisions. *See* Fed. R. Civ. P. 4(d). With the exception of certain defendants (e.g. the United States, infants, incompetents), the rules provide a mechanism wherein a plaintiff may send a form to the defendants requesting they waive service. The defendants, if they waive service, are entitled to 60 days to respond to the complaint, as opposed to the twenty day period if service is required. As further incentive to waive service, the rule mandates the Court to assess costs against the defendant for the expense of the service unless defendant has "good cause" for refusing to waive service. As a practical matter, if the suit is filed in Federal Court, counsel should readily agree to waive service to avoid the sanctions and enjoy the additional time in which to respond to the complaint.

Conflict of interest: Section 1983 plaintiffs frequently allege that the individual defendants were acting within the course and scope of employment when they committed the alleged misconduct, and that the acts were pursuant to an official and/or unofficial custom, practice or policy of the municipality. Defendants in a police misconduct suit may include the municipality, individual police officers, the officers' supervisors, the chief of police, city council or other governmental board members, and the mayor or municipal manager. The existence of a conflict of interest depends on the facts and circumstances of each case. Counsel must review the alleged facts and potential defenses at the outset of the case to determine whether a potential conflict of interest exists. Of course, counsel has a continuing duty to assess whether a conflict exists during the course of the case, as revealed by later acquired information. Should an actual or potential conflict of interest exist, ordinarily separate counsel must assume the defense of parties to the conflict, unless the circumstances permit the parties, upon advice and consent, to waive their right to conflict-free counsel.

A conflict of interest for the defense attorney may be presented by the joint representation of a municipality and individual police officers. For example, this conflict may arise if defense of the municipality requires counsel to assert the individual police officers were acting outside course and scope of employment at the time of the incident, and thus their conduct may not be imputed to municipality. Making arguments which shift (or whose effect may be perceived as shifting) liability for damages between or among the municipality and the individual defendants creates a conflict of interest. Similarly, joint representation of multiple individual police officer defendants may present a conflict of interest, especially where the defense of one or more officers may require asserting their fellow defendant officers were liable instead. Similarly, counsel's knowledge of damaging information pertaining to some officers may create a conflict of interest if it requires compromising the defense of other officers.

Other sources of a conflict of interest between the officer and the municipality may stem from the plaintiff's usual allegations of inadequate training and supervision. If defense counsel needs to argue that the individual police officer did the best he could, but was inadequately trained by the municipality, or in the alternative, that the municipality's training was proper, but this particular officer did not act according to his training, a conflict exists. Even supervisory officers may require separate counsel from the municipality in instances where the supervisors felt that the municipality did not provide adequate training funds, or where the municipality had refused to uphold a prior firing or suspension of the officer in question which the supervisor felt was appropriate.

Removal to federal court: If a lawsuit alleging police misconduct contains claims of federal civil rights violations and is filed in state courts, the lawsuit is subject to removal to federal court. Removal of Section 1983 actions to federal court may be tactically advantageous to the defense. The removal process is entirely a creature of statute. *See* 28 U.S.C. §§ 1441-51. Only a defendant may remove a case, and the plaintiff cannot block a proper removal. *See* 13 C. Wright et al., *Federal Practice and Procedure* § 3721; 7B J.W. Moore, *Federal Practice* § 704. If the Complaint contains both federal and non-federal claims, the federal court will generally assume pendent jurisdiction over the non-federal claims.[*] *See* Wright § 3722, Moore § 709. "[T]he principal purpose of giving federal courts original jurisdiction over federal claims is to afford parties relying on federal law a sympathetic, knowledgeable forum for the vindication of their federal rights." *Hunter v. United Van Lines*, 746 F.2d 635, 639 (9th Cir. 1984) *cert. denied*, 474 U.S. 863 (1985).

The decision to remove a police misconduct complaint to federal court is a tactical one for which defense counsel must consider a number of competing factors. Some of these factors are:

1. *The federal jury pool* (the Police Department's relationship with and reputation in the community may encourage counsel to seek jurors from the same geographical area in a state court forum or from the broader geographic area in the federal forum (further discussed below).

2. *Court case management* (counsel needs to have a working knowledge of the efficiency of the state and federal courts to assess the impact of potential delays in bringing the case to trial or the existence of restrictions on pleadings, motions, discovery and trial dates).

3. *Discovery limitations* (state privileges pertaining to discovery of police records may not apply in federal court; the federal rules provide for automatic disclosure of documents and witnesses; and federal courts often limit the number and timing of depositions and discovery requests more strictly than state court).

---

[*] Federal law, however, permits district court to remand non-federal claims to state court. *See* 28 U.S.C. § 1441(c).

4. *Judicial assignment* (knowledge of the state and federal court's procedures for assignment of judges to preside over the case, and the likelihood of assignment to a particularly favorable or unfavorable judge, may strongly impact the removal decision).
5. *Federal law issues* (if federal law or policy issues predominate, removal may be beneficial on the assumption that federal judges have greater expertise on such matters).
6. *Rules practice* (a comparison of the state and federal rules of civil procedure and of evidence may impact the management and resolution of the case).

The jury selection process in Federal Court is governed by the Jury Selection and Service Act. *See* 28 U.S.C. § 1863. The Act provides a methodology for random selection of prospective jurors, with the names of prospective jurors being selected from the voter registration lists, or lists of actual voters, within the Federal District or Division. The Federal Districts are generally the confines of the State the District serves, but for larger states there may be multiple Federal Districts designated by geographic areas (i.e. north, south, east, west, middle, central). The jury pool is thus those voters within the Federal District. In contrast, most State Court systems have jurisdiction within the county boundaries where the court is located. The jury pools are usually limited to those eligible persons residing within the county. Typically the counties are smaller geographic areas than Federal Districts and therefore State Courts have a smaller jury pool.

The federal law strictly limits the timing for removing a case to federal court. The defendant or defendants must file in U.S. District Court within thirty days "after receipt [of summons and complaint] by the defendant, through service **or otherwise**." 28 U.S.C. § 1446(b) (emphasis added). Thus even if the Complaint has yet to be served, the clock for removal starts running when the defendant becomes aware of the federal claims. The procedure for removal, including the notice required and the content of the petition for removal, is governed by federal statute. *See* 28 U.S.C. § 1446. If there are multiple defendants, the written consent of all defendants must be obtained and attached to the removal petition.

Meeting with client: Once the lawsuit has been received and reviewed, the defense attorney should meet the client police officer immediately. This is true even if there is a thorough investigation file received from the client or the insurance company. There are a number of things the defense attorney should seek to accomplish in the initial client meeting. Defense counsel should first review the allegations in the Complaint with the client. Many police officers will only skim the Complaint when they receive it and will not pay much attention to the details. The attorney should then discuss the nature of the case. The police officer's experience is predominately in the criminal arena, and it is important to point out the significant difference of civil litigation. Next counsel should emphasize the necessity for cooperation and assistance of the officer to successfully defend the lawsuit. If need be, defense counsel should affirm his or her independence and duty of loyalty to the police officer as client.

After these initial discussions, the facts of the case must be addressed. The officer should state in detail what happened on the date in question. The attorney should take thorough notes, and then go back over the notes and ask specific questions about specific points. The discussion may then return to the allegations contained in the complaint. In consultation with the client, counsel should determine what can be admitted, what must be denied, and what is uncertain for purposes of drafting the Answer to the Complaint. Defense counsel should be certain to discuss the officer's background, including the officer's education and prior employment. If previously employed as a police officer in another municipality, counsel should follow up and write to obtain a copy of his prior personnel file, training records, complaints, and reprimands.

At this first meeting it is imperative to begin identifying and cataloging documents. Counsel should review with the officer what documents are in his possession and what documents need to be obtained from the police department or elsewhere, either by the officer or by counsel. The officer should have copies of the incident report, witness statements, diagrams of the scene, and other relevant documents. If not, he needs to obtain them. If the officer has any field notes, those should be obtained. Copies of all of the documents from the police department regarding this incident are needed. These may include any citations, dispatch tapes, dispatch logs, photographs, shooting review board hearings or findings, or other internal investigation documents. If the client is aware of any newspaper articles, the attorney should obtain copies of those, which are often relied upon by plaintiffs' attorneys as a source of information.

If possible, during this first meeting, the attorney should obtain the officer's training records and commendations. If he does not have them with him at the first meeting, counsel should make sure he gets this material as soon as possible. This is also true for the officer's personnel file. These and other documents related to the individual officer may be maintained by the Police Department. In police-shooting cases, the officer's firearms training often becomes a central issue, therefore obtaining those records is critical. Additional documents include results of any psychological testing not included in the personnel file. The attorney needs to find out about any prior complaints, lawsuits, or reprimands against the officer, and should discuss them with the officer at their first meeting.

At the conclusion of this meeting, the attorney should advise the client how to contact counsel. The attorney should be sure to get the officer's home address and home phone number, because many officers have their numbers unlisted. The attorney should caution the officer not to discuss this situation with anyone other than counsel. The attorney should explain to the officer how the litigation will proceed and provide him with an overview and timetable of the case, which may be markedly different from that of a typical criminal case. The attorney should conclude by stressing to the officer that the litigation is a serious matter, regardless of what he thinks about the merits of the case. It needs to be brought home to the officer that no matter how meritless the case is, it will require no small effort on his part as well as on the part of counsel to win the case.

If counsel is representing the municipality, a meeting should be scheduled with the city manager or other responsible official on behalf of the city. If the police chief and/or other police supervisors have been named, the attorney should meet with them as well. The attorney should explain the theories of liability against the city and supervisors. The police supervisors may be held vicariously liable for acts of subordinates under Section 1983 only if they directed, ordered, participated in, or approved of the officer's actions. *Gentry v. Duckworth*, 65 F.3d 555 (7th Cir. 1995). It is important to advise supervisory officials, however, that actual personal involvement is not necessary for them to be liable on other theories, such as grossly negligent supervision. *See, e.g., Colon v. Coughlin*, 58 F.3d 865 (2d Cir. 1995). They should also know that certain defenses available to the individual officer might be unavailable to municipal defendants. Counsel should point out, for example, that the defense of qualified immunity for a police officer acting in good faith is not available to a municipal defendant in a Section 1983 action. *See Camfield v. Oklahoma City*, 248 F.3d 1214 (10th Cir. 2001). Yet, it is important for the city and the supervisors to understand that many times their defense rises or falls with the defense set forth by the police officer, because if there is no underlying civil rights violation by the officer, there can be no other liability.

Municipal officials should be reminded of the need for cooperation among the municipality, the supervisors, and the police officer. If the facts reveal this is not a case of liability against the individual police officer, the municipality and the supervisors should avoid blaming, reprimanding or terminating the officer. On the other hand, if the officer engaged in misconduct, the officials should take whatever disciplinary measures are justified, despite the potentially adverse consequences in the civil litigation.

Responding to the Complaint

The Rules of Civil Procedure permit a defendant to respond to a complaint either by way of an Answer, which is a pleading affirmatively admitting or denying the allegations in the Complaint, or by way of a Motion seeking Court rulings as to the content or viability of the Complaint.

Motion for a more definite statement: A motion for more definite statement, pursuant to Fed. R. Civ. P. 12(e), may be appropriate where a pleading is so vague or ambiguous that a party cannot reasonably be required to frame a responsive pleading. Rule 12(e) is designed to strike at unintelligibility rather than the want of detail. If the pleading meets the requirements of Rule 8, by fairly notifying the opposing party of the nature of the claim, a motion for a more definite statement will not be granted. *See* Fed. R.Civ.P. 8; 2A *Moore's Federal Practice* §12.18.

A motion for a more definite statement may be vital in defending many cases brought by *pro se* litigants, meaning those plaintiff's who represent themselves. Often *pro se* litigants, unfamiliar with the art of legal pleading, produce unintelligible complaints. The motion for a more definite statement may also be useful in multiple plaintiff/multiple defendant cases where the pleadings make it impossible to discern which allegations pertain to which defendants. In deciding whether to file a motion for a more definite statement, counsel should assess whether tactical advantages might be lost or gained by early exposure of weaknesses in plaintiff's case. It is often more advantageous to attack these shortcomings at the close of discovery by way of a Motion for Summary Judgment rather than give plaintiff the opportunity to redraft the pleadings.

Motion to strike: Rule 12(f) of the Federal Rules of Civil Procedure permits a party, or the court, upon its own initiative, to move for an order striking "from any pleading any insufficient defense or any redundant, immaterial, impertinent, or scandalous matter." A party must make the motion "within 20 days after the service of the pleadings upon that party." A motion to strike is disfavored by the federal judiciary and objectionable matter will not be stricken from a pleading if it has any bearing on the subject matter of the litigation. 2A *Moore's Federal Practice* § 12.21(2).

Although disfavored, counsel should consider moving to strike certain allegations which may harm the defendants if permitted to remain in the complaint. Such harm may occur if jurors are permitted to read the allegations, or if the press publishes articles based on the unfounded allegations, which press reports may in turn taint potential jurors. In excessive-force cases, allegations of unrelated violence or sexual misconduct not connected to the case at issue should be stricken. Any indecent or repulsive language will certainly be stricken upon a Motion.

Motion to dismiss: A defendant may move for dismissal of an action or claim against him in a federal district court for failure of the plaintiff to comply with the Federal Rules of Civil Procedure. Under the Federal Rules of Civil Procedure, a motion to dismiss may properly raise the defenses of lack of jurisdiction over the subject matter, lack of jurisdiction over the person, improper venue, insufficiency of process, insufficiency of service of process, failure to state a claim on which relief can be granted, and failure to properly join a party. The most significant Motion to Dismiss is that brought under Rule 12(b)(6), wherein the moving party asserts the complaint fails to state a claim for relief.

The Rule 12(b)(6) motion to dismiss tests the legal sufficiency of the complaint. Ordinarily the Court looks to the four corners of the complaint, however, if matters outside the pleadings are presented to and considered by the court, it may treat a Rule 12(b)(6) motion as a motion for summary judgment brought under Rule 56. In judging the sufficiency of a complaint, the court must accept the factual allegations in the complaint as true, construe them in the light most favorable to the plaintiff, and then determine if the complaint shows any set of facts which could entitle the plaintiff to relief.* *Gooley v. Mobil Oil Corp.*, 851 F. 2d 513, 514 (1st Cir. 1988). However, the court must "eschew any reliance on bold assertions, unsupportable conclusions and 'opprobrious epithets.'" *Chongris v. Board of Appeals of Town of Andover*, 811 F. 2d 36, 37 (lst Cir. 1987). A Rule 12(b)(6) dismissal is a judgment on the merits and res judicata barring later claims. *Stewart v. U.S. Bancorp*, 297 F.3d 953 (9th Cir. 2002).

To state a claim for section 1983 relief against a Municipality, the complaint must allege the violation was caused by a pattern, practice, policy or custom of the municipality. *Monell v. New York Department of Social Services*, 436 U.S. 658 (1978), *Oklahoma City v. Tuttle*, 471 U.S. 808 (1985). Conclusory, unspecific allegations unsupported by a factual foundation fail to meet the minimum pleading requirements for municipal liability under Section 1983. *Monell, supra*, at 694. "To allow otherwise would be tantamount to allowing suit to be filed on a respondeat superior basis." *Strauss v. City of Chicago*, 760 F.2d 765, 768 (7th Cir. 1985). Under *Monell*, municipalities cannot be held liable under section 1983 on a respondeat superior basis. *See* footnote 1 *supra*. A single act or decision may be sufficient to impose municipal liability only if made by a high level "policymaker." *Pembaur v. City of Cincinnati*, 475 U.S. 469. This official must have "final policymaking authority." *City of St. Louis v. Praprotnik*, 485 U.S. 112 (1988). A municipal policy of inadequate training of police officers, however, cannot be inferred from a single finding of excessive force, even if the officer acted egregiously in inflicting the injury. *City of Oklahoma v. Tuttle, supra.*

To state a claim for relief under Section 1983 for individual officers, a different standard applies. Essentially, in a civil rights action under Section 1983, the plaintiff must prove, by a preponderance of the evidence, that a person acting under color of state law deprived him of a Constitutional or federally protected right. *Tatro v. Kervin*, 41 F.3d 9, 14 (1st Cir. 1994). The plaintiff must identify a specific right derived from a specific provision of the Constitution or federal law. *Id.; see also,*

---

* There is some authority for the proposition that in civil rights cases, there is a heightened pleading standard. *See, e.g. Dartmouth Review v. Dartmouth College*, 889 F. 2d 13, 16 (1st Cir. 1989) (stating the need for plaintiffs to set forth factual allegations, either direct or circumstantial, regarding each element of a specific actionable legal theory "is perhaps greater where allegations of civil rights violations lie at the suit's core"); *see also Krohn v. United States*, 742 F. 2d 24, 31 (1st Cir. 1984) (given the Supreme Court's "strong condemnation of insubstantial suits against government officials" as expressed in *Harlow v. Fitzgerald*, 457 U.S. 800 (1982), "[a] plaintiff, before commencing suit, must be prepared with a prima facie case of defendant's knowledge of impropriety, actual or constructive"); *Albany v. Fridovich*, 862 F. Supp. 615, 620 n. 8 (D. Mass. 1994) (calling the First Circuit rule a "heightened standard for specificity in pleading").

Albright v. Oliver, 510 U.S. 266 (1994). Allegations that individual police officers acted negligently are not sufficient to state a claim under section 1983. *Daniels v. Williams*, 474 U.S. 327 (1986), *Davidson v. Cannon*, 474 U.S. 334 (1986).

Defense counsel should exercise restraint when contemplating a Motion to Dismiss for Failure to State a Claim for Relief. Federal courts liberally construe the pleadings, and in close cases will deny a Motion to Dismiss. Often then the Motion merely serves to educate plaintiff's counsel as to the weaknesses of plaintiff's case or as to defense strategy. Furthermore, even if the Complaint is defective in failing to state a claim for relief, under the Rules of Procedure, a plaintiff may amend the Complaint as of right prior to the filing of a responsive pleading. The Motion to Dismiss is not considered a "responsive pleading" for this purpose, thus the Motion may only prompt a corrective amendment to the Complaint.

There are, of course, certain circumstances where a Motion to Dismiss should be vigorously pursued. For instance, if plaintiff's counsel sues the current police chief or current municipal officials who were not in office at the time the incident occurred, a Motion to Dismiss as to those defendants may be filed. A claim for punitive damages against a municipality are subject to dismissal. Another possible basis for a motion to dismiss is the expiration of the statute of limitations. There is no express limitations period set forth in Section 1983, however, federal courts look to comparable state statutes of limitations. While the applicable statute of limitations is that of the forum state, federal law governs in determining which limitations statute of the forum state is to be applied. Because claims under section 1983 are best characterized as personal injury actions, the state statute governing personal injury actions usually controls. *Wilson v. Garcia*, 471 U.S. 261 (1985).

Answer and affirmative defenses: Assuming a motion to dismiss is not warranted or unsuccessful, the defendant must file an Answer to the Complaint, and include in that Answer any applicable affirmative defenses. The Answer typically requires the defendant to admit or deny each of the allegations of the Complaint with specificity. If uncertain as to any allegation, the answer must state that defendant is without knowledge to admit and therefore must deny the allegation at this time. Under the Rules of Civil Procedure, counsel's signature on the Answer certifies, among other things, that to the best of counsel's knowledge, after having made reasonable inquiry, the claims, defenses, and other legal contentions are warranted by existing law, and the denials of factual contentions are warranted on the evidence. *Fed.* R. Civ. P. 11. Federal common law and federal statutory immunities are affirmative defenses which must be pleaded by the defendant. *Harlow v. Fitzgerald*, 457 U.S. 800, 815 (1982). The case law pertaining to recovery for police misconduct is continually expanding, and it will be necessary for the attorney to research the current applicable substantive law prior to filing the answer to determine the availability of certain affirmative defenses. If pendent state law claims exist, counsel should plead any available affirmative defenses to each specific tort. Most police misconduct cases arise out of situations in which the initial contact between the officer and plaintiff ostensibly was for legitimate law enforcement purposes. In many cases, the municipality and individual officer will likely be able to raise as a defense the claim that the officer only used reasonable force to enforce the law and effect an arrest. It is recognized that a police officer has the right and the duty to use such force as is necessary to carry out his duties, and the defense of reasonable force, if established, would preclude any recovery by the plaintiff in an action under state law. The question as to whether the officer used reasonable force usually is a question of fact for the jury's determination, with the issue to be decided in the light of all the circumstances as they appeared to the officer at the time of the encounter in question.

The affirmative defense that the police officer acted in good faith during the incident should be pled. In claims alleging wrongful arrest, the existence of probable cause for the officer's challenged actions is an affirmative defense. The affirmative defenses of res judicata or collateral estoppel assert that a plaintiff's claims are barred because the claims were previously resolved against the plaintiff in a prior action involving the identical parties and claims. *See Allen v. McCurry*, 449 U.S. 90 (1980) (holding state court judgments in Section 1983 actions are binding and plaintiffs are precluded from re-litigating the same causes of action in federal court). For a municipal client, counsel should remember to raise the affirmative defense of the *Monell* standard that the acts complained of were not done pursuant to a municipal custom, policy or practice.

Qualified immunity is perhaps the most important affirmative defense to preserve. It may be helpful to briefly discuss the doctrine of qualified immunity. The law concerning immunity from liability distinguishes between "absolute" immunity (i.e. absolute judicial immunity for official acts of the judiciary) and "qualified" immunity (i.e. the good faith immunity for public officials performing discretionary functions). As it relates to the defense of police-misconduct claims, the doctrine of qualified immunity has given rise to a large body of case law and legal commentary. Under federal law, "government officials performing discretionary functions, generally are shielded from liability for civil damages insofar as their conduct does not violate clearly established statutory or constitutional rights of which a reasonable person would have known." *Harlow v. Fitzgerald*, 457 U.S. 800, 818 (1982). "Qualified immunity, which is a question of law, is an issue that is appropriately decided by the court during the early stages of the proceedings and should not be decided by the jury." *Tatro v. Kervin*, 41 F.3d 9, 15 (1st Cir. 1994); *see also Anderson v. Creighton*, 483 U.S. 635, 646 n.6 (1987) (motions for summary judgment based on qualified immunity should be favored). This is so because "[t]he entitlement is an immunity from suit rather than a mere defense to liability." *Mitchell v. Forsyth*, 472 U.S. 511, 526 (1985).

The standard for a government official (including police officers) seeking qualified immunity is "whether a reasonable official could have believed his actions were lawful in light of clearly established law." *Febus-Rodriguez v. Betancourt-Lebron*, 14 F.3d 87, 91 (1st Cir. 1994). The doctrine of qualified immunity "requires a constitutional right to be clearly established so that public officials are on notice that this conduct is in violation of that right." *Frazier v. Bailey*, 957 F.2d 920, 930 (1st. Cir. 1992). The focus should be not on the merits of the plaintiff's underlying claim, but instead on the objective legal reasonableness of the official's conduct as measured by reference to clearly established law and the information the official possessed at the time of the allegedly unlawful conduct. *Lowinger v. Broderick*, 50 F.3d 61, 65 (1st Cir. 1995). The qualified-immunity standard "gives ample room for mistaken judgments by protecting all but the plainly incompetent or those who knowingly violate the law." *Lowinger* at 65. The doctrine anticipates and accommodates "reasonable error...because officials should not err always on the side of caution" for fear of being sued. *Hunter v. Bryant*, 502 U.S. 224, 229 (1991) (internal citations omitted).

Prior to determining whether a constitutional right was "clearly established" at the time of the alleged violation, a court must first decide "whether the plaintiff has asserted a violation of a constitutional right at all." *Seigert v. Gilley*, 500 U.S. 226, 232, 111 S.Ct. 1789, 1793, 114 L.Ed.2d 277 (1991). As a prerequisite to that threshold decision, a plaintiff must state with particularity the exact nature of the constitutional infringement alleged so the court can properly focus its efforts. Merely stating a constitutional provision will not suffice: "[t]he right to due process of law is quite clearly established..., and thus there is a sense in which any action that violates that Clause (no matter how unclear it may be that the particular action is a violation) violates a clearly established right....But if the test of 'clearly established law' were to be applied at this level of generality, it would bear no relationship to the 'objective legal reasonableness' that is the touchstone of the qualified immunity inquiry." *Anderson v. Creighton*, 483 U.S. at 639 (1987); *see also, Borucki v. Ryan*, 827 F.2d 836, 838 (1st Cir. 1987) ("it is not sufficient for a court to ascertain in a general sense that the alleged right existed").

In the context of a police-shooting case, the constitutionality of the use of deadly force incident to arrest depends solely on whether the officer's conduct was "objectively reasonable" under all of the facts and circumstances confronting him/her. *Graham v. Connor*, 490 U.S. 386, 397 (1989); *see also Napier v. Town of Windham*, 187 F.3d 177, 183-184 (1st Cir. 1999); *Roy v. Lewiston*, 42 F.3d 691, 694 (1st Cir. 1994). The reasonableness of an officer's use of force must be judged from the perspective of a reasonable officer on the scene, rather than with the 20/20 vision of hindsight. *See Graham*, 490 U.S. at 396. The Supreme Court's standard of reasonableness is "generous to the police in cases where potential danger, emergency conditions or other exigent circumstances are present." *Roy, supra* 42 F.3d at 695. "The calculus of reasonableness must embody allowance for the fact that officers are often forced to make split-second judgments—in situations that are tense, uncertain, and rapidly evolving—about the amount of force that is necessary in a particular situation." *Graham*, 490 U.S. at 396-97. The First Circuit has interpreted *Graham* "to surround the police who make these on-the-spot choices in dangerous situations with a fairly wide zone of protection in close cases." *Roy*, 42 F.3d at 695; *see also Medeiros v. Town of Dracut*, 21 F. Supp. 2d 82 (D.Mass. 1998) (summary judgment for police officer on qualified immunity grounds in shooting of unarmed suspect). Consequently, courts in the First Circuit do not "second-guess" officers, even if, in retrospect, a situation could have been handled differently. *See St. Hilaire v. City of Laconia*, 71 F.3d 20, 28 (1st Cir. 1995). Qualified immunity must operate in this case "to protect officers from the sometimes 'hazy border' between excessive and acceptable force, and to ensure that before they are subjected to suit, officers are on notice their conduct is unlawful." *Saucier v. Katz*, 533 U.S. 194, 206 (2001).

Discovery

Case investigation and informal discovery: Just as it is important, at an early stage, to know the law applicable to the case, early investigation of the incident is critical. The attorney should not rely on the police department's investigation alone. For example, witnesses should be interviewed by the attorney to determine credibility and strength of testimony. A visit to the scene of the incident with the involved officers is most helpful. If possible and when appropriate, the scene should be viewed with defense experts and an opportunity provided to the expert to talk and question the officer (bearing in mind that any such conversations may, or may not, ultimately be discoverable).

Claims alleging police misconduct generally arise out of a single confrontation between the plaintiff and the police. The plaintiff and the police officer involved typically give dramatically different versions of the facts surrounding the incident, and often there are no other available witnesses–at least disinterested witnesses–to the encounter. In this setting, the attorney's investigation may reveal more than one version of the "facts," and evidence that may be susceptible of two different interpretations, one favoring the plaintiff and the other benefitting the defendants. The defense attorney should seek evidence tending to corroborate the police officer's version of the facts, and evidence most likely to decrease the plaintiff's credibility. Counsel should also search for facts concerning the municipality's negligence in the operation of the police department and the supervision and training of its officers.

Locating and interviewing witnesses: By the time an answer has been filed and responses to defendant's interrogatories and requests for production have been received from plaintiff, witnesses will have been identified from two sources: the client, and the plaintiff's discovery responses. Counsel will have been aware of some of the witnesses from the beginning. These will be witnesses that the client knew because their names were obtained at the scene of the incident. The second source will be the plaintiff's answers to interrogatories. When plaintiff's answers to interrogatories are received they may reveal the names of people who witnessed the incident, but were unknown to the officer. There may also be names of individuals who will say that there were prior incidents of misconduct by the officer or prior similar shootings by other police officers in the same department.

From the outset, the attorney should make a list of all witnesses and their anticipated testimony, along with current addresses and phone numbers. Some easy sources to find addresses are the water department records or other utilities. An often overlooked source of information is the phone book. The defendant police officer also should be asked to help locate witnesses by sources to which he has access. If witnesses cannot be located, counsel should hire a private investigator to find them.

Important witnesses should be personally interviewed by counsel. Another important, but often overlooked aspect of informal discovery is taking statements from witnesses. Although counsel should anticipate encountering some difficulty in locating and obtaining cooperation from witnesses, persistence and perseverance pays off in this key area of discovery. Before any initial contact is made to seek an interview, it is advisable for defense counsel to learn as much as possible about the attitudes and background of each person sought to be questioned. It is probably best for a private investigator, rather than defense counsel to contact a potentially hostile witness. An investigator may seem much less an "enemy," or authority figure, to a lay witness who is noticeably antagonistic to the defendant.

Any interview by defense counsel ordinarily should be witnessed by a third person. It is helpful to take someone along, such as an investigator to act as a witness to any statements made. The third person may also document the fact that the witness would not cooperate if the witness refuses to talk. Also, if the witness consents to an interview but refuses to sign a sworn statement or allow the interview to be recorded, another individual is available to impeach the witness in court should the witness later change his/her version. The third person protects counsel from becoming a potential witness at trial.

If the witnesses are neutral, they probably will not be hesitant to talk. Once a cooperative witness is found and an interview begun, the attorney should explain to the witness the purpose of the visit, the nature of the lawsuit, and the reason a statement is taken and recorded, assuming the interviewee consents to some form of making a permanent record of the interview. The interviewee should be told that it is necessary to preserve the witness' testimony in the event his or her memory fades. Of course, counsel also hopes to obtain a record for later use in impeaching the witness and attacking his or her credibility, if necessary.

Viewing scene and preserving evidence: There is no substitute for seeing the actual physical evidence or scene of a shooting. Even though an attorney can read a description of the scene and perhaps get a mental picture, it is far superior to have personally viewed it. Once counsel has a clear mental picture of the scene, and the physical evidence associated with the incident, it is much easier to convey that to the jury.

Photography, of course, is one of the best means of preserving physical evidence in place, and adequate photographic coverage of the evidence relating to the incident is a necessity. The key to this process is compiling a comprehensive photographic record of the scene of the incident. Typically, the district attorney's office will have investigated the incident, and can provide defense counsel with accurate photographs taken shortly after the incident. The photos will put the jury at the scene and show it what the officer faced at the time of the incident.

Videotapes of the scene and even videotaped interviews of key witnesses, made contemporaneous with the incident, can be invaluable. If there was media coverage of the incident or its immediate aftermath, it is necessary to obtain copies of any existing television videotapes or newspaper photographs. In some instances the police department itself may have videotaped the incident. Counsel should be cautious in relying upon the lighting of the scene as portrayed in videos or photographs, which often distort the actual lighting at the time of the incident.

Formal discovery: There are a number of mechanisms for discovery equally available to both plaintiffs and defendants. The Rule governing the scope of discovery in federal court provides that "[p]arties may obtain discovery regarding any matter, not privileged, that is relevant to the claim or defense of any party, including the existence, description, nature, custody, condition, and location of any books, documents, or other tangible things and the identity and location of persons having knowledge of any discoverable matter." *See* Fed. R. Civ. P. 26(b)(1). The rule further provides an expansive definition "relevant" in that " [r]elevant information need not be admissible at the trial if the discovery appears reasonably calculated to lead to the discovery of admissible evidence." *Id.* The mechanisms available for formal discovery include depositions, interrogatories, production of documents and things, entry upon land for inspection, physical and mental examination of persons, and requests for admissions. This section will address the more significant aspects of formal discovery.

Effective discovery is critical to defense of section 1983 actions. These cases are fact intensive and witness credibility is often a critical factor in jury's determination of issues relating to fact resolution and state of mind. Generally, counsel should undertake written discovery in the form of interrogatories and requests for production of documents prior to the

taking of deposition. Interrogatories are useful for background information and claimed damages, but are not as effective in eliciting detailed
factual information as are depositions. Favorable deposition and
interrogatory responses may often be followed up by requests for
admissions. It is sometimes an extremely effective deposition technique
to have plaintiff disclose each and every material fact underlying each
and every allegation in the complaint. Contention interrogatories may
also be used in this manner.

Discovery Propounded to Plaintiff

Interrogatories: Interrogatories should be submitted to the plaintiff
in the initial stages of the case. These should be based on a careful
review of the specific allegations of plaintiff's complaint and should focus
on the factual basis for each allegation. In addition, interrogatories
should inquire into the plaintiff's background, including previous encounters with the police, his or her alleged injuries, and any expert
witnesses or witnesses to the incident.

One potentially objectionable area of inquiry concerns prior
encounters with the police not leading to convictions. Plaintiff's counsel
may object on the ground that mere encounters are not relevant or
discoverable. However, prior convictions, as well as misconduct not
leading to conviction, may be admissible evidence for impeachment
purposes. The extent to which a witness' criminal record and other
misconduct may be used to impeach him varies widely among jurisdictions. The current view under the Federal Rules is that it is a legitimate
purpose of discovery to obtain information for use on cross- examination
and for the impeachment of witnesses, and it can be successfully argued
that these items are relevant and discoverable in this type of litigation
to show bias, prejudice or motivation in filing the lawsuit.

Interrogatories are helpful in identifying the plaintiff's background.
They may be used to inquire how plaintiff is currently employed, his job
history, former addresses, and educational background. Questions as to
the plaintiff's prior arrest history, whether he has any convictions, or has
had any type of altercations with police in the past are important. The
filing of prior civil suits or any claims against anyone for money in the
past may also lead to admissible evidence.

Of course the incident giving rise to the complaint should be the
subject of interrogatories. Interrogatories should inquire as to the name
and address of the eyewitnesses regarding this incident and a summary
of their anticipated testimony. Although the federal rules provide for

automatic disclosure of expert witnesses, it may be useful to pose interrogatories as to the name and address of any expert witnesses and a summary of their anticipated testimony. Identifying damages is often the most fruitful area for interrogatories. Regarding the plaintiff's injuries, interrogatories should ask the name and address of each doctor, hospital and or other medical health care provider, and specify the dates of treatment, the nature of treatment, and the prognosis for future treatment. In a police shooting case where there is a fatality, the damages interrogatories may focus on evidence of claims for lost income and future earning capacity.

There are a number of other areas of inquiry for defendants' interrogatories to plaintiff. The interrogatories should ask plaintiff to specify the factual basis for allegations in the complaint. For example, if the complaint alleges a lack of training, an interrogatory should ask what is the factual basis for the allegation of insufficient training, and ask plaintiff identify what witnesses or documents will support this allegation. Similarly, if the complaint contains a *Monell* claim against the municipality, counsel should serve an interrogatory as to the factual basis for the custom or policy, including the names of any prior "victims" of the custom and how the "policy" resulted in unconstitutional conduct. *See Monell v. Dept. of Social Svcs.*, 436 U.S. 658 (1978) (discussed *supra* in the section entitled "A Typical Lawsuit Arising from a Police Shooting).

Once answers to these interrogatories are obtained, the attorney should forward a copy to the clients and, if possible, schedule a meeting to discuss the interrogatory answers with them. Many of the names or incidents referred to in the answers will not be familiar to counsel and can be explained by the client. If eyewitness names are given in the interrogatory answers, the attorney should locate them and, if possible, take sworn statements from them. If prior allegations of misconduct are referred to in the answers, it will be necessary to obtain from the police department the reports and documentation on these prior incidents.

Requests for production of documents: The attorney should request all relevant documents and other tangible evidence from plaintiff's counsel. Defense counsel should request all physical evidence in the possession of plaintiff or plaintiff's counsel regarding this incident. The attorney should specifically request any photographs of the scene, photographs of the plaintiff's injuries, photographs of defendants and photographs of any other relevant evidence.

The request should include all of the plaintiff's medical bills and medical records. However, the attorney should not rely exclusively upon the request for production because plaintiff may not have or may refuse to release all of the relevant records. Counsel may need to obtain copies directly from the doctors via an authorization from plaintiff, a subpoena to the medical provider's Keeper of the Records, or a court order. Copies of the plaintiff's tax returns should be requested if lost income or impairment of earning capacity is alleged. Counsel should also request any documents evidencing plaintiff's substantive claims in the complaint, such as prior misconduct, a "policy" on the part of the city, or inadequate training of the officer. In shooting cases, it is often important to obtain the articles of clothing worn by the plaintiff, if these were not seized as evidence after the shooting. Similarly, if a vehicle is involved it may be important to examine the plaintiff's automobile and photograph it. If the plaintiff does not possess photographs of the vehicle, counsel will have to obtain them, by a court order if necessary.

Requests for admissions: Rule 36 provides a procedure by which a party may request another party to admit, for purposes of the pending action only, the truth of any matters within the scope of discovery set out in the request, including the genuineness of any documents described in the request. Rule 36 has not been used as much as some of the other discovery rules, although it is a valuable time saver when properly used. Its function is to define and limit the matters in controversy between the parties. The rule is intended to expedite the trial and to relieve the parties of the cost of proving facts that will not be disputed at trial, the truth of which is known to the parties or can be ascertained by reasonable inquiry.

In civil rights cases, requests for admissions are often employed by plaintiff's counsel to require the defendants to admit or deny elements of proof in the case such as that the individual police officer was acting under the color of state law at the time of the incident. Defense counsel may use the requests as a means to narrow some of the facts for trial (i.e. requesting an admission that the plaintiff was speeding prior to a traffic stop) or to alleviate burdens of producing evidence at trial (i.e. requesting an admission that plaintiff was terminated from his employment may obviate the need to call witnesses to prove this). Most often, however, the requests for admission are employed as a means to verify the genuineness of documents to avoid having to lay an evidentiary foundation for the admission of the documents at trial.

Responding to Plaintiff's Discovery Requests

Interrogatories: At the outset, the attorney should explain to the client the importance of answering discovery inquiries correctly and truthfully. It will be necessary to explain the adverse results that an incomplete or untruthful answer could have during litigation. Responding incorrectly to an answer to interrogatories under oath also can have a severely adverse impact on credibility. On the other hand, there is no necessity to volunteer information, and discovery requests should be read fairly but narrowly.

Most plaintiffs' attorneys put forth interrogatories similar to those used by the defendant. For example, usually the plaintiff's counsel will ask background questions on the officer, just as the defendant will of the plaintiff. It is important to explain to the client the necessity for sitting down and taking time to answer these, thinking of all the things in his background that are responsive. For example, if an interrogatory inquires what training the police officer has had, it is of vital importance that he sit down and recall all his training. If the person cannot recall, he needs to obtain all records to refresh his memory.

A second area of inquiry from the plaintiff's attorney will usually be regarding the witnesses to this incident. All known witnesses should be listed, as well as stating that discovery is not complete and additional witnesses will be listed as they are discovered. Another area of interest to the plaintiff that may be the subject of interrogatories involves prior instances of alleged misconduct on the part of the officer. Proof that the officer "had a propensity for violence" or that he has committed other acts of "police brutality" in the past potentially may be the most damaging evidence the plaintiff can present. Such evidence not only may persuade an otherwise doubting jury that the plaintiff is more worthy of belief than the officer, but also that the municipality was negligent in hiring or retaining the officer, or in otherwise failing to take appropriate steps to prevent a recurrence of past acts of misconduct. In jurisdictions with a liberal discovery approach, it is best to list all the prior allegations of misconduct and later try to exclude them from evidence by way of a motion in limine. If the jurisdiction has a more conservative discovery approach, it may be advisable to object on grounds of burdensomeness, irrelevancy, and prejudice in answering this interrogatory and seek a protective order. Counsel should remember that any information given to the plaintiff's attorney concerning dates and names of prior incidents of misconduct must be thoroughly investigated in advance. This will enable counsel to defuse these prior incidents of misconduct or prior allegations of misconduct before the plaintiff can turn them into evidence that is damaging to the defense.

Responding to document requests: Under the Federal Rules, parties have obligations to make required disclosures, which include initial disclosures providing "a copy of, or a description by category and location of, all documents, data compilations, and tangible things that are in the possession, custody, or control of the party and that the disclosing party may use to support its claims or defenses, unless solely for impeachment." *See* Fed. R. Civ. P. 26(a)(1)(B). As a practical matter, rather than providing mere descriptions of the relevant documents, often counsel simply produces copies of the documents. For the most part, the so-called "automatic disclosure" rules have had their intended effect of eliminating the adversary conduct regarding discovery and keeping the parties focused on advocacy concerning the merits of the case.

This is not to say that there are no longer disputes concerning disclosures or production of documents. These disputes often arise when issues of privileged documents are implicated. Discovery in section 1983 police misconduct cases frequently involves requests for information conditionally privileged under state law, such as police officer service records, citizen and officer complaints against individual officers and intra-departmental confidential correspondence. Discovery disputes frequently arise from confusion as to whether state or federal law governs the privilege. In section 1983 cases (or any civil rights case brought under federal statutes), questions of privilege are resolved by federal law. "Questions of privilege that arise in the course of the adjudication of federal rights are 'governed by the principles of the common law as they may be interpreted by the courts of the United States in the light of reason and experience.'" *United States v. Zolin*, 491 U.S. 554, 562 (1989) (quoting Fed. R. Evid. 501). As one Court stated, "[i]t obviously would make no sense to permit state law to determine what evidence is discoverable in cases brought pursuant to federal statutes whose central purpose is to protect citizens from abuse of power by state and local authorities. If state law controlled, state authorities could effectively insulate themselves from constitutional norms simply by developing privilege doctrine [making it] impossible for plaintiffs to... prosecute their claims." *Kelly v. City of San Jose*, 114 F.R.D. 653, 656 (N.D. Cal. 1987).

Even if there is no federal privilege protecting the defendant's sensitive records from disclosure, counsel should still seek protection arguing the federal courts should recognize applicable state privileges as a matter of comity. Courts often adopt a balancing test to determine which, if any, police records should be disclosed. Categories of competing interests in Section 1983 discovery proceedings include: interest of law enforcement, privacy interest of police officers or citizens who provide information to or file complaints against police officers, interests of civil rights plaintiffs, the policies underlying the national civil rights laws, and the needs of the judiciary.

When balancing the claim of privilege against the opposing party's need for discovery in a civil rights case, the federal court will consider a number of factors. As set forth by the District of Columbia Circuit Court of Appeals, relevant factors are "(1) the extent to which disclosure will thwart governmental processes by discouraging citizens from giving the government information; (2) the impact upon persons who have given information of having their identities disclosed; (3) the degree to which governmental self-evaluation and consequent program improvement will be chilled by disclosure; (4) whether the information sought is factual data or evaluative summary; (5) whether the party seeking discovery is an actual or potential defendant in any criminal proceeding either pending or reasonably likely to follow from the incident in question; (6) whether the police investigation has been completed; (7) whether any interdepartmental disciplinary proceedings have arisen or may arise from the investigation; (8) whether the plaintiff's suit is non-frivolous and brought in good faith; (9) whether the information sought is available through other discovery or from other sources; and (10) the importance of the information sought to the plaintiff's case." *Tuite v. Henry*, 98 F.3d 1411, 1417 (D.C. Cir. 1996) (citing *Frankenhauser v. Rizzo*, 59 F.R.D. 339, 344 (E.D.Pa.1973)). Counsel should keep these factors in mind when invoking any privilege. Should counsel strenuously object to disclosure despite the plaintiff's demonstrated need for the disputed documents, the defense attorney may do well to request an "in camera" inspection of the documents by the court prior to disclosure. The Court's inspection of the documents may be sufficient to preclude or limit their disclosure.

An advisable middle ground for counsel to seek concerning the disclosure of potentially privileged documents is to persuade plaintiff's counsel to agree to a protective order prohibiting re-disclosure. Often defense counsel recognizes that the disputed documents are highly relevant to the plaintiff's case, yet does not wish the documents to be published to the press, disclosed to non-parties, or used as fodder in unrelated litigation. A legitimate fear exists that members of the plaintiff's bar may circulate damaging documents for use in other police misconduct claims, particularly where there is an allegation of "custom, policy or practice" liability on behalf of the municipality. Plaintiff's counsel may wish to avoid a contentious discovery dispute and agree to assent to the entry of a protective order prohibiting the disclosure of the confidential information to anyone except parties, their attorneys, witnesses and experts. The assented-to order may further provide that upon termination of the case, the original and all copies of the documents, and portions of the deposition transcripts and deposition exhibits containing the confidential information, shall be returned to the defendant.

As a practical matter it is extremely difficult to successfully resist discovery of most police records in section 1983 actions. In cases asserting municipal liability by way of a "custom, policy or practice," the focus of discovery is often on rules, regulations, orders, policies, and citizen complaints of police conduct "similar" to that alleged in the action. Complaints of "similar conduct," though ordinarily not admissible against individual defendants, will be a necessary part of the action against the municipality, and are thus frequently ordered disclosed to plaintiff, and may be ruled admissible at trial.[*] Potentially a defendant may be required to conduct a series of 'mini trials' during the actual trial, to determine the adequacy of the investigation and the underlying facts of each civilian complaint file disclosed to plaintiff.

Depositions: The deposition is one of the most potent, best recognized, and often utilized discovery tools. One of the critical steps in preparing the defense is to depose the plaintiff. Other persons whose depositions must be taken include adverse witnesses who have not been previously interviewed and given sworn statements, and potentially the plaintiff's expert on police procedures.

Preparation is vital for conducting an effective deposition. The preparation should include having propounded the discovery requests discussed above and become thoroughly familiar with the responses. Defense counsel should prepare a chronology of events, and also identify and organize deposition exhibits. Counsel should then prepare an outline of the areas to cover, carefully thinking about the order of questions. For the key issues, it may be helpful to draft specific questions.

---

[*] This is one of the bases for moving to bifurcate the trial as discussed below.

Deposing plaintiff: There are multiple goals in the taking of plaintiff's deposition. Primarily counsel should seek to obtain the plaintiff's version. In a police misconduct case, the defense attorney wants to obtain every fact that the plaintiff has to support his or her claim, including the name of every witness who has information and all documents that plaintiff contends supports the claim. Questioning should be designed to limit the plaintiff from later adding additional facts or allegations to the case. Thus, after asking the specifics about each fact. counsel should confirm the completeness of the answer by inquiring whether there is anything else.

Another goal of the deposition is to evaluate the plaintiff as a witness. The deposition is an opportunity to gauge how a jury will react to the plaintiff and the plaintiff's version. The defense attorney should pay attention to body language and how plaintiff answers the questions. Factors such as whether the plaintiff is easily provoked, rambles, listens poorly to questions, or has disjointed answers may affect the prospects for success on the merits. In contrast, if plaintiff's testimony is persuasive, or the plaintiff pleasant and helpful, it may encourage a settlement. The deposition also is an opportunity to evaluate the plaintiff's lawyer as to both the lawyer's style and knowledge of the case.

Substantive goals of the deposition are to get admissions from the plaintiff to things that are helpful to the defendant's case and set up a motion for summary judgment. Depositions are also used to lock in the facts by having the plaintiff testify to things counsel already knows and which the plaintiff cannot deny. Counsel should seek to identify impeachment material, which may vary from implausible narrations of fact to inconsistencies with prior statements. It is also important to establish what the witness does not know and to elicit this testimony to preclude plaintiff from later asserting memories that just came to mind. In addition, depositions may lay the foundation for admissibility of documents, to eliminate authenticity disputes later.

Other collateral goals of the deposition may be to test the strength of defendant's case by exploring plaintiff's knowledge of facts that favor the defendant and determining if the plaintiff has any contrary evidence. Confronting the plaintiff and the opposing counsel with facts that are harmful to the plaintiff's case may also be used as a tool in encouraging the other side to settle. The stress of submitting to depositions can have the benefit of making plaintiff less inclined to pursue the case through trial. Counsel should not hesitate to ask hard questions, or questions which may embarrass plaintiff or expose weaknesses. Making the plaintiff confront inconsistencies or admit that he or she does not have support for a particular claim can be a very effective deposition technique.

As for the conduct of plaintiff's deposition, counsel should begin with general questions on the plaintiff's background and then make inquiry into the incident that gave rise to the lawsuit and the alleged damages. In preliminary questioning, the attorney should explore previous encounters with the police, especially arrests and convictions. Then the attorney should take plaintiff through the entire events of the day of the incident that gave rise to the lawsuit, culminating with inquiry regarding the incident itself. Counsel should address events on the date of incident leading up to the critical event—what had plaintiff been doing earlier in the day and where was plaintiff coming from and going. When discussing the critical events, a detailed inquiry should be made. It is defense counsel's job to pin the plaintiff down in detail on everything that happened that night. It is important to remember that at trial the plaintiff may tell a different story. In addition, any friends who were with plaintiff during the incident may testify to a different version of what happened. The same is true with respect to damages. Occasionally, plaintiffs will allege damage to their reputation and impairment of earning capacity. Once they are committed to these two items of damages, this will open the door for inquiry into their reputation before the shooting, as well as their earning capacity before the shooting.

Although the rules permit parties to the case to be present during depositions, counsel should hesitate before having the individually named officers present for plaintiff's deposition. Defense attorneys want to elicit admissions from the plaintiff that may be helpful to the case, and the presence of the officers may make the plaintiff less likely to narrate long answers or concede unfavorable points. Of course, it is sometimes helpful to have the client present at the plaintiff's deposition, or any other deposition, for a variety of reasons. The officer's familiarity with the facts of the case may provide insight to the answers given by the plaintiff and may be able to suggest further questioning as a result. The officer's attendance may "pressure" the plaintiff to be more forthright in his or her testimony or may be used to "rattle" the plaintiff, if that is the objective. The officer may want to assess the credibility and appearance of a particular witness. The officer's attendance at the deposition of a key adverse witness may open the officer's eyes as to the weakness or strength of the case and result in a more reasonable attitude toward settlement. In addition, the officer's attendance may signal the seriousness with which the case is being treating. The officer's attendance will also enable him or her to learn of the details of plaintiff's version of events prior to the officer's deposition.

After a thorough deposition of the plaintiff, everything plaintiff can testify to at trial should be known. There should be no surprises. In addition, there should be ample material from which to cross-examine him, both as to the believability of his story and comparing his version to the testimony of the other witnesses.

Deposing non-party witnesses: Essentially, the same approach taken in deposing plaintiff should be taken in deposing adverse witnesses. Counsel should go through the same line of questioning, beginning with background questions, leading up to questions about the critical events of the incident, and ending with questions about the witness' knowledge of any "policy" on the part of the city or prior misconduct on the part of the officer. It may be preferable to obtain a sworn statement from the witness in lieu of a deposition to preclude opposing counsel from interposing objections, or manipulating the testimony or cross-examination. As a practical matter, however, most adverse witnesses will not give such a sworn statement.

An additional area for questioning non-party witnesses concerns the reputation and background of the plaintiff. In particular, counsel should inquire as to whether the witness used drugs or was drinking on the night of the incident or if he knows whether plaintiff did. Regardless of what a witness says, the attorney should always probe for some bit of information that might be helpful to the client. When this proves impossible to get from a witness who is extremely hostile toward the client, counsel should seek to expose the obvious bias of the witness and to pin down the witness on every factual detail surrounding the events in question. The attorney will then be well armed to impeach the antagonistic witness at trial. Bias on the part of the witness is readily apparent if the witness refuses to say anything that might favor the defendant. The more objective testimony of other witnesses, and circumstantial evidence that contradicts the absolute pronouncements of the prejudiced witness will further reduce the credibility of such a witness. If the witness being deposed would not talk to defense counsel before the deposition, the attorney should ask him why he would not consent to an interview, and if he talked to plaintiff's counsel to establish bias.

Defending the police officer's deposition: Equally important as deposing the plaintiff and plaintiff's witnesses is the preparation of the defendant police officer for being deposed by the plaintiff's counsel. It is critical that the officer be thoroughly counseled on what to expect and thoroughly familiar with all the relevant evidence in the case. A skillful plaintiff's counsel is going to want to take the deposition of the defendant police officer immediately after collecting all relevant documentary information. Prior to presenting the officer for deposition, he should be thoroughly advised of the potential questions from plaintiff's attorney. He should have read any report of the incident he prepared and be thoroughly familiar with it. He should have read any other witness reports, and any other documents generated by a shooting-review board or by supervisors concerning their investigation into the incident. Likewise, the officer should be thoroughly familiar with the allegations of the complaint, and the theory of the plaintiff's case.

It is best if all alternative courses of conduct for the incident are discussed with the police officer prior to his deposition so that he can explain why he acted as he did and not in some other manner. The attorney should run the officer through a series of questions to see how he handles them. In essence, the defense counsel must become a "devil's advocate" and play the part of the plaintiff's attorney in preparing the client for deposition. If possible, it may be helpful to actually take a practice deposition of the client.

It is also important to advise the client prior to the deposition about some general rules of depositions. For example, the attorney should explain the basic format of a deposition and how it is used, emphasizing that the client will be under oath and must tell the truth, and how damaging it can be if he shades the truth or gives a wrong answer and tries to change his version later. On the other hand, the attorney also should explain to the officer that while it is imperative that he tell the truth, he does not need to volunteer anything. The officer should make his answers as short as possible, confining the response to the question asked, while at the same time telling the truth. The officer can elaborate on the answers at trial in front of a jury.

Many officers are trained and experienced in testifying in criminal cases, and may take the deposition lightly. The officer should be made to understand that testimony in a civil case is significantly different from a criminal case. Use of police jargon should be avoided. The police officer should also be advised ahead of time that the plaintiff, as a party to the case, has a right to be present during the conduct of the deposition. In addition, the witness needs to understand that the plaintiff's attorney may try to get him angry or confused. If the officer does not understand a question, he should be told to say so and not guess. The plaintiff's attorney will be forced to repeat or rephrase the question. Likewise, if the officer begins to get angry, he should request to take a break, because a loss of temper, may harm his credibility and his clarity. If the officer follows these simple rules, he will do a better job of testifying during the deposition and make a better and more believable witness.

Expert discovery: The Federal Rules of Evidence permit opinion testimony from qualified experts in certain circumstances. "If scientific, technical, or other specialized knowledge will assist the trier of fact to understand the evidence or to determine a fact in issue, a witness qualified as an expert by knowledge, skill, experience, training, or education, may testify thereto in the form of an opinion or otherwise." *See* Fed. R. Evid. 702. Rule 702 has two main policy goals: first, to permit expert testimony to promote the triers-of-fact's search for truth by helping them to understand other evidence or determine the facts in dispute; and second, to preserve the trier of fact's traditional powers to decide the meaning of evidence and the credibility of witnesses. The benefits of expert testimony are evident by the Rules of Evidence Advisory Committee statement that "An intelligent evaluation of facts is often difficult or impossible without the application of some scientific, technical, or other specialized knowledge." On the other hand, a potential danger of expert testimony is that experts are not subject to the requirement that their testimony be based on personal knowledge. The rationale permitting admission of the testimony is that an expert's testimony still will have a reliable basis, but in something other than personal knowledge. The problem behind this rationale is that often experts testify about complex and obscure matters concerning which neither the judge nor jury may be capable of critically evaluating the reliability. Another danger is that expert opinions may pertain to the ultimate issues in the case, and the jury may improperly defer to the expert opinion, despite the judge's instructions not to do so.

It may be helpful to briefly address the landmark Supreme Court decision concerning the admissibility of expert testimony in *Daubert v. Merrell Dow Pharmaceuticals*, 509 U.S. 579, 113 S.Ct. 2786 (1993). The *Daubert* decision focused on the appropriate analysis trial courts must undertake in scrutinizing expert testimony under the Federal Rules of Evidence. Rule 702 of the Federal Rules of Evidence provides, "if scientific, technical or other specialized knowledge will assist the trier of fact to understand the evidence or to determine a fact in issue, a witness qualified as an expert by knowledge, skill, experience, training or education, may testify thereto in the form of opinion or otherwise." The *Daubert* court pronounced a framework for the trial judge to act as gatekeeper to screen purportedly scientific evidence for the purpose of ensuring that scientific evidence or testimony is not only relevant, but reliable under Rule 702. The *Daubert* court explained that "scientific" as provided in the rule implies grounding in the methods of science, and the term "knowledge" implies more than subjective belief or unsupported speculation. Thus experts in a police shooting case must have a basis upon which to offer any opinion evidence.

An expert on either side of a case should be competent, informed and objective. The expert should be qualified by education and experience to give opinions not just on "police misconduct," but on the particular problem involved, whether it be jail deaths, excessive force, swat tactics, or other police action. The expert should possess all pertinent information on the incident, the parties, the training and supervision of officers and any other relevant issues. The expert should give the impression of being an objective, knowledgeable third party, and not an advocate.

Preparation of the defense expert begins with his selection early in the litigation. Bearing in mind the qualities enumerated above, the best defense expert is one who is at ease with his competence in the area of expertise to be addressed. Therefore, the attorney should select an individual who is qualified by education and experience. The expert should furnish defense counsel with his resume, list of representative clients, a sampling of other cases in which he was involved, and any relevant publications. The expert should be furnished with as much evidence and information as he requests, bearing in mind that all such information, whether written or verbal, is discoverable. Written contact between the expert and counsel should be limited and the expert should be advised that his notes, items underlined or jotted in the margins of exhibits, as well as his entire file would be subject to discovery if the expert is testifying at trial.

The expert should be advised of the defense theory and theme of the case to determine whether the lawyer's view is practical. The defense expert may be utilized to outline for counsel necessary items for early investigation; to research and provide background on the plaintiff's expert; visit the scene and review facts with the involved officer; review all depositions, exhibits, and physical evidence from an expert-professional standpoint; critique the officer's conduct, offer alternative methods which could have been used, point out weaknesses in the case; and provide background from personal knowledge or experience of similar incidents.

The most frequent source of expert testimony in litigation is that of medical experts. The nature, extent, and permanence of plaintiff's injuries is often the subject of expert opinion by both sides of a lawsuit. In a police-shooting case, there are a number of other areas where defense counsel may seek expert testimony. In a garden-variety Fourth Amendment lawsuit, such as one alleging excessive use of force during a misdemeanor arrest, there may be no need for expert testimony as the jury is competent to determine if the force used in effecting the arrest was reasonable. Where there is the use of specialized weapons during the arrest, such as night-sticks, pepper spray, or police dogs, expert testimony may be used to assess the propriety of the force used. *See Kopf v. Skyrm*, 993 F.2d 374 (4th Cir. 1993) (The decision discusses the admissibility of expert testimony on the use of slapstick and police dog). As for use of lethal force, the ultimate question of reasonableness of the use of force is one for the jury to decide. Case law does support the admission of expert testimony to testify on subsidiary issues such as prevailing standards for the use of lethal force. *See Samples v. City of Atlanta*, 916 F.2d 1548 (11th Cir. 1991). If there is a claim against the municipality, there is a need for expert testimony as to whether the police department's recruitment, training, supervision, or discipline meets the generally accepted standards in those areas. If there are commonplace police activities at issue, such as executing search warrants, using police pursuits, or preventing custodial suicides, expert testimony may be admissible to describe how law enforcement agencies throughout the country address these issues.

In the context of the phenomenon of SbC, the use of experts may be sought by both plaintiff and defendant in a civil-rights lawsuit. Defense counsel may seek to admit expert testimony to explain the SbC phenomenon to substantiate the police officer's testimony that the suspect's conduct escalated the need of lethal force. In contrast, plaintiff's counsel may seek expert testimony concerning the prevalence of the phenomenon to argue that the police department's training (or lack thereof) concerning how to respond to such issues was Constitutionally inadequate. Other experts often employed in police-shooting cases are those qualified to testify as to visual perception in low light levels, and/or the psychological and physiological impact of stress on police marksmanship.

Defense counsel should consider deposing plaintiff's expert only after the expert has completed all work on the case and has formed an opinion. This usually occurs after the close of discovery and shortly prior to trial. In federal court, expert disclosures are governed by the Federal Rules of

Civil Procedure, and are required to be made at least 90 days before trial. *See* Fed. R. Civ. P. 26(a)(2)(C). The rules do not permit the deposition of the expert until after submission of the expert's disclosure report. *See* Fed. R. Civ. P. 26(b)(4)(A). The party seeking to take the deposition of the opposing expert must pay the expert a fee for time spent responding to the discovery, and pay the other party a fair portion of the fees and expenses reasonably incurred in obtaining facts and opinions from the expert. *See* Fed. R. Civ. P. 26(b)(4)(C). A deposition of plaintiff's expert may not be required, depending on the detail of plaintiff's expert disclosures, defense counsel's knowledge of the assigned judge's preferences in permitting experts to testify outside the scope of their disclosures, and the defense expert's feedback concerning the plaintiff's disclosures.

Should counsel decide to proceed with deposing plaintiff's expert, the first area of inquiry should be what material has been furnished to him concerning this litigation. The expert witness should be required to bring with him the entire file concerning this matter, including correspondence with plaintiff's counsel, invoices for services, as well as all factual data upon which he relies. It should be established on the record that defense counsel has obtained his complete file on the case. If not, counsel must inquire as to what has been removed from the file and why. If necessary, counsel should adjourn the deposition so the witness can retrieve the entire file. Assuming the expert has brought with him his entire file, the attorney should go through and mark each item in the file as a defendant's exhibit to the deposition.

The deposition should proceed with defense counsel inquiring into the work the witness has done on the case, what he intends to do in the future, what authoritative treatises he relied on, his ultimate opinions and the bases for his opinions. Defense counsel should explore every possible and conceivable area of potential testimony, preventing any surprises when this expert testifies. Furthermore, the deposition is a means to identify material with which to cross-examine the expert. Fertile areas of cross-examination material might be found in authoritative treatises in the field and testimony given in depositions or at trial in other cases by the expert.

Other areas of inquiry include the expert's background and credentials. Prior to the deposition, defense counsel should have already researched the witness' background and obtained a copy of his curriculum vitae. If the expert is a former or current law enforcement officer, counsel may find material for cross-examination in training manuals and course material utilized by the witness. An additional area of potentially rewarding inquiry concerns any allegations of misconduct which have been leveled against the expert as an officer. Counsel should obtain all information on any such allegation and subpoena any supporting documentation.

Motion for summary judgment: Summary Judgment is a procedure to dispose of all or part of the case prior to trial. To obtain a summary judgment, the defendant must establish that there is no triable issue of material fact as to the action, and that the defendant is entitled to a judgment as a matter of law. The Motion for Summary Judgment must be supported by sworn affidavits or declarations, or discovery material, such as answers to interrogatories and deposition testimony. Any issue or cause of action that can be avoided by a partial summary judgment will enhance the prospects of the defense at trial.

Summary Judgment must be granted if "the pleadings, depositions, answers to interrogatories, and admissions on file, together with the affidavits, if any, show that there is no genuine issue as to any material fact and that the moving party is entitled to judgment as a matter of law." Fed. R. Civ. P. 56(c). Once the moving party avers "an absence of evidence to support the nonmoving party's case,...the latter must adduce **specific facts** establishing the existence of at least one issue that is both 'genuine' and 'material.'" *See Celotex*, 477 U.S. at 325; *Anderson v. Liberty Lobby*, 477 U.S. 242, 248 (1986) (emphasis added). "The mere existence of a scintilla of evidence in support of the [non-moving party's] position will be insufficient; there must be evidence on which the [fact finder] could reasonably find for the [non-moving party]." *Local 48 v. United Brotherhood of Carpenters & Joiners*, 920 F.2d 1047, 1051 (1st Cir. 1990) *Garside v. Osco Drug, Inc.*, 895 F.2d 46, 48 (1st Cir. 1990). "[W]here elusive concepts such as motive or intent are at issue, summary judgment may be appropriate if the nonmoving party rests merely upon conclusory allegations, improbable inferences, and unsupported speculation." *Smith v. Stratus Computer, Inc.*, 40 F.3d 11, 12 (1st Cir. 1994) (citations omitted).

Careful preparation of the factual aspects of a police misconduct case, along with a good working familiarity with the applicable law, provides a sound basis for summary judgment motions. Only motions that are well founded in law and fact should be presented, but in nearly every police misconduct case, there is some aspect that can be disposed of by way of summary judgment. It is highly recommended that defense counsel carefully analyze his or her case to determine the propriety of summary judgment, thereby narrowing the issues for trial. Often plaintiff's diverse claims against multiple defendants can be narrowed by way of Motions for Partial Summary Judgment. The successful attorney must research and grasp the current state of the law, which is continually changing in civil-rights litigation, to persuade the Court to grant summary judgment.

Perhaps the most prevalent basis for summary judgment in a police shooting case is the doctrine of qualified immunity. As discussed previously, qualified immunity is available for police officers if their conduct, when viewed objectively, was reasonable under clearly established law. The fact that there was a shooting, or even a fatality, does not preclude a Court from granting summary judgment based upon qualified immunity. Indeed, the case law is replete with examples of Court decisions granting summary judgment in such circumstances. *See, e.g. Marquez v. Gutierrez*, 322 F.3d 689 (9th Cir. 2003) (The court granted the correctional officer summary judgment in the officer's shooting of an inmate during an assault on another inmate because reasonable officer could have believed that shooting one inmate in the leg to stop an assault that could have seriously injured or killed another inmate was a good faith effort to restore order, and was thus lawful); *Easley v. Kirmsee*, 235 F.Supp.2d 945 (E.D.Wis. 2002) (The Court held that officers were entitled to qualified immunity where officers were dispatched to search for the decedent, who had left his home in a rage, inebriated, spattered with blood from self-inflicted cuts, and armed with a knife. When the officers closed in on him, he refused to relinquish the knife and began to charge an officer who, fearing for his life, shot and killed the decedent); *Dorsey v. Ruth*, 222 F.Supp.2d 753 (D.Md. 2002) (The Court held that an officer was entitled to qualified immunity from liability under § 1983 arising from his shooting of motorist after a high-speed chase when motorist attempted to back his/her vehicle into another officer. It was clearly established that the police officer's use of deadly force was not excessive, because he had probable cause to believe that the suspect posed a threat of serious physical harm to the officer or others).

Furthermore, the denial of a Summary Judgment Motion on basis of qualified immunity in § 1983 action is subject to an immediate interlocutory appeal. *See, e.g. Finsel v. Cruppenink*, 326 F.3d 903 (7th cir. 2003). Ordinarily, a denial of a motion for summary judgment is not a reviewable final decision, and the defendant must wait until after a trial on the merits to obtain review of the denial. The right of interlocutory appeal from the denial of qualified immunity is due in part to the fact that qualified immunity is an immunity from suit rather than a mere defense to liability, and immunity is effectively lost if a case is erroneously permitted to go to trial. *Mitchell v. Forsyth*, 472 U.S. 511, 526-27 (1985). Given the availability of interlocutory appeal, and the case law upholding the use of lethal force in many circumstances, counsel is strongly encouraged to file a Motion for Summary Judgment on these grounds.

Another common basis for a Summary Judgment Motion is that there is insufficient evidence of a "policy or custom" on the part of the city. As discussed above, a municipality cannot be held liable for civil rights violations as *respondeat superior*, but may only be liable upon a showing that the deprivation of rights was pursuant to a municipal custom, policy or practice. Counsel for the municipal defendant should review the deposition testimony in the case and all the other evidence obtained through discovery to determine whether there is any support in the record for plaintiff's allegations of a municipal "policy or custom." A single isolated incident of the use of excessive force by a police officer cannot establish an official policy or practice of a municipality sufficient to render the municipality liable for damages under Section 1983. *Oklahoma City v. Tuttle*, 471 U.S. 808 (1985). Typically, plaintiff's counsel seeks to establish municipal liability by alleged failure to train, supervise, or discipline its police force. This should require more than simple negligence in the areas of recruiting, hiring, training, supervision, or discipline of individual officers to impose liability. The Supreme Court set out the framework for establishing municipal liability on a failure to train theory in *City of Canton v. Harris*, 489 U.S. 378, 390 (1989). A City's failure to train its police officers must reflect a deliberate or conscious choice by policymaking officials, such that one could call it the City's policy or custom. The failure to train must "amount[ ] to deliberate indifference to the rights of persons with whom the police come into contact." *Harris*, 489 U.S. at 388; *see also Bd. of County Comm'rs of Bryan County v. Brown*, 520 U.S. 397, 404 (1997). Moreover, the City's decisions must be the "moving force" behind an actual Constitutional violation. *Harris*, 489 U.S. at 389. "The scope of failure to train liability is a narrow one." *Brown v. Muhlenberg Tp.*, 269 F.3d 205, 215 (3d Cir. 2001). "To survive summary judgment on a failure to train theory, the [plaintiffs] must present evidence that the need for more or different training was so obvious and so likely to lead to the violation of constitutional rights that the policymaker's failure to respond amounts to deliberate indifference." *See Id.* at 216 (citation omitted). Given these parameters, summary judgment on behalf of the municipality should be sought, and if allowed may eliminate a significant portion of the plaintiff's case.

Another ground for a summary-judgment motion may be any supervisory defendant's lack of personal involvement in the incident. As previously noted, Section 1983 does not impose liability under vicarious liability or respondeat superior theories; the law is clear that liability of supervisory personnel under Section 1983 must be based on more than merely the right to control subordinate officers. Rather, a plaintiff must show either the supervisor personally was involved in the constitutional violation or that there is a "sufficient causal connection" between the supervisor's conduct and the constitutional violation. *Thompkins v. Belt*, 828 F.2d 298, 303-04 (5th Cir. #1987); *see also Southard v. Texas Bd. of Criminal Justice*, 114 F.3d 539, 550 (5th Cir. #1997) ("[T]he misconduct of the subordinate must be affirmatively linked to the action or inaction of the supervisor"). A supervisory official is held to a standard of "deliberate indifference," which requires proof that the supervisor "disregarded a known or obvious consequence of his action." *Southard*, 114 F.3d at 551 (internal quotation marks omitted). A supervisor will not be held liable for unintentional oversights. *Id.*

In addition, counsel may move for summary judgment on various other grounds, and may move for summary judgment as to any pendant state law claims accompanying the civil rights-claim. Defense attorneys should not ignore specific tort defenses while concentrating on the civil-rights aspects of the lawsuit. A motion for summary judgment as to the state-law claims against the defendants is an effective tool for paring down the plaintiff's claims, and it seems to have a demoralizing effect on the plaintiff as portions of his lawsuit are dismissed. This technique is effective in helping to settle the claim and narrow the issues for trial.

Settlement and Offers to Compromise Judgment

Offer of judgment: The prospect of an award of attorneys' fees to a prevailing plaintiff is a frequent encouragement, and at other times an obstacle, for settlement in civil-rights cases. Reasonable attorney's fees are generally awarded to the prevailing plaintiff in a Section 1983 suits through the operation of 42 U.S.C. § 1988 (The Civil Rights Attorney's Fees Award Act of 1976). Attorney's fees may far exceed the damages awarded in police-misconduct cases, though this is unlikely in a police-shooting case. The successful use of an Offer of Judgment under Rule 68 of the Rules of Civil Procedure may reduce attorney's fees and litigation costs.

Rule 68 permits a defendant to offer judgment to be taken against it in a specified amount. If the plaintiff fails to accept the offer and later obtains a judgment less favorable than the offer, then the plaintiff must pay the defendant's costs incurred from the time of the offer. The plaintiff is also barred from recovering its own costs from the time of the offer. Rule 68 will operate only when the plaintiff is the "prevailing party," but the total judgment is less than the offer. Rule 68 will not shift the costs if the defendant is the "prevailing party" (i.e. a defense verdict). *Delta Airlines, Inc. v. August*, 450 U.S. 346, 355 (1981). Nominal or 'token' offers serve little purpose since Rule 68 operates only when the plaintiff prevails but for a lesser amount than the offer. *Id.*

The purpose of Rule 68 is to promote settlement. *See Marek v. Chesny*, 473 U.S. 1, 6 (1985). This is accomplished through two related devices. First, a plaintiff who rejects an offer under the rule risks having to pay the costs the defendant incurred after the offer. Rule 68 does not permit a defendant to recover its attorneys' fees. *See Poteete v. Capital Eng'g, Inc.*, 185 F.3d 804, 807 (7th Cir. 1999); *but see Staples v. Wickesberg*, 122 F.R.D. 541, 544 (E.D. Wisc. 1988) (dicta). Second, the same plaintiff will be unable to recover its own post-offer costs even if it prevails in judgment. *See Marek*, 473 U.S. at 6. Furthermore, Rule 68 will bar the plaintiff's recovery of attorneys' fees incurred after the date of the offer in actions in which a plaintiff is ordinarily entitled to recover its post-offer attorneys' fees as costs. *See Id.* at 10. As the Supreme Court explained: "Rule 68's policy of encouraging settlements is neutral, favoring neither plaintiffs nor defendants, it expresses a clear policy of favoring settlement of all lawsuits. Civil-rights plaintiffs–along with other plaintiffs–who reject an offer more favorable than what is thereafter recovered at trial will not recover attorney's fees for services performed after the offer is rejected. *Id.* In civil-rights cases, Rule 68 is a powerful settlement device, because it can negate Section 1988 and operate to stop the accrual of plaintiff's post-offer attorney's fees. *Marek v. Chesny*, 473 U.S. 1 (1985); *Real v. Continental Group, Inc.*, 653 F.Supp. 736, 738 (N.D.Cal 1987).

Settlement tactics and techniques: By the time discovery is complete, the defense counsel should have a grasp of all the evidence that will be heard at the time of trial, both for the plaintiff and the defendant. The case should be continuously evaluated, however, and counsel should not wait until the eve of trial to consider recommending a settlement offer. Often the best settlement bargains are struck early in the proceedings, when defense counsel has thoroughly reviewed the case facts but prior to discovery revealing some harmful aspects of the case. Defense counsel should try to be impartial and look at the case as an objective jury would. Discussing the facts of the case with other attorneys and laypersons may give an impartial view of the potential liability.

Based on a demonstrated ability on the part of the plaintiff to prevail at trial, a realistic appraisal of the merits of the case, and the plaintiff's readiness and determination to try the case, defense counsel may recommend settlement. Certain aggravating circumstances in a police misconduct case, such as a video of the incident, or a high volume of rounds fired, may influence settlement based on the potential jury's likely perception of the circumstances, rather than the legal merits of the case. Counsel must advise his client of the risks of an adverse judgment to enable the client to assess the benefits of settlement. In determining the risk of an adverse judgment, an experienced trial counsel will include knowledge of similar past cases, as well as a review of recent jury verdicts and reported settlements in other litigation.

The defense attorney should propose a range of possible settlement. In determining the range of a settlement, the attorney must consider the plaintiff's chances of winning at trial, the amount of a possible jury verdict, the length of the trial, and the cost of litigation, including the expense of expert witnesses and the amount of attorney's fee that could be assessed against the defendant if the plaintiff prevailed. A great number of specific factors must be taken into account by the attorney when making this evaluation, including such things as the particular court before which the case will be tried if it proceeds to trial, and the appearance and demeanor of all of the witnesses. Taking all of these factors into account, there will always be a judgment call to be made. Different lawyers place different values on the same case. The best determiner of settlement value comes from evaluating and comparing the case at hand with similar lawsuits tried in the same jurisdiction.

Whatever is the attorney's evaluation of the possible range of settlement, once it has been established, the evaluation should be communicated in writing to the client and the insurance carrier, if there is one. A letter should be sent explaining the range of possible jury verdicts and counsel's opinion of the chances of winning or losing the case. The attorney should provide this evaluation well in advance of trial, so that the settlement discussions can be commenced in a timely fashion. If the client extends authority to settle the case, counsel should then contact the plaintiff's attorney and negotiate a particular figure and the terms of an agreement.

Defense counsel may be able to evaluate the case and recommend a settlement, but if the client refuses to settle, the case will have to go to trial. The attorney should be aware that in police misconduct cases the emotions on both sides are sometimes more important than the money involved, and a recommended settlement may not be approved if the governmental entity is either self-insured or has the right to approve or disapprove a settlement recommended by its insurer.

Once counsel obtains the client's consent, the settlement negotiations may begin aimed at reaching an agreement with the plaintiff within the settlement range. Because of the contentious nature of civil rights suits and especially in police-shooting cases, a third party mediator is a useful resource to facilitate settlement. Many courts now have mediation programs and there are numerous private providers of alternative dispute-resolution services. Negotiating a settlement is more art than science, and counsel may learn this craft through the many legal treatises on the subject and through personal experience.

In the event a settlement is reached, defense counsel should prepare the settlement documents to best control their content. The settlement documents include a release of all claims, a settlement agreement (often incorporated in the release), and a stipulation of dismissal of the action with prejudice. The settlement agreement should provide that no liability is admitted and that the settlement covers all claims and all theories of liability. If possible, defense counsel should negotiate for plaintiff to agree that the settlement is under tort theory, not under civil rights; and that the individual officers are dismissed with prejudice in exchange for their agreement not to seek attorney's fees from plaintiff. These items may eliminate the negotiated case from becoming part of a "pattern and practice" of the municipality. The outright dismissal of the officers may psychologically satisfy the officer who believes he has done nothing amiss and lends an aspect of success in the eyes of the public, other officers, and municipal officials.

Trial Practice

Preparing for Trial

    The theme of the defense: After evaluating the factual and legal positions and determining that the case will not or cannot be settled, counsel must determine the manner and method of trial. The tone and tenor of the defense presentation is nearly as important as what information is given to the jury, so consideration should be given to the method of communicating the theme or theory of the case. Every lawsuit has a theme or theory that runs throughout the case and ties disjointed facts together in a coherent package. Most jurors are in an unfamiliar legal environment and will welcome any assistance counsel can give them to make order out of the chaos. Presenting the "theme" of the case will assist the jury in comprehending and evaluating the evidence and provide cohesion to the presentation of the defense.

    Police misconduct cases combine elements of tort and constitutional law. It is, therefore, important to tailor the case to play both themes to the jury. The attorney will need to focus on the Constitutional propriety of the officer's conduct, as well as the commonsense propriety of that conduct. A jury may forgive a slight, technical violation of constitutional rights so long as the officer's actions were sensible, but a case is much less palatable to a jury if technicalities of the law were obeyed, but the policeman acted unreasonably. The type and order of proof at trial must incorporate both legal and logical justification for the police action.

    Whatever theme or theory is chosen, it should recur throughout all aspects of the trial, including the trial briefs and other preliminary motions (introducing the theme to the court); during voir dire by counsel, if permitted (counsel's use of a theme must be very subtle at this stage); in the opening statement (direct announcement of the theme when framing the evidence); in the testimony of the major witnesses (reinforcing the theme); in arguments to the bench (to assert the need for admission of particular evidence); and in both jury instructions and closing argument.

    Pretrial motions: Because police-misconduct trials are fraught with legal issues, pretrial motions can simplify, and in some cases eliminate, legal issues. Two of the most helpful motions are the motion in limine and the motion to bifurcate.

● Motion in limine. The motion in limine is a motion made before trial seeking the court to preclude the admission of evidence or prejudicial statements or questions in front of the jury. A motion in limine should be filed when appropriate so that the lawsuit is limited to relevant issues and kept within manageable bounds. Even if the court ruling on such a motion is advisory, it will often give the parties a preliminary reading on the judge's view of the evidence. A successful motion in limine may also foster settlement, as plaintiff's counsel recognizes that certain evidence may not be admissible.

Particularly in police-misconduct cases, evidence may be introduced which is relevant to the liability of one defendant, but irrelevant and highly prejudicial to another. It is in this type of situation that the motion in limine is most critical. For example, in a police-misconduct case, plaintiff may attempt to introduce evidence of prior incidents of similar misconduct by other members of the police agency. A motion in limine may be aimed at precluding plaintiff from offering this evidence, which is detrimental to the defense case for the individual officer. While such information may be relevant to the municipal policy issue, it is irrelevant and highly prejudicial to the individual officer. In these circumstances, however, bifurcation may be the most appropriate solution.

● Motion to bifurcate. The motion to bifurcate is a request to cut the trial into two parts, literally, either along party lines or between damages and liability. A motion to sever or severance, on the other hand, divides the lawsuit into two or more separate independent causes. This should be distinguished from a bifurcated trial, which leaves the lawsuit intact but enables the court to hear and determine one or more issues without trying all controverted issues at the same hearing.

Bifurcation is an infrequently occurring event, but is often sought in civil-rights cases where there is a municipality as a defendant and to individual public officials. Bifurcation also may be granted to try the issue of liability separately from the issue of damages. Under federal rules, a trial may be divided along the liability-damages issues, with each issue tried separately before the same jury. Often, state rules-of-practice also have provisions making this possible. A case ripe for bifurcation along these lines occurs when the liability issues can be resolved in a relatively brief, straightforward fashion, but issues of damages are more complicated. To be successful, the judge must be convinced that either prejudice or efficiency requires bifurcation.

A motion to bifurcate also may be called for when one defendant's liability is predicated, at least in part, on another's, or when one defendant's case would be irreparably damaged by the proof offered against a codefendant. This occurs most often when an individual officer and the municipality are both sued under tort and constitutional theories. As noted, proof may be offered against the municipality which is irrelevant and prejudicial to the officer. Additionally, the municipality's liability is predicated upon the officer having committed a wrongful act. Both of these considerations mitigate in favor of bifurcation. The manageable procedure to follow is to try the case against the officer first, permitting no evidence of prior police misconduct incidents, and, if liability is established, try the municipality on the issues of "policy and custom" to the same jury.

The Jury Trial

To secure a jury trial, a jury demand must be made within 10 days after service of last pleading. It is common practice to include a jury demand with the answer. The court may order a jury trial even if all parties have waived it, although this is a rare occurrence. *United Press Association v. Charles*, 245 F.2d 21 (9th Cir. 1957). The demand for jury trial may not be withdrawn without the consent of all parties. *See* Fed R. Civ. P. 38(d); *Goldman, Sachs & Co. v. Edelstein*, 494 F.2d 76 (2d. Cir. 1974).

In federal court the size of the jury is no fewer that six members and no more than twelve members. *See* Fed. R. Civ. P. 48. The vote of the jury must be unanimous unless the parties otherwise stipulate. *Id.* Federal court jurors are selected from the territory of the district, which usually includes more than one county. Jurors most likely will be selected from areas not unreasonably far from the location of the trial. *See* 28 U.S.C. §§ 1861-1874 (Jury Selection and Service Act).

Voir dire: The Latin phrase voir dire, meaning "to speak the truth" is legal term referring to the Court questioning a witness or a juror. It also refers to the selection process for empaneling a jury. The federal judge has wide discretion to conduct the examination, or to allow the attorneys to conduct the examination. *See* Fed. R. Civ. P. 47. Procedure may vary markedly from judge to judge.

One of the most important and sensitive processes in any trial is the selection of the jury. Although there are few universal guidelines that are applicable, there is no question that plaintiffs' attorneys are greatly concerned with jury selection in police misconduct litigation, and this concern is manifested by the effort and expense put into jury selection. Likewise, defense counsel must be similarly concerned with jury selection.

The question of a juror's biases and prejudices is always a paramount concern for defense counsel, for challenging for cause and peremptory challenges. Accordingly, in selecting a jury through voir dire in police-misconduct litigation, it is important to consider the attitudes of the jury panel towards the police, both generally and in light of the information that will be presented. Most jurors will have had some contact with police, and many may have residual resentments–for example, from receiving an "unjustified" traffic ticket. Additionally, jurors are constantly exposed to television shows, movies, and news reports detailing incidents of police "brutality." For these reasons, it is important to learn as much as possible about the jury panel.

Wise judgment in jury selection depends on solid, concrete information. As a result, the more defense counsel knows about a particular panel member, the more effectively he or she can judge the juror's attitudes. However, the time to make such an investigation at trial is limited. In most cases, the attorney will not learn the identities of the prospective panel members until the impanelment of the jury begins. It is difficult to elicit jurors' true feelings about police and police misconduct cases. The use of so-called "mock" juries–that is, the use of people serving as jurors for test purposes–may be helpful in determining the attitudes of individuals with similar demographic traits to the jury panel. Psychologists often are used in the selection of individuals for the jury or in helping review the best means of ascertaining the attitudes of potential jurors, particularly in large-exposure to monetary damages. Rather than relying on intuition, counsel should consider retaining experts to analyze the panel and select the jurors.

The practice of jury selection varies as to whether the jurors are to be examined collectively or individually. Furthermore, while it is generally the more convenient and better practice to allow the examination of the jurors to be conducted by counsel, rules of court giving the trial judge either exclusive or discretionary power to conduct the voir dire examination have been promulgated in various jurisdictions. Jury selection in the federal system permits the judge to do the bulk of the questioning, and the trial judge ordinarily will permit only a limited amount of questioning by the attorneys.

The problem of potential juror prejudice is compounded in federal court and those state courts where trial counsel is rarely permitted to directly conduct voir dire. A judge-conducted voir dire is the least satisfactory kind to a trial lawyer. Federal trial court judges often ask too few questions to permit counsel for either side to determine a juror's prejudices or leanings, and they almost always avoid challenges for cause by simply asking an apparently prejudiced juror whether, despite the juror's feelings about the matter, the juror could set aside his or her feelings and render a fair verdict. A juror is more likely to put on a favorable impression before a judge and to give him a less candid answer, than would a person being questioned by an attorney.

Where the trial judge conducts the voir dire, the court may allow attorneys to submit written questions they wish to be posed to the jurors. The judge will then ask those questions that he deems necessary. When confronted with this federal-type voir dire, it is important to submit written, requested voir dire questions to the court in advance and then urge the court to cover those areas of inquiry with the panel.

Whether the attorney or judge conducts voir dire, there are some significant areas of inquiry in a police misconduct case. Counsel should determine if the jurors had any prior encounters with law enforcement, personal or professional, and the juror's feelings about those encounters. The juror's attitudes about "civil rights" are important, as are attitudes about money damages. Jurors' employment in law enforcement or government, any experience as victims of crime, and prior experience as a juror, witness or party in a lawsuit should be considered. The relevant experiences of the jurors' spouses, immediate family members may also be important.

Opening statement: In every case, civil or criminal, the opening statement has been determined to be one of the key points of jury persuasion. Although, technically, the opening provides only an opportunity to preview the case and not for argument, the skilled advocate must begin persuasion at this point. Counsel should make effort to personalize individual police officers and portray the department as favorably as possible

The theme of the defense case must be clearly presented in the opening. Recalling that the defense must present both logical and legal justification for any action taken, counsel must set forth the reason-ableness of police action. Additionally, as in any trial, defense counsel must elicit and minimize any damaging evidence. The opening should also address the issue of damages and conclude with a short statement of the desired result.

In opening, as throughout the case, defense counsel should exhibit a concern over the seriousness of the allegations, but confidence that the client will ultimately be exonerated. Counsel should keep in mind the "theme" of the case, what will be offered in evidence which helps and hurts defendant's position, and statements that plant "seeds of curiosity" about key pieces of evidence (that is, telling the jury what to look for without completely revealing what will be offered). The opening statement presentation should be made from the officer's viewpoint of the evidence. It is important to have an attention-getting start and a compelling conclusion. An important aspect of the opening statement is to make some reference that can be picked up again in the closing argument. The opening statement's final remarks in opening should lead the jury to the conclusion counsel wants it to reach: a verdict for the defendants.

Cross-examination of witnesses by defense: In civil cases the plaintiff begins the presentation of witnesses, as plaintiff has the burden of proof. Much of the plaintiff's case will be presented through the use of adverse witnesses, the individual defendants and municipal personnel. Defense counsel should be prepared to cross-examine these witnesses, who are obviously favorable to the defense, when they are called as witnesses by plaintiff. Of course defense counsel needs to prepare to cross-examine the plaintiff's own witnesses, who are adverse to the defense. Cross-examination of the plaintiff's experts will require special preparation.

By checking the court's file, counsel can determine which of the defense's favorable witnesses have been subpoenaed by the plaintiff. What may not be as easily determined is whether the plaintiff will call one of the named defendants as an adverse witness. Accordingly, any subpoenaed, favorable witness and all named defendants should be prepared for this possibility.

Often a plaintiff will call a named defendant as a first witness. This can be unnerving to the defendant--a fact not overlooked by plaintiff's counsel. The purpose of putting such witnesses on the stand is not to let them "tell their story." The questions will be leading and designed to elicit only adverse facts. All witnesses should be instructed to expect this and not to argue with the lawyer. They should be aware there will be an opportunity for defense counsel to present his/her version of events.

When a defendant or favorable witness is called as a witness by opposing counsel, a decision must be made whether to examine that witness partially, fully, or at all. In most instances, it is recommended that the witness be fully examined and not later recalled unless facts developed in trial warrant it. Generally a judge will appreciate counsel's attempt at expediency and permit full examination. By presenting a defense witness fully at this time, counsel also gains two other important advantages:

1. It limits the opponent's opportunity at cross- examination during the defense case in chief; and
2. The defense version is before the jury at an earlier, persuasive stage of the trial, in accord with the primacy theory of persuasion. In any event, defense witnesses should be prepared to testify at any point in the trial.

Cross-examining adverse witnesses is an important aspect of the police-misconduct case. Trial preparation should include the creation of a separate file or binder on each adverse witness that should contain the background on the witness, including criminal records; any statements or depositions of the witness; any documents or evidence showing bias, interest, or prejudice; and any exhibits counsel may wish to introduce through the adverse witness

Cross-examination of the adverse witness should be limited to leading questions, although defense counsel's tact and demeanor is critically important. The attorney must control the witness without appearing "authoritarian," especially in a police-misconduct case where the authoritarian conduct of the police is a central issue. The cross-examination should be limited in scope and duration with little or no opportunity for the witness to retell his/her direct testimony.

Generally, the plaintiff will testify either toward the beginning or toward the end of trial. Most plaintiff's counsel do this so that the plaintiff's case may begin or end on a strong note. If the plaintiff makes a very weak appearance as a witness, the testimony may be sandwiched in the middle. Whenever the plaintiff appears on the stand, his/her testimony is singularly important.

Many plaintiffs in police misconduct cases present stories rife with inconsistencies and either incorrect or untenable statements. The key to effective cross-examination is not to flail away at each inconsistency but to focus on the key ones. Defense counsel should limit the scope of questioning to three or four major areas that dovetail with the theme of the case. Establishing the plaintiff as credible is important, but no less important is showing that even portions of plaintiff's testimony supports the defendant's theme of the case. Cross-examination of an adverse witness generally requires inquiry into some or all of the following areas: (1) opportunity to objectively observe or gain knowledge of the incident; (2) bias or prejudice against police or in favor of the plaintiff; and (3) consistency of testimony with the witnesses' prior statements, the testimony of others, or the physical evidence.

The most fundamental aspect of cross-examining the plaintiff's expert witness on police procedures is knowledge of the adversary. In federal court, the Rules of Procedure require counsel to make comprehensive automatic disclosures to include a written report containing the expert's opinion and reasons therefore data or other information considered by the expert witness, any exhibits to be used as a summary of or support for the opinions, the witness's publications within last 10 years, the qualification of the witness, the expert's compensation for testifying, and a listing of other cases and their outcomes where witness testified as expert within last four years. *See* Fed. R. Civ. P. 26(a)(2)(B). plaintiff's police experts often engender strong reactions from the named defendants, and counsel must be careful not to lose objectivity and professional tact when cross-examining this type of witness. Only leading questions should be asked with little or no opportunity for the expert to wax eloquent. If the expert's qualifications are suspect then the counsel should attack them. If not, the attorney can turn the witness' expertise to his own advantage by establishing points of agreement which confirm defendant's theme of the case. The weakness of the plaintiff's case and the strength and reasonableness of various aspects of the defense case can be elicited effectively through the plaintiff's expert. There are occasions when the plaintiff's expert cannot be finessed, has nothing good to say for the defendant, and sees nothing wrong in the plaintiff. This may permit questions of the expert focusing on his/her failure to be fair and objective in his/her review of the officer's actions.

Presenting defense witnesses: The two types of witnesses are the defense expert and police witnesses. In preparing the defense expert for actual testimony, much will depend on the expert's courtroom experience. For those unfamiliar with the judicial system, a trip to the courthouse may be in order, along with mock direct and cross-examinations. The expert should be prepared to explain and defend his/her qualifications in a way that bespeaks neither modesty nor bravado. The quality of objectivity should be emphasized with the idea of the expert "teaching" the jury. Eye contact and rapport with the jury are particularly important, as well as the timely use of charts, graphs, or other audio/

visual aids. For example, the evidentiary use of a "shoot-don't-shoot" film, through an expert, not only addresses the frequently recurring theme of police training, but personalizes for the jurors the split-second judgment required of officers.

The quality of expert objectivity must also be shown in responding to cross-examination. The expert should be directed never to argue with plaintiff's counsel. In a manner which is not condescending, the expert must patiently explain why his own viewpoint is the correct one and plaintiff's attorney's viewpoint is in error. The considerations for background investigations of the plaintiff's expert apply equally to the defense expert, and counsel should prepare the expert for possible attack in this area by plaintiff's lawyer.

Police officer witnesses, despite their familiarity and frequent contact with criminal court, must prepare for their testimony at both deposition and trial. Police officers must approach testifying in a police-misconduct case differently than when testifying as investigating officers. As a defendant in a civil case, it is the officer's acts which are being examined, and the officer should understand that his testimony will be subject to rebuttal. The defendant officer should be impressed with the fact that civil lawsuits are significantly different than criminal trials, and the stakes involved for the officer himself are personally greater.

When testifying, the officer should be cautioned to avoid police jargon. Furthermore, it is important for the officer to maintain objectivity to the maximum extent possible. The officer must never lose patience despite inciting tactics by plaintiff's counsel. Most often, it is recommended that the defendant officers wear civilian clothes at trial, and nonparty police witnesses may wear a uniform. This dress maximizes jury identification with the defendant while lending extra credibility to nonparty witnesses. This rule is flexible and much depends on the particular jury.

Police witnesses, whether named as defendants or not, should be prepared for testimony in several areas. The officers need to be familiar with their educational and practical training, including schools, seminars, in-house and on-the-job training. They must be familiar with the department's chain of command and policies (written and unwritten) that relate to the incident involved. A working knowledge of procedures for citizen complaints and internal affair investigations is important. Knowledge of similar incidents of misconduct by the officers involved or in the department may be necessary; however, this information will be subject to a Motion in limine or Motion to Bifurcate discussed previously. The officers should be familiar with any reports they wrote and reports written by others who saw the incident. The officers should be able to make a chronological recitation of the facts. Familiarity with the applicable criminal and constitutional law is also critical for the testifying officer. As noted earlier, all witnesses should be prepared to testify at any time and to answer questions forthrightly and respectfully. Any documents to be used with a witness should be reviewed in advance, including any documents anticipated in cross-examination.

Special effort should be made to ensure that the demeanor of police officers at trial does not prejudice jurors and/or the judge. Trial preparation should include critique and instructions regarding body language, facial expressions, utterances and general demeanor that may send jurors signals that the officer is insensitive, capable of committing the complained of conduct, dislikes plaintiff, is emotionally unstable, hostile or inflexible in dealing with the public. Conversely, try to have the officer project a professional image (consistent with the officer's personality) of the type of peace officer the juror would feel comfortable calling in an emergency.

Directed verdict/motion for judgment as matter of law: Under the Rules of Civil Procedure, after the taking of testimony, the case need not be submitted to the jury at all. The court has the power to direct a verdict if the evidence is such that reasonable persons could not differ about the result. A verdict may be directed for the plaintiff, though this is much less common than a directed verdict for the defendant. A directed verdict is obtained by way of a Motion brought at the close of plaintiff's case, or at the close of the evidence. The terminology for the motion was changed by the 1991 amendments to the Rule so that instead of "directing a verdict" the court now grants a "motion for judgment as a matter of law." In common practice, however, many attorneys and judges continue to use the former term of "directed verdict."

When confronted with a Motion for a Directed Verdict, the Court may rule on the motion immediately, or reserve decision. Often the court will reserve decision on the motion for directed verdict, submit the case to the jury, and then pass on the legal sufficiency of the evidence on a later submitted motion for judgment notwithstanding the verdict. This course avoids the need for a second trial if an appellate court should hold, contrary to the view of the trial court, that the evidence was sufficient to raise a jury issue. It also saves the court from being second-guessed on appeal where the jury finds for the defendant, mooting the need for a directed verdict. The standard of sufficiency of the evidence is the same whether on a motion for directed verdict or a motion for judgment notwithstanding the verdict.

Closing argument: Closing argument should be just that–a persuasive argument. It differs, at least in theory, from opening in that it is not simply an overview of facts; it is a compelling argument about what conclusions should be drawn from those facts. The closing should reemphasize the theme or theory of the case, review the facts, and reassert the reasonableness of the defendant's actions. The closing argument is the last opportunity for counsel to appeal to the jury, and it is of crucial importance. It should be dignified and positive, delivered with sincerity and with belief of the advocate in the client's cause. The closing argument needs to be cogent and forceful, stressing the strengths of the defense case and the weaknesses of the other side.

The subject of damages should also be addressed in closing argument. Because juries will often be unaware of the true significance of giving one dollar as nominal damages (the availability of attorney's fees to the prevailing party under 42 U.S.C. § 1988), trial counsel must impress on the jury that even one dollar as nominal damages is significant and should not be lightly awarded. If a claim for punitive damages remains in the case, this too should be addressed in closing argument. If plaintiff's counsel made claims in his opening statement that the evidence would show that the officer acted recklessly or intentionally, and the evidence does not support such strong accusations, the plaintiff's overall credibility will be undermined. Even if the judge fails to direct a verdict for the officer on punitive damages and the issue goes to the jury, defense counsel should remind the jury of plaintiff's promise to prove reckless or intentional conduct. Again, if the proof fails the promise, plaintiff's credibility will suffer. Thus defense counsel should attack damages not only as an item by itself, but also as an issue of the plaintiff's overall credibility.

Closing argument should personalize the officers and the department, such that the jury recognizes it is deliberating on the liability of individuals and not on un-sympathetic institutions. By applying the facts to the law as set forth in the jury instructions, instructions counsel will have already confirmed during the charging conference with the judge, would be given to the jury, the defense attorney can bring added emphasis to favorable instructions. A good trial attorney carries on an amicable and straight forward discussion with the jury, but is not afraid to use some drama. The highlighting of exhibits admitted into evidence may help ensure they are considered during deliberations.

Jury instructions: In the manner and method of instructing the jury, federal courts follow their own rules, regardless of state practice and legislation. The judge instructs the jury orally at the conclusion of the trial after the closing arguments of counsel to the jury. When a state-created right is to be enforced, the state law must be examined for the substance of the instructions, but the form of instructions and the method of objecting to them are procedural questions on which the federal court is not bound by state concepts.

In an action to recover damages for police misconduct, counsel for both sides should present requested instructions to the court. Although the jury is instructed following the closing argument, the usual practice is for all requested instructions to be presented to the court prior to the argument. The court will inform counsel of its proposed action on requested instructions prior to counsels' arguments to the jury. Astute counsel will incorporate the facts applying to the judge's instructions into the closing argument.

Jury instructions in a typical police misconduct case can be a source of confusion to most juries. The most difficult aspects of instructions in these cases are sorting out the different theories of liability available against different defendants, and the defenses available to each. Bifurcation of the trial between the municipality and the individuals alleviates some of the problems of jury instructions. Additionally, filing dispositive pretrial motions can be invaluable in simplifying issues.

Even with the issues limited, the instructions may be difficult to comprehend. Carefully worded and understandable instructions are therefore critical. Counsel is reminded that police misconduct litigation is a rapidly changing area of the law, and instructions must be drafted taking into account the latest case law bearing on the facts of the case.

The verdict: In most federal cases, the traditional general verdict is used, by which the jury merely finds for one or the other of the parties. Two other procedures are made available by the rules. Under Rule 49(b) the court may, in its discretion, submit along with the general verdict one or more issues of fact upon which the verdict necessarily depends. This course requires the jury to give close attention to the more important issues and their answers serve to check the propriety of the general verdict. Another procedure is made available by Rule 49(a), where the jury returns no general verdict at all but makes special written findings on each issue of fact. It is becoming a more common practice for counsel to seek that the jury make special verdict findings.

Many trial attorneys submit proposed special verdict questionnaires for Court approval, carefully drafting the questions to assist in a fair, but favorable, outcome.

Post-trial Practice (Appeal)

Post-trial Motions

The party dissatisfied with a jury verdict, as the losing party usually is, may attack the verdict in either of two ways. The party may assert that the proceeding was in some fashion so tainted with error that the party should be given a new trial, or it may assert that its opponent's evidence failed to create an issue on which reasonable persons could differ, and that the dissatisfied party should be awarded judgment as a matter of law. Though these two motions are very different in what they seek, and in the standard to be applied in passing on them, the losing party may, and usually does, move in the alternative for both kinds of relief.

Rule 59 does not list the grounds for which a new trial may be granted, but says only that this action may be taken for any of the reasons for which new trials have heretofore been granted in actions at law in federal courts. The usual grounds for a new trial are that the verdict is against the weight of the evidence, that the damages are excessive, or that, for other reasons, the trial was not fair. The motion also may raise questions of law arising out of substantial errors in the admission or rejection of evidence or the giving or refusal of instructions. It long has been understood that if the trial judge is not satisfied with the verdict of a jury, the judge has the right--and indeed the duty--to set the verdict aside and order a new trial. Many will object, however, to the judge usurping the fact-finding role of the jury. A motion for a new trial, stating grounds therefore, must be filed within 10 days after the entry of judgment. *See* Fed. R. Civ. P. 59(b). Though the tendency in the courts has been to apply this strictly, however, a doctrine has developed allowing relief when a party has been misled by action of the court purporting to enlarge the time, even though the court lacks power to make the order.

Where the damages assessed by the jury in the event of a plaintiff's verdict are considered too high, defense counsel can move for a remittitur to lower the amount. If, as is common, there is conflicting evidence as to the amount of actual damages, one of the grounds for a defense motion for new trial should be the award of excessive damages. The court has the power and may decide to deny the motion unless the plaintiff refuses to agree to a reduction of damages, in which case a new trial will be granted. Such an order operates as an effective remittitur to reduce the amount of damages without foreclosing defendant's right to appeal on the issue of liability.

Awards of Attorney's Fees

In the event of a successful verdict for the defendant, the defense should consider filing an application for costs and attorney's fees. Costs are routinely granted to prevailing parties, and if the case is determined to have been frivolous, attorney's fees may also be granted. Although most plaintiffs are unable to respond financially, a successful motion for attorney's fees and costs can serve as a bargaining deterrent to an appeal by the losing plaintiff. Local rules should be consulted to determine the time within which such a motion must be filed, what costs are recoverable, and what documentation must be submitted. The standard for awarding prevailing defendant's attorneys' fees is a high one, the Court must make a finding that the plaintiff's action was frivolous, unreasonable, or without foundation, even if plaintiff did not bring the case in subjective bad faith. *See Commonwealth v. Flaherty*, 40 F.3d 57 (3d Cir. 1994). Where the case proceeded to trial, it presumptively had sufficient merit to survive a Motion to Dismiss and/or a Motion for Summary Judgment, thus it unlikely will be deemed "frivolous" or "without foundation."

An award of attorney's fees to prevailing plaintiffs, however, is the rule rather than the exception. The Civil Rights Attorney's Fees Awards Act of 1976, codified at 42 U.S.C. § 1988, provides that in any action to enforce certain civil rights statutes, including Section 1983, the court in its discretion may allow the prevailing party, other than the United States, a reasonable attorney's fee as part of the costs. The Fees Act was a legislative response to the Supreme Court decision in *Alyeska Pipeline Service Company v. Wilderness Society*, 421 U.S. 240 (1975), which prohibited federal courts from awarding attorney's fees in civil-rights cases without express congressional authority. The intent of the Act is to encourage private litigation to correct abuses of civil rights in lieu of the government having to seek enforcement. It is this intent, coupled with the Act's legislative history, which permits plaintiffs, nearly as a matter of right, to recover attorney's fees if they prevail on "any significant issue" in the litigation.

Notably, a plaintiff's success on "any significant issue" may cause plaintiff to become a prevailing party entitled to attorney's fees. The plaintiff may be considered to be the prevailing party even if the plaintiff does not win on all the issues, or even the central issue. *Hensley v. Eckerhart*, 461 U.S. 424 (1983). The plaintiff may be entitled to attorney's fees even if the claim is settled or mooted prior to trial. *Maher v. Gagne*, 448 U.S. 122 (1980); *see also Chicano Police Officers Assoc. v. Stover*, 624 F.2d 127 (10th Cir. 1980). A more frequent occurrence is an award of attorney's fees where only nominal damages are awarded by the jury. *Skoda v. Fontani*, 646 F.2d 1193 (7th Cir. 1981).

Two U.S. Supreme Court decisions set forth the criteria and the method of calculating attorney's fees under Section 1988. *Hensley v. Eckerhart*, 461 U.S. 424 (1983); *Blum v. Stenson*, 465 U.S. 886 (1984). The *Hensley* and *Blum* decisions held that the starting point to calculate fees is "hours times current market rate." Adjustments can be made to the fee from that point, either upward or downward, depending upon the circumstances. The factors to be considered include the time and labor required; the novelty and difficulty of the questions involved; the skill requisite to perform the legal service; the preclusion of other employment; the customary fee; the type of fee; the amount of legal fees involved and the results obtained; the experience, reputation, and ability of the attorneys; the undesirability of the case; and awards in similar cases. The prevailing party bears the burden of submitting adequate documentation in support of the hours claimed. Courts will look for contemporaneous time records which should be of sufficient detail and probative value to enable the court to determine that the hours were reasonably expended. Some courts have permitted discovery of one's opponent's time records to determine the reasonableness of time expended, although there is a split of authority on this issue.

Appeal

Not every judgment or order of a trial court can or should be appealed. Defense counsel must consider a variety of legal and practical issues before undertaking an appeal. As a threshold matter, the judgment or order must be an appealable final decision of the Court. "Final orders" are immediately appealable, whereas "interlocutory orders" are not. Final orders are rulings that end the litigation on the merits and leave nothing for the Court to do, but execute the judgment. Interlocutory orders are interim rulings that do not end the litigation and contemplate some further action by the court. For example discovery orders or denials of motions to dismiss are not ordinarily appealable. As discussed above, however, a denial of a motion asserting qualified immunity may be appealable immediately. Rule 58 of the Federal Rules of Civil Procedure sets forth the procedure for entry of judgment, which requires the filing of a separate document and triggers the time for making post-trial motions and for taking an appeal.

The decision to take an appeal requires a weighing of the client's ultimate objectives, whether the objectives can be met by taking an appeal and the likelihood of success on appeal. Counsel must consider the types of appellate relief available. For example, if the most that a successful appeal may obtain is a new trial (because the appealable error was an evidentiary ruling or erroneous instruction) and the prospects of achieving a significantly better result upon retrial than that already obtained are slim, there may be little value in pursuing an appeal. Sometimes, however, the appeal is pursued with the strategy of negotiating a settlement during its pendency that is more favorable than the trial outcome. Another factor impacting the decision to appeal is the long-term effects of creating a potentially adverse precedent by the appellate court's decision. This is especially true for municipal defendants that may have other similar cases pending and strategically want to take an appeal from another case which presents a more inviting fact pattern for a favorable appellate decision.

Because of the expense of an appeal in the form of attorney's fees, obtaining a transcript, and the accumulation of post-judgment interest, defense counsel should scrutinize the likelihood of success prior to advising the client to pursue the appeal. In considering the likelihood of success, the attorney should evaluate the adequacy of the record below to determine if the issues presented have been preserved for review (by being sufficiently raised, or objected to, in the trial court), assess the applicable standard of review on appeal, and measure the strength of the legal position to be argued in light of established case law, statutes or commentary on the issue.

Plaintiff has 30 days from the date of judgment to file a Notice of Appeal under the Federal Rules of Appellate Procedure. *See* Fed. R. App. P. 4. The time for the appeal is mandatory and jurisdictional. A failure to timely appeal will forfeit that party's right of appeal. The time for taking the appeal may be tolled by the timely filing of certain post-trial motions. The most common post-trial motions that suspend the time for taking an appeal are Motions for Judgment as a Matter of Law under Rule 50(b), Motions for a New Trial under Rule 59, and Motions for

Relief from Judgment or Order under Rule 60. Once the District Court grants or denies the post-trial motion, the time for the appeal begins to run. If the Notice of Appeal is timely, and the plaintiff has paid the filing fees for the appeal, the appellate procedure begins. The appellant has 10 days in which to designate and order parts of the record from the District Court. The appellant also should place an order for a transcript of the proceedings. The next step is to await the transmittal of the record from the District Court to the Circuit Court of Appeals. Once the District Court notifies the parties that the record is filed, the timetable for assembling the Joint Appendix to Briefs and the Briefs of the parties begins to run. Once the briefs of the parties are filed, the Circuit Court will notify the parties of a date for oral argument, or may decide the matter on the briefs in certain circumstances.

After the decision of the Circuit Court of Appeals, if a party wants further review, the party has 90 days from the entry of judgment to apply for a writ of certiorari to the U.S. Supreme Court. *See* 28 U.S.C. § 2101(c). The Supreme Court review of cases on certiorari is discretionary, and due to the volume of cases, usually limited to those few cases that present issues meriting a Supreme Court opinion. Statistics show the Supreme Court denies more than 98 percent of the petitions for certiorari, thus such review is indeed a rare event.

Conclusion

In defending police misconduct cases, the challenges facing counsel are varied and oftentimes daunting. Defense counsel must be knowledgeable of the substantive law and proficient in the courtroom. This area of law is constantly changing, and counsel is obligated to keep abreast of new developments. There are few areas of the law, if any, that equal the challenges and diversity of cases one finds in civil-rights litigation. The demands of successfully defending such a case are certainly rewarded with the professional satisfaction derived from ably representing police officers and securing a just and resolution to the lawsuit.

Cites Listed

13 C. Wright et al., *Federal Practice and Procedure* § 3721
28 U.S.C. § 2101(c)
28 U.S.C. §§ 1331, 1332
28 U.S.C. §§ 1441-51.
28 U.S.C. §§ 1861-1874 (Jury Selection and Service Act)

2A *Moore's Federal Practice* § 12.18.

2A *Moore's Federal Practice* § 12.21(2).

42 U.S.C. § 1863

42 U.S.C. § 1983

42 U.S.C. § 1985

42 U.S.C. § 1986

42 U.S.C. § 1988

7B J.W. Moore, *Federal Practice* § 704

Albright v. Oliver, 510 U.S. 266 (1994)

Alexis v. McDonald's Restaurants of Massachusetts, Inc., 67 F.3d 341,352 (1st Cir. 1995)

Allen v. McCurry, 449 U.S. 90 (1980)

Alyeska Pipeline Service Company v. Wilderness Society, 421 U.S. 240 (1975)

Anderson v. Creighton, 483 U.S. 635, 646 n.6 (1987)

Anderson v. Liberty Lobby, 477 U.S. 242, 248 (1986)

Garside v. Osco Drug, Inc., 895 F.2d 46, 48 (1st Cir. 1990).

Gaudreault v. Salem, 923 F.2d 203, 205 (1st Cir. 1990).

General Tel. Co. of the Northwest, Inc. v. EEOC, 446 U.S. 318, 333, 100 S.Ct. 1698, 64 L.Ed.2d 319 (1980)

Gentry v. Duckworth, 65 F.3d 555 (7th Cir. 1995).

Goldman, Sachs & Co. v. Edelstein, 494 F.2d 76 (2d. Cir. 1974)

Gooley v. Mobil Oil Corp., 851 F. 2d 513, 514 (1st Cir. 1988).

Graham v. Connor, 490 U.S. 386, 109 S.Ct. 1865 (1989)

Hafer v. Melo, 502 U.S. 21, 25 (1991)

Harlow v. Fitzgerald, 457 U.S. 800, 815 (1982)

Hensley v. Eckerhart, 461 U.S. 424 (1983)

Hunter v. Bryant, 502 U.S. 224, 229 (1991)

Hunter v. United Van Lines, 746 F.2d 635, 639 (9th Cir. 1984) *cert. denied*, 474 U.S. 863 (1985).

Kelly v. City of San Jose, 114 F.R.D. 653, 656 (N.D. Cal. 1987).

Kentucky v. Graham, 473 U.S. 159 (1985).

Kopf v. Skyrm, 993 F.2d 374 (4th Cir. 1993)

Local 48 v. United Brotherhood of Carpenters & Joiners, 920 F.2d 1047, 1051 (1st Cir. 1990).

Lowinger v. Broderick, 50 F.3d 61, 65 (1st Cir. 1995).

Maher v. Gagne, 448 U.S. 122 (1980)

Marek v. Chesny, 473 U.S. 1, 6 (1985).

Marquez v. Gutierrez, 322 F.3d 689 (9th Cir. 2003)

Mass. Gen. L. ch. 12 §§ 11H, 11I

Medeiros v. Town of Dracut, 21 F. Supp. 2d 82 (D.Mass. 1998)

Mitchell v. Forsyth, 472 U.S. 511, 526 (1985)

Monell v. Dept. of Social Services of the City of N.Y., 436 U.S. 658, 665 (1978).

Moore § 709

Napier v. Town of Windham, 187 F.3d 177, 183-184 (1st Cir. 1999)

Newport v. Fact Concerts, Inc., 453 U.S. 247 (1981)

Oklahoma City v. Tuttle, 471 U.S. 808 (1985)

Pembaur v. Cincinnati, 475 U.S. 469, 483 (1986)

Poteete v. Capital Eng'g, Inc., 185 F.3d 804, 807 (7th Cir. 1999)

Real v. Continental Group, Inc., 653 F.Supp. 736, 738 (N.D.Cal 1987)

Roy v. Lewiston, 42 F.3d 691, 694 (1st Cir. 1994)

Samples v. City of Atlanta, 916 F.2d 1548 (11th Cir. 1991)

Saucier v. Katz, 533 U.S. 194, 206 (2001)

Seigert v. Gilley, 500 U.S. 226, 232, 111 S.Ct. 1789, 1793, 114 L.Ed.2d 277 (1991)

Skoda v. Fontani, 646 F.2d 1193 (7th Cir. 1981)

Smith v. Stratus Computer, Inc., 40 F.3d 11, 12 (1st Cir. 1994)

Smith v. Wade, 461 U.S. 30, 56 (1983)

Southard v. Texas Bd. of Criminal Justice, 114 F.3d 539, 550 (5th Cir. #1997)

St. Hilaire v. City of Laconia, 71 F.3d 20, 28 (1st Cir. 1995)

Staples v. Wickesberg, 122 F.R.D. 541, 544 (E.D. Wisc. 1988)

Stewart v. U.S. Bancorp, 297 F.3d 953 (9th Cir. 2002)

Strauss v. City of Chicago, 760 F.2d 765, 768 (7th Cir. 1985)

Tatro v. Kervin, 41 F.3d 9, 14 (1st Cir. 1994)

Thompkins v. Belt, 828 F.2d 298, 303-04 (5th Cir. #1987)

Tuite v. Henry, 98 F.3d 1411, 1417 (D.C. Cir. 1996)

United Press Association v. Charles, 245 F.2d 21 (9th Cir. 1957)

United States v. Zolin, 491 U.S. 554, 562 (1989)

Wilson v. Garcia, 471 U.S. 261 (1985)

Wright § 3722

PART FOUR

TACTICAL AND NEGOTIATION STRATEGIES

Chapter 6

NEGOTIATING WITH THE SUICIDE BY COP SUBJECT

Mark S. Lindsay & Delmar Dickson

Introduction

One of the most complex negotiations that police officers will be required to conduct is with the individual who is attempting "suicide by cop (SbC)." As with all suicides, the mental state of the subject is complicated. The individual is operating from a mindset of "crisis." Rupple (1985) describes a crisis state as:

> A precipitating event has occurred within the last 24 hours and the subject's normal coping mechanisms have not worked to resolve the situation.
>
> The subject is acting and responding from an intense emotional level rather that a rational/thinking level, in response to a highly stressful situation.
>
> The situation is perceived to be a threat to the emotional, psychological and physical needs of the subject. (1)

Think of a crisis as an electrical circuit that is overloaded. The system shorts out, and basic, everyday tasks cannot be accomplished until the system has been repaired. In a SbC incident, not only is typical suicidal ideation coming into play, but also other social factors that cause the subject to see the police not as people there to help, but as the instruments of his/her destruction. By maintaining the police as inanimate objects, the individual is easily able to make the transition to suicide. In order to get the responding officers to adapt to his/her suicidal plans, the individual must create a heightened level of intensity that forces the officers to fear for their lives or the lives of innocent hostages or bystanders. In most instances, the individual will perform a precipitating event of such magnitude as to prompt an "all out" response from the police department. This event usually involves a weapon and a crime of violence. e.g. armed robbery, discharging a firearm etc, allowing the individual to control the incident and increase the heightened threat level of the responding law enforcement.

The subject will deliberately continue to escalate the incident through such actions as refusing to drop the weapon, advancing on the officer, pointing weapons at the officer, or threatening hostages. If the subject at any time allows a de-escalation of the intensity of the incident, then it is likely that the police will be able to successfully resolve the incident.

Police negotiators are trained from the beginning to contain the incident as soon as possible and then begin using proven defusing techniques. In most incidents, these techniques work, but in SbC incidents, these techniques run counter to the needs of the subject. The SbC individual cannot allow the police to gain control.

The information about the incident possibly being a suicide by cop will develop from many sources. The individual may tell the negotiator that he or she wants the police to kill him/her, or the information may come from intelligence officers as they process the background of the individual. To determine if this is going to be a suicide, murder/suicide, or a suicide by cop, it is vital that the police are aware of the warning signs of suicide. A person doesn't wake up one day and think, "Today I'm going to kill myself."

Suicide evolves over time, the process to arrive at suicide as a viable option can take as long as a year. A person who begins to look at suicide as a viable option, has been under numerous stressors. Suicide is the culmination of both chronic and acute stressors; therefore, the investigator must look at the individual's whole life, not just one part of it or just one stressor.

The principle point for the police to remember is that this is a suicide. The only difference is the weapon of choice. In a regular suicide the weapon may be a gun, drugs, knife or car etc. In a SbC, the weapon is the police officer. There are many reasons that people decide to use the officer as their weapon. Their religion may prohibit suicide. They may wish to be seen as a martyr. They may be afraid that they will mess up the suicide and have this as one more failure in life. The negotiators, to resolve these types of incidents, must rely on their crisis intervention training.

There are seven warning signs of suicide:

1. Previous suicide attempts
2. Talks or thoughts of suicide or death
3. Changes in personality or mood

4. Changes in eating or sleeping patterns
5. Withdrawal from friends and activities
6. Substance abuse
7. Final arrangements.

Certain interpersonal or social stresses are particularly common in suicide (Morgan, 1979). They include:

1. Social isolation
2. Estrangement
3. All kinds of loss, including bereavement or concerning finance, status, esteem, separation, divorce, or religious belief.

As a street officer and an investigator, the author's experience helped develop the "The Crisis Negotiation Threat Assessment Scale." Standards were needed to meet "the four in the morning test." In other words, what information is available to make life or death decisions. Generally time is not on the side of the police during these incidents; these incidents are fluid. In the direct attack type of incident, the shooting is over within approximately 10 minutes. In the barricade situation, the incident rarely lasts more than four hours.

The Crisis Negotiation Threat Assessment Scale

The Crisis Negotiation Threat Assessment Scale diagnostic criteria takes into account two different fields, suicide and criminal justice. In investigating these incidents, one factor that affects the determination of SbC or any other type of suicide is the investigators' unwillingness or incapabilities to ask the appropriate questions. Police Officers are taught the "Joe Friday rule," or "Just the facts, ma'am or sir." What the investigator and the legal community must understand is that some times the facts are hidden. Because suicide is more of a psychological event than a physical event, the individual has mentally accepted suicide as the most viable option before he/she attempts to commit suicide.

This preparation will be seen in changes in the individual's daily actions. The investigator, having never met the subject, must allow those who know the individual to speak about these changes in character. These changes are the pointers to the acceptance of suicide as a viable solution.

The Crisis Negotiation Threat Assessment Scale diagnostic criteria, now a part of the FBI's HOBAS scale, is a dynamic tool that can be used and modified. After reviewing hundreds of cases, Mark Lindsay, one of the two authors, found discrete factors that existed in Hostage/Barricade/Suicide incidents. If three of the five history factors and eight of the 12 event factors are evident, there is a high probability that the subject is likely to attempt and involve the police in a SbC incident.

Crisis Negotiation Threat Assessment Scale

I. History (3 of the 5 required)

1. **Mental or chronic physical illness:**	The subject may have either diagnosed or undiagnosed mental illness. Some of the symptoms of physical illness may not be found until the autopsy.
2. **Drug or alcohol abuse:**	May be either legal or illegal substances.
3. **Low social economic background:**	When individuals commit suicide, they use the means with which they are most familiar. These people have extensive interaction with the police.
4. **Suicide attempts:**	As with most suicides, there may be prior attempts.
5. **Criminal history:**	The subject will have a history of some type criminal background, most often of the impulsive nature.

II. Events (8 0f 12 required)

1. **Incident initiated by subject or third party:**	The subject approaches the police, or causes an action that will lead others to call the police.
2. **Event to ensure police response:**	The subject wishes to die at the hands of the police. He or she will create an incident that is designed to bring the police to him or her.
3. **Subject forces confrontation:**	Instead of surrendering, the subject will take actions that cause the incident to escalate.

4. **Initiates aggressive action:**   The subject will become aggressive in order to heighten the officer's level of fear. Again, the purpose is to cause an escalation of the incident.

5. **Threatens officer with weapon:**   The subject needs the officer to kill him. Therefore the officer must be placed in fear.

6. **Advances towards officer:**   The subject will make some attempt to approach or appear to advance towards the officer. This is designed to reinforce the confrontation and the belief of aggressiveness on the part of the subject to the officer. Again this is part of the escalation of the incident.

7. **Refuses to drop the weapon:**   The subject will not heed commands from anyone to drop the weapon. To do so would cause an immediate de-escalation of the incident and interrupt the suicide process.

8. **Threatens citizen with harm:**   The subject needs to be killed by the officers and will use citizens (hostages) to maintain pressure on the police.

9. **Presence of deadly weapon:**   The subject will maintain the weapon to ensure that the officers will kill him or her. This could also be by implied actions that cause the police to believe that the subject is armed.

10. **Recent stressor:**   As with all suicides, there needs to be a crisis or other catalyst for the suicide. This will generally have occurred within the last 24 hour, but it could be as long as 72 hours prior to the incident.

11. **Injured officer or citizen:**   Normally, if there is only one officer, that officer will not be harmed, as the officer is the instrument of death. If there are citizens or additional officers present, the subject may attempt to harm them in order to escalate the incident.

12. **Retreat by Officers:**   The officers retreat out of fear for their lives. Unlike regular shootings where the retreat is for cover/concealment, officers have stated that they knew someone was going to die.

Negotiating with the SbC Subject

Most often the individual who commits suicide will do so in a place where he/she feels comfortable, such as home, car or a location that has sentimental value. The individual who commits suicide in a public place may be saying to the world, "Look, I am in control."

The negotiator then needs to ask the right questions about the individual and have a viable plan. Some questions the negotiator needs to ask are: How do I know if this is a suicide by cop? How do I control it? What will provoke the individual? If the negotiator or the intelligence officer suspects suicide by cop, confront the individual. Ask why he wants the police to kill him. Make it personal; make sure the individual understands that he is asking another human being to kill him. Make the individual understand the emotional and psychological trauma that the officer and his family will go through.

One negotiator told a subject that his children would never again respect the police because they had killed their father. To which the subject asked the hostage who he had taken, "Why did he have to say that?" The hostage who was a mental health professional told the police during the debriefing that he felt this was the turning point in the incident. Within a half hour the subject surrendered. The individual must understand that he is dealing with humans, not inanimate objects.

Two building blocks of suicide are: (1) The subjects are in crisis and (2) They are not thinking rationally; they are thinking with their emotions. Until such time as they return to rational thinking, they are unable to problem-solve. The longer it takes them to return to rational thinking, the more likely they are to successfully commit suicide. Remember, a successful suicide in this instance means having the police kill them.

What process allows a person to arrive at the point where suicide is a viable option? Most people can handle two chronic stressor (affecting the person for six months or longer) and one or two acute stressor (affecting the person for less then six months) at any one time. When stressors become too overwhelming, they will send the person into crisis. Once in crisis, they help identify the most pressing matter. Often the intervener wants to tell the subject what is the most pressing matter, but it's their crisis. When interveners are negotiating with a subject, they need to avoid giving him or her the decision to make. The subject is in there because his or her decision-making process has been overloaded. The intervener need only work on one stressor. The objective is not to resolve all the issues at this time, but to assist the subject in moving to a rational state of mind.

Case Study I

At 9:34 P.M. on February 15, 1994, police officers received a call about the discharge of firearms. Upon arrival, the officers parked their marked vehicle in front of the location and were confronted immediately by the subject who was armed with a .25 caliber semi-automatic handgun. The subject was holding a one-year old child and pointed the gun at the child's head. The subject told the officers "They had better get in here." When the officers asked what the problem was, the subject ran up the stairs and into the apartment. The subject came to the window and pointed his weapon at the officers, who took cover behind some trees. The officers then requested assistance.

At 10 p.m., the Quick Response Team (QRT) and Crisis Negotiation Team were requested. The QRT secured the perimeter while negotiators contacted the subject. While the perimeter was being secured, the subject came to the window and fired two shots at police. The subject stepped back inside and fired one more round in the apartment. During this time, the subject spoke to the negotiator. At various times during the negotiations, the subject placed the phone down and came to the window with the one-year old hostage in his hand (the subject was holding the hostage by the neck) and made threatening gestures with the gun towards the child.

Based on advice from the negotiation team and the team psychologist, the on-scene commander ordered a tactical resolution to the event. Again, the subject stopped negotiations and came to the window with the one-year old in his arms. This time the subject placed the barrel of the gun in the child's mouth. Fearing that the child was about to be killed, the police marksman fired a single shot at the subject. At the last moment, the subject turned his head and the round, instead of hitting the subject in the bridge of the nose and killing him, entered his mouth and exited the opposite side. The subject came to the phone and told the negotiator that he had been shot. The negotiator told the subject that the police would come in and take him to the hospital. The subject stated "come in." Once the police QRT entered the apartment, the subject pulled out a handgun he had hidden behind him and engaged the police in a shoot-out. The subject was hit more times, but did not die. The subject was subdued, and the hostage rescued. Investigation revealed that the subject had been fighting with his girlfriend, who called the police. The hostage was the child of the girlfriend and another male. The subject had an extensive record for assault and weapons violations and narcotics usage.

Case Study II

On March 25, 1992, a man entered a trailer in Anchorage, Alaska. He then proceeded to take his girlfriend and four other people hostage. The girlfriend was able to escape and call the police. The suspect, who was armed with a 9mm handgun and two to four pounds of C-4 explosives strapped to his chest, held the police at bay. During the negotiations with the police, the suspect had only one demand, "He wanted his girlfriend returned to the trailer, at which time he would give her the gun and have her shoot him." As the incident continued, the subject released one adult hostage and two children that he held as hostages. Eventually, the suspect came out of the trailer with the remaining hostage. The subject attempted to force his way with the hostage to his truck parked outside. Once the hostage got into the truck, a police sniper fired a .223 round at the suspect striking him. The hostage fled out the driver's door of the truck. The suspect was shot three more times and still managed to pull the detonating cord on the explosives, killing himself and causing an explosion and subsequent fire. The suspect had been wanted on kidnapping and sexual assault charges.

As often occurs in SbC incidents, the police never gain complete control of the incident. The suspect escalates the incident as needed to force the police to kill him/her. The dynamics of the incident remain fluid. The suspect is able to maintain the intensity of the incident.

As with many suicides, the SbC subject will often have some type of plan. It may be something as simple as running out the front door with a weapon pointed at the officers. A more complex plan may be to create an environment of terror for the hostages by holding them in front of the window or glass door and threatening them with a weapon in front of the police.

Impulsiveness in a suicidal individual is possibly the most dangerous trait with which the negotiator will have to deal. The objective of the negotiation is to have the individual surrender without harm to any one. Unfortunately, when dealing with an impulsive person the desired outcome, may not be surrender. How can the negotiator or the intelligence officers identify a person, who may be impulsive? Indicators of impulsivity include a history of "common" assault, especially a history of increasingly violent assaults and tendency to be quick to anger, cry, and agitate. Crying by the individual in a crisis situation could cause the negotiator to put his or her guard down. Crying may mean that the negotiator has begun the process of moving the subject from crisis to resolution, but it could also cause the subject, who has not totally committed to the act of suicide or police assisted suicide, to make the final commitment. The emotion of crying as the individual comes to understand the total ramifications of his /her action could lead to shame and embarrassment.

These impulsive individuals also verbally strike out at people. They are described by acquaintances as being "thin-skinned" and "short-fused" and cannot stand having someone "in their face." They often drink heavily when stressed, drive recklessly when angered, and go on gambling, drinking, spending, and or sex sprees, exhibiting behavior mental health professionals have described as "manic." Traffic offenses include speeding, accidents, and parking violations are also indicators of impulsivity. The negotiator needs to control the subject in such a way that the likelihood of impulsive reaction decreases as the incident unfolds.

Tactical Strategies

There are certain actions of which the negotiator can apprise the on-scene commander that will also lessen the likelihood of an impulsive action on the part of the subject. In those cases where the SbC situation has become a hostage/barricade incident, those officers likely to be the weapon of choice are the tactical team members. A standard SWAT practice is to never give up ground once it has been taken. Generally, that is a good rule of thumb, but not when the incident is a SbC. In these incidents, the on-scene commander needs to remove the weapon of choice, (his tactical people). By moving the tactical team back, the on-scene commander has accomplished two events. First, he has made it difficult for the subject to readily attack the police, thus reducing the subject's chance to act impulsivity. Second, he has removed the principle weapon of suicide from the reach of the subject.

The on-scene commander also has an obligation to his or her officers on the scene, not to place them in harm's way needlessly. This covers both psychological and physical harm. A failure on the part of the on-scene commander to protect his/her officers could result in an officer firing the fatal shot, only to have that officer's action reviewed by his/her department, the district attorney's office, the FBI, or the U.S. Attorneys' office. This could cause the officer who pulled the trigger on this case to be the next case with whom the negotiators and tactical teams are dealing. Don't believe that police officers don't commit suicide. Each year in America about 300 officers commit suicide (Douglass 2002).

There will be political and social second-guessing when an officer kills a minority SbC subject. The agency needs to train for these incidents with its negotiation and tactical teams prior to an incident. Each police agency needs to be aware that incidents of SbC occur. No agency is protected from an incident of this type. Prior planning will help with all aspect of the recovery from a suicide by cop, from community understanding of the incident to intervention by the officer who fired the fatal shot.

As they become familiar with the dynamics of SbC, and as they train for it, police agencies will begin to see successful resolutions. There will always be the one that the police are forced to kill, but that one will be the exception.

References

Hagan, Ronald LT. NCOIC conflict management team: Delaware State Police. Interview 2002.

Lindsay, M. Kutzer, D, MD & Tress, S. (1993) Crisis Negotiations threat Assessment Scale. Scale used as the basis of the FBI HOBAS Database.

Morgan, D. (1979) Death Wishes: The understanding and management of deliberate self-harm. New York: John Wiley and Sons.

Rupple, S. (1985) Lecture notes: Negotiation team seminar, Baltimore MD.

Chapter 7

COMPARISON OF SITUATION AND TACTICAL STRATEGIES OF SUCCESSFUL AND UNSUCCESSFUL SbC INCIDENTS

Vivian B. Lord, Ph.D.

Introduction

arlier chapters describe the personal characteristics of SbC subjects, but another important component of situations that involve law enforcement is the surrounding environment and situational characteristics. To expand our limited knowledge on individuals who use law enforcement officers in their attempts to kill themselves, the current chapter describes one study that examined the characteristics of SbC incidents and the law enforcement tactical strategies used in their intervention.

Method

SbC Defined

For the purpose of this research, law enforcement assisted suicides, or "suicides by cop" (SbC) were defined as those individuals who, when confronted by law enforcement officers, either verbalized their desire to be killed by law enforcement officers and/or made gestures, such as pointing weapons at officers or hostages, running at officers with weapons, or throwing weapons at officers. This study included completed law enforcement-assisted suicides **and** attempts in which the officers averted the shooting of the subject, bringing him or her out of the situation alive. The study also contained a few subsequent suicides, but only in which the initial gestures and/or verbalizations were observed, and the officers were able to prevent the subject from initiating an assault on them. After an extended period of time, the subject ended his* own life.

SbC victims are considered successful in their attempt to have the officer shoot them if they are killed or injured by officers; the subjects were able to carry out their intentions. Subjects who killed themselves

---

* *Suicide and Law Enforcement:* 607-626 (2001), Reprinted with permission of the publisher, Behavioral Science Unit, FBI Academy, Department of Justice

during the SbC incident are also considered successful. If the SbC subjects were apprehended by the officer or the officers effected a surrender, they were categorized as unsuccessful.

An example of one of the SbC cases was a white male subject, age forty, who had been committed several times to a mental institution for depression, hallucinations and delusions. He had also been charged with assault against his parents on several occasions. The SbC complaint was received by law enforcement as a hostage situation. The subject's brother had observed the subject forcing his parents to enter his house at gun point. Although the subject never made any contact with the negotiator, he did allow his parents to leave. After several hours, the officers introduced OC chemicals into the house. The subject came out on the front porch with his shotgun. He was yelling such statements as, "somebody is going to die out here today." He then walked straight at the officers' patrol cars with his shotgun pointed. He was shot and killed by the officers.

Selection of Cases

Thirty-two local North Carolina county and municipal law enforcement department administrators were personally contacted by the researcher. The officer responsible for the department's tactical unit or the department's negotiator(s) was interviewed. The researcher provided the definition of SbC to the responsible officer, and the officer was asked to select cases between the years of 1991 and 1998 that met this definition. To maintain the anonymity of the subject and officers involved, the interviewed tactical officer or negotiator read information from the selected case files to the researcher.

Procedure

Although the law enforcement departments contacted include both municipal and county departments and range in size, they cannot be considered a representative sample. For this reason, and because the research on this phenomenon is so new, this study is primarily descriptive in nature. This information is comprised of specific personal, historical, behavioral, and situational factors of the suicidal subject and the incident. Personal information of the subject includes gender, race, age, employment status, use of drugs and alcohol, length of residence in the area, prior law enforcement contacts, criminal and mental health history, social support such as family and friends, and disruptions in his or her life. Situational factors are type, season and time of call; indication of planning; previous suicide attempts; length of incident; substance abuse during incident; weapon used by the subject; environmental factors; conversation of subject during the incident; and outcome of the incident. In addition, the officers were asked to supply information related to their intervention with the subject. Intervention information included the use of mental health professionals or family members in negotiation with the subject, tactical strategies, and verbal interactions between the negotiator and subject.

Sample: Sixty-four SbC cases from 32 law enforcement agencies were examined. The departments represented a variety of different size towns and cities, as well as both police and sheriff agencies from across North Carolina. As described in Table 7-1, SbC subjects were primarily white males between the ages of 25 and 40. The SbC cases included 16 subjects killed by officers, five suicides committed during the standoff with police, and 43 attempts in which officers either negotiated a surrender or managed an apprehension. These attempts can be further categorized by action taken after the SbC incident. Eighteen subjects were committed to a mental hospital, 15 were arrested for assault on officers or other family members, and nine were injured by officers. As noted within the definition of SbC, subjects killed or injured by officers are considered successful and are merged in the current study's analysis.

Table 7-1

Demographic Variables of All SbC Subjects

Variable	Number	Percentage
Sex		
Male	60	93.8
Female	3	4.7
Race		
White	48	75.0
Black	14	21.9
Latin American	1	1.6
Unknown	1	1.6

Variable	Number	Percentage
Age		
Under 25	9	14.1
25-39	36	56.3
40-59	18	28.1
Over 60	0	0
Unknown	1	1.6
Outcome		
No action	1	1.6
Committed to hospital	18	28.1
Arrested	15	23.4
Injured by officer	9	14.1
Killed by officer	16	25.0
Suicide during SbC incident	5	7.8

Results

Characteristics of the SbC Incident

The most frequent time that SbC incidents were reported was between 1700 and 2100 (43.5%) (Table 7-2), which is also the most common time for assaults against law enforcement in general (State of North Carolina Uniform Crime Report 1998 Annual Report, 1999). Unlike other suicides which are likely to occur more often in spring and winter, SbC complaints seem to occur most frequently in fall (36.5%) and least frequently in winter (11.5%). Although seasons do not seem to play an important role in the decision to attempt SbC, one of the departments reported an incident that occurred in February. A forty-four year old man had barricaded himself in his house. After several hours of negotiations, the subject went downstairs to get some tobacco. A tactical team member, who was stationed outside a window, saw the subject reach for the tobacco and yelled to him, "I sure would like some of that tobacco. Come on, buddy, it's cold and rainy out here, just give up." The subject surrendered.

Interference of environmental factors is quite often cited as an obstacle to overcome (McMains & Mullins, 1996). Although a large percentage of these incidents occurred without any interference from people, media, or other stimuli (29.4%), in approximately the same percentages of cases law enforcement did have to contend with people (29.4%) and media (23.5%) (Table 7-2). Contending with the public and the media can be a problem for law enforcement officers attempting to negotiate with SbC individuals. In Case #2, law enforcement received a complaint about a domestic dispute between an impaired subject and his girlfriend. When the police arrived, a crowd was encouraging him to kill himself or attack law enforcement. The officers commanded him to stop and drop the knife. He did not, but rather ran at the police and was killed.

Table 7-2

Situational Characteristics of SbC Incidents

Variable	Number	Percentages
Time of Call		
0500-1100	2	3.6
1100-1700	17	30.9
1700-2100	25	45.5
2100-0500	10	18.2
Total	**55**	
Season		
Spring	16	25.8
Summer	16	25.8
Fall	22	35.5
Winter	8	12.9
Total	**62**	
Environment		
No Stimuli	15	49.2
People/Crowd	15	17.5
Media	8	12.6
Physical Barrier	1	1.6
People & Noise	12	19.0
Total	**63**	

The length of time that an incident lasted appeared to differ between those subjects who were successful in their attempt to get officers to shoot them and those who were not. Those incidents that ended quickly were most likely to result in injury or death of the subject; 61% of those subjects who were in incidents that lasted less than an hour were injured or killed (Table 7-3).

More than likely officers were surprised by the subject and unlikely to be able to protect themselves. In nine of the incidents that ended in injury or death of the subject, no tactical strategies were used, and the incident lasted less than one hour.

Intervention Tactics

Law enforcement officers have a number of tactical strategies at their disposal when intervening in SbC or other barricaded incidents (McMains & Mullins, 1996). Although this researcher does not propose to suggest that a subject's decision is based on specific strategies, it is worth examining what strategies are used and their relationship to the outcome of the subject.

Negotiators must consider the use of mental health professionals especially as an additional resource if the subject has a mental health history. Most of the incidents did not include the use of such a professional (89.1%). If a mental health professional was used, it was most frequently the subject's psychologist (10.9%).

Use of family members is also a consideration, but primarily for providing additional information to the negotiator about the subject and the precipitating factors. Although family members were not used very often (75.0%), when used, it was primarily a parent (15.6%).

Potential tactical strategies included: (1) the establishment of a safe perimeter around the subject usually confining him or her to a building or vehicle, (2) distraction devises such as "flash bangs," (3) physical restraint, and (4) introduction of gas to force the person into one area or out of an area. The main purposes of such strategies are to confine the individual safely in order to allow negotiation, to distract the subject so that tactical members might entered his facility and restrain him, or to move him from area into another potentially safe one. Establishing a perimeter was the primary tactical strategy (40.6%) used by officers in the current study. Physical restraint (7.8%), distraction devises (1.6%), OC gas (12.5%) were used to lesser extent. As noted earlier in cases in which officers were unable to utilize any tactical strategies at all, a higher percentage of subjects were shot or killed by officers (36.0%) than were unsuccessful in their attempt (Table 7-3). Negotiation tactics included (1) building rapport with the subject (17.2%) and (2) discussing the subject's problems (43.8%). Just focusing on the weapon was utilized in over twenty percent of the cases (25.0%). Interestingly in those cases in which officers only focused on the weapon ("put the weapon down"), over half of the subjects were injured or killed (52.0%) (Table 7-3). On the other hand, in those cases in which negotiators were able to discuss the problems of the subject, most incidents did not result in injury or death (66.7% unharmed).

Table 7-3

Comparison of Intervention Variables of SbC Incidents*

Variable	Unsuccessful %	(n)	Outcome Successful %	(n)	Total %	(n)
Duration						
Less than 1 hr.	19.4	(7)	45.8	(11)	30.0	(18)
Less than 3 hrs	33.3	(12)	29.2	(7)	31.7	(19)
Less than 5 hrs.	36.1	(13)	20.8	(5)	30.0	(18)
Between 5 and 24 hrs.	11.1	(4)	4.2	(1)	8.3	(5)
Total		(36)		(24)		(60)
Tactical Strategies						
None	20.5	(8)	36.0	(9)	26.6	(17)
Perimeter	38.5	(15)	44.0	(11)	40.6	(26)
Negotiation	10.3	(4)	12.0	(3)	10.9	(7)
Gas	17.9	(7)	4.0	(1)	12.5	(8)
Physical Restraint	10.3	(4)	4.0	(1)	7.8	(5)
Nonlethal Force	2.6	(1)	0		1.6	(1)
Total		(39)		(25)		(64)
Verbal Intervention						
None	12.8	(5)	16.0	(4)	14.1	(9)
Deal with Weapon Only	7.7	(3)	52.0	(13)	25.0	(16)
Build Rapport	12.8	(5)	24.0	(6)	17.2	(11)
Discuss Problem	66.7	(26)	8.0	(2)	43.8	(28)
Total		(39)		(25)		(64)

*   SbC subjects who were successful in their attempt to be shot by officers are compared with those who were unsuccessful in their attempt

In cases in which officers were unable to utilize tactical or negotiation tools, the SbC incident was likely to be short-lived with lethal results. On the other hand, in cases in which the subject was willing to negotiate, and the negotiator was able to discuss the subject's problems with him, the subject was usually restrained without harm. In making these conclusions, it is important to realize that the subject controls his or her own life. Officers are unable to utilize tactical tools or negotiate with SbC subjects when they are surprised by the subject and must quickly protect themselves and others. Given time to establish a perimeter, develop rapport with the subject, and discuss issues with him or her, the officers are better prepared to intervene with the subject.

Conclusion

When officers are able to negotiate safely with the subject, discussing what issues are bothering him or her, officers are usually able to prevent injury to the subject. Unfortunately a large number of SbC incidents begin as an unrelated complaint to a suicide attempt. When the officers are attacked without warning, they only have time to protect themselves and others.

Law enforcement officers are becoming more aware of individuals who attempt to use police to kill them. Tactical officers and negotiators also are beginning to comprehend the need for some subjects, especially in barricaded situations, to maintain control. Understanding these subjects will continue to help officers successfully intervene.

It would be helpful for officers to expand the interview of SbC attempters who live to include information that would help law enforcement's understanding of the motives behind SbC incidents. This is not to say that law enforcement officers can control the choices that the subject makes; only the SbC subject can make the decision to use a weapon to confront officers and get injured or killed. Future research focusing on successful intervention strategies, particularly in the area of negotiation approaches, will also be helpful.

Notes

The current study only discovered male SbCs who ended their own lives.

References

Crime in North Carolina 1998: Uniform Crime Report (1999). Raleigh, North Carolina McMains, M. J. & Mullins, W. C. (1996). Crisis negotiation. Cincinnati, Ohio: Anderson Publishing Co.

Chapter 8

USE OF LESS LETHAL FORCE IN
SUICIDE BY POLICE INCIDENTS

Robert J. Homant

Overview

"Suicide by cop (SbC)" makes up a substantial proportion of the incidents that result in police use of deadly force. Various sources have attributed anywhere from 10% to 50% of police use of deadly force to the problem of dealing with subjects who prefer to die at the hands of the police, either as an alternative to regular suicide or to being captured (cf. Kennedy, Homant, & Hupp, 1998; Oyster, 2001). Differences in the percentages involved from study to study are partly a matter of the level of evidence needed to classify an incident as SbC, and even more so a function of an area's violent-crime rate. If an area has a relatively low crime rate, especially if gun-related crimes such as armed robbery are rare, then a higher percentage of police activity is likely to be involved with domestics, disturbed persons, and suicide threateners, who collectively produce the most SbC incidents (Homant & Kennedy, 2000b; Lord, 2001).

As police trainers and supervisors become more aware of the issue of SbC, various recommendations for possible tactical responses have been put forth. These responses have the dual purpose of saving the lives of all involved, including the person who initiates the SbC incident, as well as protecting the police from undue criticism, both in the media and in the courtroom. There are two possible problems here, however. One is that various tactics will be too uncritically accepted, simply because they would seem to have face validity. The other is that police officers who deviate from these tactics may find themselves even more vulnerable to second guessing and lawsuit than they normally are in use-of-force situations. The disturbed person attempting suicide by cop is often a more sympathetic person than the escaping felon.

The purpose of this chapter, therefore, is to examine the status of various police tactics in responding to SbC situations, with special attention to the use of "less lethal" technology. Two terms, "less than lethal" (LTL) and "less lethal," have been used to describe a variety of use of force technologies, such as the baton, tear-gas, beanbag bullets, etc. In an earlier version of this research (Homant & Kennedy, 2000a), the term "less than lethal" was preferred because it clearly distinguished the officer's intent. My impression, however, is that "less lethal" is fast becoming the preferred term. "Less lethal" signifies that any use of force has the potential to be lethal, and various technologies should be viewed on a continuum from manual holds through traditional deadly force. This helps to alert the officer to the risk involved in deploying force, and it also tells the courts that when a subject dies or is seriously injured, it was not necessarily because of the misuse of some supposedly non-lethal technique.

I will use the term "less lethal" throughout this chapter to refer to all those technologies outside of deadly force (shooting) that are used to restrain subjects or induce compliance with police commands. In the present research, the less lethal weapons that were found to be used in actual SbC situations included: baton or nightstick, pepper spray (oleoresin capsicum) or mace, tear gas, Taser, beanbag bullets, and rubber, plastic, or wooden bullets.

The term "nonlethal" will be used to refer to any non-technological force, such as tackling, pushing, grabbing, etc., that involves direct police-to-subject contact without use of a weapon or other instrument (cf. Bailey, 1966; International Association of Chiefs of Police, 1998).

As pointed out in Chapter 4, the threat to use force, such as pointing a weapon at someone, can also be legally construed as the use of force (cf. *Robinson v. Solano*, 2002). This makes sense in a legal context. In the context of evaluating tactics, however, the "threat" of force needs to be kept conceptually separate from the use or attempted use of force.

Use of Less Lethal Force

The civil disorders of the 1960s gave impetus to the goal of substituting police use of less lethal for lethal force (Robin, 1996). As police develop and refine various use of force continua for training purposes (Desmedt, 1984; Garner, Shade, Hepburn, & Buchanan, 1995), federally-sponsored research continues in an attempt to provide police departments with weapons that can bring certain inherently dangerous police-citizen encounters to a non-fatal conclusion (Anonymous, 2001; Heal, 2001; IACP, 1998).

While less lethal weapons include such technological advances as disabling nets, sticky foam, electronic auto arrester systems, and disorienting pulsed light, traditional less lethal weapons such as batons, chemical irritants, electronic stunning devices, and beanbag, rubber, or wooden bullets are in more common use (cf. Hayeslip & Preszler, 1993; Trostle, 1990). The efficacy of even these more common measures, however, has not been sufficiently documented (Scott & Copeland, 2001).

Although both law enforcement personnel and concerned citizenry remain hopeful that the use of less lethal force will reduce shootings by police, there is no conclusive evidence that justifiable homicides by police have been reduced by the availability of less lethal weapons (Bailey, 1996), though there certainly would seem to be anecdotal evidence of success (Button, 2001). Geis and Binder (1990) have suggested that there may still not be an effective substitute for the standard police firearm. On the positive side, Kaminski, Edwards, and Johnson (1998) found that the use of pepper spray significantly reduced assaults on police in Baltimore County, Maryland.

The varieties of equipment options and deployment strategies even for a single less lethal weapon, such as bean-bag bullets, can be overwhelming. Different combinations of bag type and caliber interact with different distances, weather conditions, terrain, crowd size, officer training, etc. to make generalization from one instance to the next problematic (Anonymous, 2001). Therefore, in examining how various tactics and technologies have been used in SbC situations, we must take a primarily qualitative approach. By this I mean that it is premature to look for cause and effect relations using objectively categorized variables; at best we will try to discern patterns that can provide some insight into why certain approaches were associated with a positive or negative outcome.

Legal Implications of Less Lethal Force

One of the driving forces in motivating the development of less lethal technologies has been concern over deadly force lawsuits (Dorsch, 2001; Hopper, 2001; Scott & Copeland, 2001). Above, Chapter 4 reviewed court rulings specific to SbC cases. At this point it will be helpful to briefly review recent rulings and dicta specific to less lethal technologies (see also Miller, 1995).

In *Headwaters v. Humboldt* (2000), a key issue involved use of pepper spray as a compliance technique. That is, police were not using the spray in response to danger to themselves or others, but to induce environmental protesters to comply with a lawful police order to release themselves from a self-imposed "locking device" in order to be removed from the site. The protesters were given clear warning about what was to happen, and the chemical was directly applied to their closed eyes using a Q-tip. Among other points raised, the police argued that the alternative, cutting through the locking device, presented a risk of fire, as well as injury to the protesters.

The District Court found this use of force reasonable and granted summary judgment to the defense, but, on appeal, the Ninth Circuit Court disagreed. A unanimous court first stressed that the "reasonableness" of this use of force should normally be a matter for the jury to decide. Because the District Court had granted qualified immunity, however, the Circuit Court proceeded to examine the issue of reasonableness. The Court concluded, "Thus, where there is no need for force, any force used is constitutionally unreasonable." (*Headwaters v. Humboldt*, 2000, p. 1199) The opinion went on to state that a compelling state interest could justify force, but the state is clearly obligated to use less intrusive methods (even if substantially more costly and inconvenient), if feasible. If less forceful tactics were available, then the reasonableness of the pepper spray is for a jury to decide.

One key factor distinguishes *Headwaters* from most SbC situations. In *Headwaters*, the protesters were non-violent, posing no immediate threat to anyone. The Circuit Court favorably cited *Monday v. Oulette* (1997) to the effect that pepper spray could be used to thwart a suicide attempt (see below).

However, in cases where an ambivalently suicidal person has created a stand-off with no immediate threat, or where a slowly advancing knife wielder can be "easily" evaded, the reasonableness of the use of less lethal technologies would appear to be in the hands of the jury. While various appeals courts wax eloquent about reasonableness being a jury's call, this would seem to overlook the approach of many risk managers, which is to "settle" in those cases where the city fails to win summary judgment. (This is especially true in cases such as *Headwaters*, where there are no real disputes as to what happened.) It should be noted that the ruling in *Headwaters* was briefly put in doubt by *Saucier v. Katz* (2001; see Chapter 4). The Circuit Court, however, had no difficulty in finding that the right not to be pepper sprayed while passively protesting was clearly established. (*Headwaters v. Katz, Amended*, 2002)

In *Chew v. Gates* (1990), police used a dog to locate Thane Carl Chew, who had three outstanding felony warrants and had fled on foot from a traffic stop and was hiding in a large junkyard. According to plaintiff Chew, the police handler, Officer Bunch, had allowed the dog to run out of sight. Trained to bite and hold, the dog attacked Chew, causing severe injuries despite Chew's alleged attempt to surrender. In granting defendants' motions for summary judgment, the District Court cited a Sixth Circuit case, *Robinette v. Barnes* (1988), to the effect that use of a trained police dog in these circumstances was constitutional. (Summary judgment was not granted to the individual officer who allegedly ordered the dog to attack after Chew attempted to surrender; if proven, this would clearly be an excessive force violation.) A jury awarded Chew $13,000 on the claim against Officer Bunch, and Chew appealed the dismissal of the suit against the other officers and the Los Angeles Police Department.

In a long, complex opinion, the Circuit Court essentially agreed with the appellant Chew. The key points raised were: (1) the use of the dog represented "severe force"; (2) *Robinette* did not apply, essentially because it was a deadly force situation; and (3) in contrast, Chew was unlikely to escape, and (4) his dangerousness had not been established. The police had two hours to develop other tactics; the court specifically suggested a helicopter. (*Chew v. Gates*, 1994, p.1443) Therefore, a jury must determine whether the use of extreme force was objectively reasonable.

Four recent cases specifically involve the use of beanbag bullets.

1. *Deorle v. Rutherford* (2001) has been reviewed in Chapter 4. Although the use of beanbags could be considered "successful," in that it avoided the necessity for deadly force and resolved the situation without Deorle committing suicide, it did result in serious injury to Deorle. The Circuit Court ruled that a jury could find this use of force to have been excessive.

2. *Bell v. Irwin* (2002) was also reviewed in Chapter 4 In this case, the police officers were granted summary judgment, but only because the use of deadly force would have been justified in stopping Bell from blowing up his trailer; otherwise, a jury would have had to determine what level of force was represented and whether it was reasonable.

3. In *Omdahl v. Lindholm* (1999), police officers were in a standoff with a 15-year-old suicidal male. The youth had a rifle but had not directly threatened officers. As it was getting dark, officers tried to coax Omdahl to leave his rifle and come out of a wooded area. Unwilling to leave the rifle, he held it behind him, pointed toward the ground. The officers fired two beanbag rounds, hitting him. As he stumbled backward, he was hit again, this time by a regular bullet. Although not killed,

Omdahl required extensive treatment. It is not clear from the court description why the focus was on the lethality of the beanbags rather than the actual bullet. I presume that the bullet was fired either by accident, or because one officer believed that the beanbag rounds meant they were being shot at. In any event, the Omdahl family sued, alleging that the use of the beanbags represented deadly force, and deadly force was unjustified. The District Court refused the police officers' motion for summary judgment and the Circuit Court agreed. The Court treated the disagreement as to the level of force represented by beanbags as a factual dispute, and thus something that a jury would have to decide. It was implied (but not stated) that even if a jury concluded that beanbags were not deadly force, they could still find them to be excessive.

4. *Medina v. Cram* (2001) was reviewed in Chapter 4. In this case, a variety of police tactics were tried. Negotiation, beanbags, a dog, and sneaking up from behind, all failed to stop Medina, and deadly force was used. Medina survived and sued on the grounds that poor police tactics prior to the shooting had led directly to the use of deadly force. The Federal District Court ruled that Medina did not have a right to have police use less intrusive means in their attempts to seize him. A dissenting opinion, however, felt that these tactics were part of the totality of circumstances leading to the shooting and should have been submitted to a jury to evaluate for reasonableness.

Two cases involving pepper spray seem especially apropos. In *Clem v. Corbeau* (2002), Officers Corbeau and Nelson responded to a wife's call for assistance with Robert Clem, a mentally ill individual who had stopped taking medication. The officers attempted to talk Clem into going with them to see his doctor. At first he seemed compliant, but then became agitated. Officer Corbeau said that Clem patted his pocket and threatened to kill Corbeau, but this threat was denied by other witnesses. There is some dispute as to how agitated Clem became. Officer Corbeau then doused him with pepper spray. After a few minutes, Clem recovered, and began advancing on Officer Nelson. Once again, Clem was pepper sprayed. Clem turned away, apparently heading toward the bathroom. Clem then advanced toward Officer Corbeau, who backed up a few feet and drew his weapon. Clem was either "rapidly charging" Officer Corbeau, or stomping forward robot-fashion. Officer Corbeau fired three times, hitting Clem in the leg and intestines.

In appealing for summary judgment, Corbeau argued among other points that the failure of two doses of pepper spray to subdue Clem was a factor in calculating his dangerousness as Clem advanced at Officer Corbeau. However, if the plaintiffs' version of what occurred is remotely accurate, this seems to be a case where the use of a less lethal weapon, pepper spray, was successful and should have prevented any need for deadly force. In reading the description of events, one wonders if Officer Corbeau himself was somehow affected by the spray, since even in the version most favorable to Officer Corbeau, there seems to be little justification for deadly force. In any event, Officer Corbeau's assertion of qualified immunity was denied.

Finally, in *Monday v. Oulette* (1997) Officers John Oulette and Thomas Mohrbach arrived at the residence of Daryl Monday, whom they believed to be committing suicide by an overdose of medication. Finding 20 pills missing from a prescription, Officer Oulette insisted that Monday accompany the officers to the hospital. After approximately twenty minutes of discussion and debate, Officer Oulette finally warned Monday that he would be pepper sprayed if he did not agree to go to the hospital. Monday persisted, and Officer Oulette sprayed him, with a blast lasting from one to eight seconds, depending on whose version of events one accepts. Monday was then taken to the hospital on a stretcher, where he remained for five days as a result of a severe reaction to the pepper spray. (Whether or not he was attempting suicide originally was unknown.) Monday filed a 1983 suit for excessive force. The case went to trial, but after hearing the plaintiffs' case the judge granted summary judgment to the defense based on qualified immunity. The Circuit Court, on appeal, commented favorably on the District Court's finding that use of pepper spray was reasonable, because it helped avoid the need for Officer Oulette to place his hands on Monday, which could easily have escalated into more serious force, including injuries to the officers as well as to Monday.

Taken together, the above cases do not offer a consistent pattern. Some courts, as in *Medina* and *Oulette*, are comfortable in making the decision as to whether a level of force is excessive. Other courts, as in *Omdahl* and *Deorle*, prefer that a jury decide exactly where a use of force fits on the continuum of lethality, as well as whether or not its use was reasonable. While most courts do not question police tactics unless the tactic itself can be construed as excessive force, both pepper spray and beanbags have been found to be excessive under some circumstances. Certainly one factor that plays a key role in determining the objective reasonableness of any use of force is the expectation that the tactic will be successful. We turn now specifically to the use of various tactics in SbC situations.

Tactics in SbC Situations

"Suicide by cop" has been defined as "Incidents in which individuals, bent on self destruction, engage in life threatening and criminal behavior in order to force the police to kill them" (Geberth, 1993, p. 105). Although police training has for some time at least noted this problem (cf. Geller & Scott, 1992; Noesner & Dolan, 1992; Van Zandt, 1993), training focused specifically on suicide by cop incidents has been rare until quite recently.

Recent training has been highly influenced by a study conducted in cooperation with the Los Angeles County Sheriff's Department (Hutson et al., 1998). The Public Safety Research Institute in California (Barry Perrou, personal communication, 9-17-98) and the California Commission on Peace Officer Standards and Training (1999), or POST, both offer modules specific to suicide by cop. The Michigan State Police has created a training module on suicide by cop (Gary Kaufman, personal communication, 4-9-99), and "In the Line of Duty" in St Louis, Missouri has developed a training video on suicide by cop (Don Marsh, personal communication, 6-8-99). Still other training has been developed for dealing with mentally ill subjects (Huntley, 2002; Nislow, 2000)

While it is difficult to generalize about these efforts, information from the POST Telecourse is probably typical. This training emphasizes recognition of the type of individual likely to be involved in suicide by cop and awareness of the danger posed to the officer. Officers are advised to avoid a confrontation as much as possible, to stall for time, and to use trained negotiators. Officers are urged to consider less lethal force options, but they are also warned that such use may trigger an attack on officers.

It should be noted that in all 11 cases (out of 46) where less lethal force was used in the Los Angeles County study, the subject was eventually killed with lethal force (Hutson et al. 1998, p. 686). However, Hutson et al. (1998) only examined cases of officer-involved shootings, and therefore any less lethal force would have been unsuccessful, at least in the sense that lethal force was eventually resorted to. In 46% of their SbC incidents, however, the subjects were wounded rather than killed. It is not clear why the (previous) use of less lethal force was associated with a higher fatality rate.

Besides Hutson et al., two other studies provide data relevant to use of force in SbC incidents. The first of these was conducted by Parent (1996; Parent & Verdun-Jones, 1998). Parent presents case synopses of 28 incidents of victim-precipitated homicide, most of which qualify as SbC incidents. Parent is optimistic about the potential of the Taser in such incidents, especially in cases where an officer is threatened by a knife-wielding, slowly-advancing subject. Parent and Verdun-Jones (1998) recommend tactical withdrawal in order to plan for use of less lethal force. Nevertheless, most of the cases cited by Parent (1996) in which the officer was able to overcome the subject without using deadly force involved rapid use of nonlethal, or physical, force by the officer, rather than reliance on technology.

Lord (2000, 2001) obtained detailed information on 64 SbC incidents in North Carolina. A significant advantage of Lord's sample is that it contains a large number of incidents that were resolved without resort to deadly force and without the subject's suicide. Lord reports that 16 subjects were killed by officers, five subjects committed suicide, and an additional nine subjects were injured by police. It is not clear how many of these injuries were the result of lethal as opposed to less lethal or even nonlethal force, but in at least 34 cases (53%), the subject surrendered or was overcome by police without resort to lethal force.

The primary tactical strategy found by Lord (2001) was some form of negotiation. In 28 cases this reached the point of "discussing the problem," and most of these cases (93%) were resolved successfully by the police. The only less lethal technology in evidence was the use of gas; in seven of eight cases where gas was used (88%), the outcome was successful (SbC was avoided). Lord is careful to point out that one cannot necessarily attribute a successful outcome to the strategy involved. Police obviously preferred to talk whenever that was possible, and subjects who were amenable to discussing the situation were likely to be less committed to dying in the first place. Indeed, Lord (2000) found numerous demographic, background, and personality differences distinguishing those subjects who were killed by police from those where police avoided lethal force. This suggests that the successful resolution of a potential SbC incident may have more to do with subject characteristics than with police tactics.

Scoville (1998), basing his analysis mainly on the Hutson et al. (1998) study, agrees that less lethal force may be appropriate with knife wielding subjects–if a safe distance can be maintained and if there is a designated shooter available should deadly force be needed. He goes on to caution that use of less lethal force may serve as a "go signal" that triggers hesitating subjects into a more committed SbC attempt.

Finally, Homant, Kennedy, and Hupp (2000) were concerned that the label of "suicide by cop" may imply that the subject is not particularly dangerous to others. They found that 22% of such incidents were actually not dangerous to police or others, and, more importantly, that these non-dangerous incidents were indistinguishable (until after the fact) from the 56% of the incidents in which police or others were either killed, injured, or placed in a high level of danger. They concluded that use of less lethal force in these situations was no more or less appropriate than with other dangerous subjects.

In summary, there is a lack of consensus about the effectiveness of various less lethal force techniques, especially in SbC situations. The research reported below represents a preliminary attempt to quantify some data involving the use of less lethal technologies in SbC situations, followed by a more qualitative analysis of their effectiveness.

Method

The rationale of the present research involved selecting all relevant less lethal force cases from a data base of SbC incidents, and examining these incidents to determine the effectiveness of the various approaches. A comparison sample of incidents was drawn in which less lethal force technologies were not used. These comparison incidents were of three types: incidents in which nonlethal (or physical) force was used, incidents in which police made some meaningful effort to negotiate with the subject, and incidents that seemed to present the opportunity for less lethal force. The selection of these incidents will be described more fully below. At this point it is important to stress one point: this methodology does not allow one to draw causal inferences. First, it cannot be determined whether less lethal force technologies were actually available in the comparison situations. Even if less lethal force options were available, it is likely that the decision to use or not use them was in part determined by the demeanor of the subject. Thus, in those cases where less lethal force was effective, it may indicate only that police did a good job of selecting appropriate situations for its use. There is no way to conclude with any confidence that a less lethal approach would have worked in those situations where it was not tried. The intention, then, is not to second guess the decisions made by officers on the scene, especially when the information is often quite incomplete. Nevertheless, it is hoped that an examination of the less lethal incidents will reveal something about the potential usefulness of various less lethal approaches.

The Database: Selection of Cases

The SbC incidents for this research were taken from a sample of 143 incidents that had been compiled during three previous research studies (cf. Homant & Kennedy, 2000b; Homant et al., 2000; Kennedy et al., 1998). These incidents come from a variety of sources, including court cases (appellate decisions and trial level materials and depositions), cases reported in the professional literature, cases sent to us for consultation or as a result of our interest in the area, and searches of various on-line newspapers and other media reports. In many of the cases information was available from more than one source. The single largest source was newspaper and other media accounts, which provided 68 of the 143 cases.

In collecting data on suicide by cop incidents, we originally compiled information on 174 incidents that raised the issue of possible SbC. In previous research (Homant & Kennedy, 2000b) we described the classification of these incidents as to whether or not they were SbC situations. In order to be considered SbC, the subject must have exposed him or herself to potential police fire while endangering police or others, and there had to be some evidence that the subject wanted to be killed by the police. Staying under cover and challenging police to "come and get me," or verbalizing a wish to die but not endangering anyone was not sufficient for an incident to be classified as SbC. Two raters, working independently, achieved 96.5% agreement as to which of the original 174 incidents qualified as SbC. (Disagreements were then resolved by discussion.)

The quality and quantity of the information varied greatly across cases. The information that was available, however, seldom contained any significant disputes as to the facts of the incidents. It is probable that our database somewhat over-represents incidents in which the subject was killed by police (72%), since these are more likely to receive media and court attention. Thus, cases in which less lethal force or negotiations resolved a barricade situation successfully are likely to be under-represented. Also, in some cases a subject's suicidal motivation becomes evident only after a barricade situation is unresolved by negotiations or by some less lethal tactic. It is important, therefore, to be clear that any results from this study are not meant to apply to barricade situations in general.

Many of the 143 SbC incidents that made up our original database were not relevant for looking at police tactics. In 70 incidents there did not seem to be any choice but for police to react as quickly as possible, using lethal force. Many of these were pre-planned incidents, where the subject simply initiated an apparently deadly attack on one or more officers. In 73 of the incidents, however, either some type of less lethal force or negotiation was used, or, in our judgment, there at least had been the possibility of using less lethal force.

These 73 incidents made up the final data base for this study. We subdivided them into four types: (a) 23 incidents in which the police used or attempted to use some type of **less lethal** force; (b) 13 incidents that involved only **nonlethal** (physical/manual) force; (c) 16 incidents in which police attempted to **negotiate** with the subject (beyond orders or pleas for the subject to drop his or her weapon); and (d) 21 **comparison** incidents (in which it seemed that some type of less lethal force might have been feasible). In these comparison cases, the subject typically escalated the threat to police in a relatively slow, deliberate manner, for example, by advancing with a knife or by reaching for a firearm that he or she had originally dropped.

The 70 cases from our original database that were **not** selected for this research typically involved a level of threat to police or others in circumstances that made anything other than lethal force impractical. Lethal force was in fact used in 100% of the 70 unselected cases, compared to 77% of the selected cases. One obvious difference was that the 70 unselected cases were much more likely to involve a pre-planned confrontation with the police (50% vs. 12%), and much less likely to involve an intervention with a disturbed person (37% vs. 77%) that evolved into a SbC situation. While it may be argued that other police tactics may have prevented some of these situations from becoming ones that required lethal force, our judgment was based on each situation as it did in fact evolve. (The Christopher Davies case reported at the beginning of Chapter 4 is a good example of the type of case we **excluded** here, despite expert testimony that various tactics might have been available.) It should also be noted that many incidents involved multiple tactics; an incident was classified "negotiation" only if neither nonlethal or less lethal force was used. Likewise, an incident was classified as nonlethal only if less lethal force was not used.

Results

To recapitulate, the main purpose of this research is to present qualitative data illustrating how various police tactics affect the outcome of SbC situations. Before presenting brief vignettes of a number of incidents, however, it will be useful to examine some summary data.

Comparison of Incidents by Type of Force

Table 8-1 gives a comparison of less lethal force incidents with incidents in which less lethal force was not used. As can be seen in the table, the four types of incidents differed in several respects.

Table 8-1

A Comparison of Four Approaches in Suicide by Police Situations

Police Approach

Variable	less-lethal	non-lethal	negotiation	comparison	p
Number of cases:	23	13	16	21	
Disturbed Intervention (%)	82.6	69.2	68.8	80.9	.70
Firearm Present (%)	30.4	53.8	75.0	23.8	.01
Knife Present (%)	47.8	38.5	25.0	57.1	.25
Brief (% under 10 minutes)	56.5	92.3	6.3	90.5	.001
Female (%)	0	30.7	6.3	14.3	---
Mean Age (% of N = 45)	36.7	33.0	37.9	29.7	.30
Drink/Drug Influence (%)	13.0	23.1	12.5	38.1	.20
Police Use Deadly Force (%)	78.2	30.8	81.3	100	.001
Subject dies (%)	69.6	30.8	87.5	90.5	.001

All tests by chi-square except for Age (ANOVA); all p values are two-tailed. (There were too few females for statistical analysis.)

Percentages are based on the number of subjects within each of the four subgroups who score positive on any given variable.

Previous research (Homant & Kennedy, 2000b) found that suicides by police can be divided into three major types: Direct Confrontations, in which the subject pre-plans the confrontation with police; Disturbed Interventions, in which police are called to deal with suicidal persons, domestic situations, or other mentally and emotionally disturbed subjects; and Criminal Interventions, in which intervention into more or less normal criminal activity results in a confrontation in which the subject attempts to force the police to shoot. As indicated above, most of the cases in this research were of the Disturbed Intervention type, and the frequency of Disturbed Interventions did not differ significantly by subgroup. The remaining incidents were about equally divided between the other two types.

The four subgroups also did not differ significantly in terms of age, gender, indication of drinking or drug use, or having a knife. Small subgroup sizes, however, makes some of these null findings difficult to interpret. With respect to gender, for example, there were only eight females in the sample. The fact that four of these happened to fall in the nonlethal group may be coincidence, or (more likely, we believe) may indicate a greater reluctance to use lethal force against a female subject, combined with confidence in one's ability to overpower the female subject manually.

Although possession of a knife did not differ significantly by subgroup, the difference in police tactic was highly significant when focusing on whether the subject possessed a firearm. Firearms were much more likely to be present in the Negotiation group. We believe that this simply reflects the fact that it is the presence of the firearm that helps the subject create the standoff that leads to the negotiations. Conversely, the very low percentage of subjects with firearms in the comparison group no doubt reflects our judgment that absence of a firearm in these situations was a factor suggesting that use of less lethal force would have been possible.

The four subgroups showed an extremely large difference in the duration of the incidents. For the most part this is an artifact of the negotiation category, where some amount of time is necessary to try to establish communications. Thus, very few of these incidents fell into the "brief" category. In contrast, the fact that most of the nonlethal force incidents ended very quickly is not an artifact as such. Rather, as will be established below, it reflects the fact that the opportunity to overpower a subject, especially using some element of surprise, is often present only at the beginning of a confrontation.

The most important variable in Table 8-1 is "Police Use Deadly Force." Obviously, the purpose of less lethal force or other police tactics is to avoid having to use deadly force. The fact that deadly force was used in 100% of the Comparison incidents no doubt reflects sampling bias to some extent. As indicated above, we believe that we were much more likely to acquire cases in which deadly force was used. However, this bias would be true for all four categories. It would have been possible for a subject in the comparison group to back down and surrender to police. Deadly force was used in all 21 comparison cases, and in all but two of these instances the subject was killed. The negotiation and less lethal force groups were associated with a somewhat lower level of (subsequent) lethal force. In one negotiation case the subject committed suicide, and two subjects in the less lethal group survived being shot, so that the subject survival rate was much higher (30.4%) in the less lethal than in the negotiation group (12.5%). The greatest outcome difference, however, is seen in the nonlethal group, where only 30.8% of the incidents resulted in use of lethal force, and subjects correspondingly survived at a 69.2% rate.

To summarize the above section, the type of incident or subject that the police faced differed in only a few respects across the four categories. Negotiation was more likely to involve subjects with firearms, while there was a trend for female subjects to be in the nonlethal force group. While use of less lethal force was often followed by use of deadly force, use of deadly force was greatly reduced for the nonlethal incidents. Both less lethal force and negotiation appeared to reduce use of lethal force to some extent over the comparison incidents.

We must repeat, however, that one should be extremely cautious about drawing causal inferences here. Police who did not use either nonlethal or less lethal force (i.e., the negotiation and comparison incidents) may have reasonably perceived a higher level of risk in their situations. Circumstances, such as the terrain and the relative distances between the actors, may have played a key role in decision making. The "element of surprise" often determined the use of nonlethal force, and this may not have been as available in the other three categories. Nevertheless, the relatively positive findings that emerge from the above comparisons suggest that a further examination of the less lethal incidents may be helpful in clarifying the relative advantages of different approaches.

Less Lethal Force Incidents

The 23 incidents that involved some level of less lethal force included five cases in which some form of less lethal bullet was used, two cases of Taser use, three cases of baton use, and 13 cases in which some form of gas or spray was used. The summary of these incidents below focuses on the aspects most relevant to use of force. Details that qualify them as SbC are often omitted.

Bean-bag and rubber bullets. The five incidents that used less lethal bullets can be summarized as follows:

1. Two beanbag rounds failed to stop a man advancing with a knife. An officer was stabbed, two more beanbag rounds failed to stop the man's advance, and the police then shot and killed him.
2. After three hours of negotiation failed to calm a man down, a beanbag gun was used, apparently to try to induce surrender. It is not clear whether being hit by the beanbag further angered the subject. He subsequently pointed a handgun at officers and was shot and killed.
3. A man was threatening police with a pick axe and a kitchen knife. He was hit with three rubber bullets from an "Arwin 37" and retreated into his house. At this point the use of the less lethal force appeared to be successful, in that it allowed the police to avoid use of deadly force. Unfortunately, however, when the police subsequently entered the house the subject was found dead. He had died of internal bleeding after one of the rubber bullets punctured a lung.
4. After a brief attempt at negotiations, a man carrying a pipe resembling a gun emerged from his house and threatened police. He was hit by both rubber and wooden bullets to no effect. He turned toward some spectators and was killed by a police sniper.
5. Several beanbag rounds combined with several hours of negotiation failed to induce a suicidal, rifle-carrying man to surrender. Because this occurred in an isolated desert campground, police determined that there was no danger to anyone else and simply left. Details are sketchy on this prolonged incident; it is possible that use of the beanbag rounds enabled the officers to avoid use

of deadly force. More likely the beanbag rounds neither helped nor hurt the situation.

In summary, the use of less lethal bullets was not very effective in this small sample. Four cases ultimately resulted in a fatality, and the fifth case did not seem to benefit from the less lethal force. (In a cross-validation study reported below, the issue of beanbag effectiveness is revisited.)

Taser. The two Taser cases can be summarized as follows:

1. Police encountered a man stabbing himself. He was probably high on PCP. One officer shot him with a Taser, and a second officer fired a handgun. The man was knocked to the ground but got up and advanced on the officers. They shot and killed him. The apparently simultaneous use of less lethal and lethal force obviously makes this a poor example from which to generalize. Nevertheless, it is clear that the use of the stun gun failed to deter the subject's advance on police.
2. A man entered a police station and stabbed an officer with a screwdriver. (A vest saved him from injury.) When other officers arrived, the man charged at them. A Taser was ineffective in stopping him, and he was shot and killed. One officer was wounded by a ricocheting bullet. Here again, the Taser gun was ineffective. Arguably, by delaying the police response, its use may have increased the risk to officers and thus contributed to the one officer being wounded.

Baton. There were three incidents involving use of a baton or nightstick:

1. A man advanced on three officers and pointed a gun at one officer's waist. The officer struck the man's hand with a baton. The subject then pointed the gun at a different officer. When the subject started to slowly squeeze the trigger, two officers shot and killed him. While use of the baton deflected the subject's aim from the original officer, this use of less lethal force was clearly unsuccessful, in that it created or at least maintained a high level of danger to the officers.

2. Two officers confronted a man high on PCP. He swung a broom handle back and forth at them as they advanced. They tried to control him by use of their batons and by wrestling the broom away. One officer appeared to be in trouble and his partner drew his gun. The subject rushed at the officer with the gun. The officer retreated, finally shooting the man nine times as he continued to advance. The subject was apparently quite disturbed and suicidal, and it seems probable that he would have charged at police regardless of the baton use. Nevertheless, it is possible that use of the batons caused police to get too close to the subject and in that sense helped to escalate the situation.

3. An officer attempted to arrest a disturbed individual. After originally complying, the subject approached the officer in a threatening manner. Apparently the officer tried to use his baton to control the subject. The subject was able to get the baton away from the officer and then began assaulting the officer. Eventually the officer shot the subject several times as the subject continued to advance.

In summary, in all three cases, use of a baton either escalated the situation, increased the risk, or at least failed to help the situation.

Chemical sprays. There were 13 cases in which police resorted to some type of chemical agent to control the subject. In five of these cases, police used tear gas to flush a subject from an apartment, house, or car, always after a lengthy standoff. All five cases resulted in the police shooting and killing the subject. (These incidents will not be further summarized.) In eight other cases, police used pepper spray, mace, or tear gas either to stop a subject from advancing on them, or to get him or her to drop a weapon.

The first three incidents seem to have a common theme:

1. Several police confronted a youth who was alternating threats to kill them with a champagne bottle with pleas for them to shoot. They doused him with pepper spray, to no effect. Finally one officer shot and wounded him.

2. After a car and foot chase, the subject stopped and confronted two pursuing officers. He had discarded his gun during the chase. He charged at the officers, who used pepper spray on him to no effect. One officer finally shot twice, wounding him.

3. A brick-wielding subject was surrounded by several officers in a small yard. Mace was used, but to no effect. He advanced on one officer, brick raised, as the officer retreated. Finally, two officers shot and wounded him.

Although all three of these incidents resulted in the subject surviving a police shooting, this probably was due to a combination of luck and the fact that the threat to the police did not result in multiple shots (as it might have had the subject been about to use a firearm). It seems doubtful that the use of a chemical spray helped or hurt these situations. The next two cases are similar to the previous three, except that outcomes were fatal:

4. The subject had cut his wrists, but paramedics could not treat him until police got two knives away from him. They doused him with pepper spray twice, but to no effect. He eventually advanced on the officers and was shot and killed.
5. Four officers cornered a man suspected of a stabbing. They used pepper spray to try to get him to surrender. Instead, he advanced on an officer with a raised knife; the officers' retreat was blocked by brush. The subject was shot and killed.

Although arguably the use of pepper spray in the two above incidents may have escalated things (precipitating the subject's advance on the officers), it seems doubtful that it made things worse. In the remaining three cases the pepper spray or tear gas worked as intended:

6. A person threatening suicide became angered at police intervention. Making threatening gestures toward police with a knife and cleaver, he moved down the street away from them. Police doused him with pepper spray and arrested him.
7. A suicidal subject emerged from a room and advanced on officers with a knife. They blasted him with tear gas, and he fell to the floor and dropped the knife. The officers grabbed him and arrested him.
8. Three officers chased a knife-wielding man who had threatened suicide. The subject eventually isolated one officer and confronted him with a knife. The officer held up a can of pepper spray, and the subject ran off. A police car blocked his path and a pursuing

officer pushed him against the car. He dropped his knife, and was arrested unhurt.

In summary, the use of less lethal force in our SbC situations was only marginally successful. If we discount the five incidents in which tear gas was used to flush out a subject (all of which "succeeded" in the immediate goal, but resulted in the subject's death), less lethal force was clearly successful in only three of 18 incidents. Because the combined success rate of the negotiation and comparison categories was even lower (two of 37 incidents), this is not necessarily bad. However, several of the scenarios raised the possibility that less lethal force either escalated the situation or at least put police officers at greater risk.

Nonlethal Force Incidents

There were 13 incidents in which police attempted to deal with the subject by using some level of simple physical force. With one exception, all of these incidents involved some attempt to overpower the subject. In the exception, several officers responded to a report of a woman who had been wandering an apartment building, pointing a gun at her head. When the officers confronted the subject, no weapon was evident. One officer attempted to search her for a possible weapon. She slapped his hand away, drew a handgun from her waistband, and aimed it at the officer. In the meantime the officer had drawn his weapon, and he shot and killed her. While it is arguable whether the officer attempted to use "force" to effect a search, the incident is included here because it seems instructive of one of the risks of attempting to deal with such incidents by using nonlethal force.

Use of Surprise. In five of the nonlethal-force incidents, officers used the element of surprise in an attempt to overpower subjects. Three times they were successful and twice they failed.

1. Two officers responded to a subject threatening suicide with a handgun. One officer deliberately stayed out of sight, and the other attempted to negotiate. While the man advanced on the negotiating officer, the other officer tackled him from behind. The subject was arrested without injury to anyone.
2. A uniformed, armed security officer encountered a man in a parking lot who was pushing a nude, bloodied woman onto the floor of a car. The man advanced on the officer, challenging him

to shoot. As the security officer retreated, gun aimed, the man acted as if he was reaching for a weapon in his pants pocket. Other security officers arrived and, surprising the subject, tackled him from behind and subdued him.

3. Responding to a call, an officer encountered a female who had cut her left arm and was clutching a butcher knife. She was distracted by the arrival of a second officer, and the first officer attempted to advance on her, presumably to grab the arm holding the knife. She noticed his advance, however, and reacted by cutting herself more deeply and warning the first officer to stay away. She then advanced on the second officer with her knife raised, challenging him to kill her. As she was advancing on him, the first officer was able to grab her right arm and disarm her. She was arrested without further injury.

4. Two police officers interrupted a woman who was holding a man at gunpoint. As they confronted her, the man slipped away into a building. The woman refused to drop her weapon and insisted that the man come out and admit to things he had done. She challenged the officers to go ahead and shoot her, as she had nothing to live for. A third officer arrived, and using the cover of a building, some brush, and a small incline, began to advance on her from somewhat behind her while the first two officers attempted to distract her with repeated commands to drop the gun. However, she spotted the advancing officer when he was still several feet away. As he unholstered and aimed his gun, she raised her gun toward him. He fired, as did one of the other two officers, killing her.

5. Several officers responded to a report of a man with a gun who had threatened to kill himself. Three of the officers attempted to sneak up on him from the rear in order to disarm him. The subject saw them, fired shots at them, and then began to advance toward them. They shot and killed him.

The first three of the above incidents represent the successful use of nonlethal force. It seems that mostly chance or luck distinguishes them from the two failures. Each of the above incidents lasted only a few minutes, so there was little time to use any negotiation skills. The decision to attempt to subdue a subject by overpowering him or her from behind will usually require an officer to make a rather quick go/no-go judgment when the opportunity appears to be there.

Physically Overpowering. There were seven other incidents in which police responded by use of physical force to subdue the subject. In only one of these incidents did the tactic clearly fail, although in two of the successful cases the officer placed himself at increased risk and could easily have been killed.

1. In the one clear failure, an officer encountered a man who had just stabbed someone. The officer attempted to arrest him by pushing him up against a fence. The man fell, but got up and stabbed the officer in the side. A second officer arrived, and both officers pointed their guns at the subject. The subject told them that he would lower his knife, if they lowered their guns. When the officers did lower their guns, the subject advanced on them, lunging at one of them. He continued to advance as they retreated, until they finally shot and killed him.

2. In one of the increased-risk incidents, an officer intervened in a suicide attempt. The man had a shotgun pointed at his own chin. Eventually, the man advanced on the officer. When he had closed to a distance of about four feet, the officer tackled him. The shotgun went off during the struggle, but no one was hurt.

3. In the other increased risk incident, an officer stopped a woman to arrest her for theft. She fired several shots at the officer, who was wearing a bullet proof vest. Despite the fact that one shot grazed his abdomen, he did not fire back. Eventually he wrestled her to the ground and handcuffed her.

4. Two police officers encountered a man holding a butcher knife. He had just killed his girlfriend. The officers jumped on him and eventually wrestled the knife away.

5. A 15-year-old, drunken youth confronted a police officer who had interrupted a family fight. The officer retreated as the youth advanced with a knife. Other officers then arrived and overpowered the youth without harm to anyone.

6. A female officer, along with a trainee, was in the process of a traffic stop. A man wearing a gun and holster walked up to her and said that he had a death wish. Ignoring her order to halt, he kept walking toward her. She kicked him away and along with her trainee wrestled him down and got the gun away from him.

7. Police surrounded a house trailer where several shots had been fired and a man was threatening suicide. During two hours of negotiation the man threatened to shoot police and said that he would not be taken alive. Finally he exited the trailer, holding

only a pocketknife. Police grabbed him and subdued him. (This was the only nonlethal-force incident that lasted more than about four or five minutes.)

To summarize the nonlethal-force incidents, nine would generally be considered to have a successful outcome, and four were failures, in the sense that the subject was killed by police. Nothing in particular seemed to distinguish the failures from the successes. Two of the failure incidents involved attempts to take the subject by surprise (or while distracted), but three of these surprise incidents were successful. Three of the failures involved subjects with a gun as opposed to a knife, but four of the successful incidents also involved a subject with a firearm. Of the four incidents involving a woman subject, two were successful and two were failures. Finally, use of nonlethal force clearly increased the risk to officers compared to the other approaches: one officer was stabbed, one was grazed by a bullet, and another had a shotgun go off right next to him. At least two other officers had guns pointed at them as result of attempting to approach the subject–although this may have occurred anyway.

Implications

This research has reviewed four types of police response to a sample of SbC situations. The results show a clear superiority of outcome associated with the nonlethal and less lethal force approaches. The death rate for subjects in these combined categories was 55.6%, compared to 89.2% in the combined negotiation and comparison categories. The outcome for subjects was especially better when nonlethal force was attempted, with the death rate being 30.8%. Several points need be made, however, before drawing even tentative conclusions.

The most successful tactic, nonlethal force, which generally involved trying to wrestle the subject, sometimes relying on the element of surprise, tended to place police at the highest level of risk. Although no officers were seriously hurt in the 13 incidents that we examined, in at least a few cases this outcome seemed largely a matter of luck. Also, it seemed probable to us that in some of the nonlethal force cases the subject was not particularly hostile; the subject's main aim was simply to die. It is likely, then, that at least some of these subjects did not wholeheartedly resist police intervention. Of course, even if officers know that they are dealing with a SbC incident, they should not count on the subject not also being homicidal (Homant et al., 2000b). Thus, even if further research should support the finding that a nonlethal force approach leads to the best bottom-line outcome for the subject, it is doubtful that such an approach should ever be recommended in dealing with armed subjects.

With respect to less lethal force, in most of the incidents, lethal force was subsequently used. Nevertheless, the subject survival rate of 30.4% was better than either the negotiation or comparison groups. Of course, as our brief case summaries indicated, less lethal force was used in a variety of circumstances, and it may be that a larger number of cases would indicate a type of suicide by cop situation in which less lethal force is more effective.

The SbC cases used in the above research were all obtained prior to January 1, 2000. While the majority were from the 1990s, many were from the 1980s, when less lethal technologies were not widely available. It seemed likely, then, that a current sample of cases would provide a higher proportion of less lethal force incidents. To determine whether the trends observed in the above research would hold up, a simple cross validation study was conducted.

Cross-Validation of Less Lethal Force in SbC

A search of the Lexis-Nexis general news data base uncovered 62 SbC incidents that occurred between January 1, 2000 and June 30, 2002. These incidents were found using the search terms "suicide by cop," and the combination of "police" and "suicide." The use of "police" and "standoff" proved to be too tedious a strategy, but did produce some incidents. While other search strategies may have uncovered additional incidents, the ones that were found seemed representative of those incidents that get newspaper coverage.

One obvious difference, in comparison to our original newspaper database searches, was the frequency with which "suicide by cop" is now used as a descriptive phrase–by police spokespersons, by reporters, and even by the subjects themselves (when they survived, or in notes or previous comments to friends).

For convenience, the cross-validation study will be referred to as Study 2, and the original research reported above as Study 1. The distribution of the 62 cases in Study 2, with respect to use of force and relative success, is shown in Table 8-2. "Success" here is defined in terms of the subject being taken into custody without life-threatening injury and without the (eventual) use of lethal force. Data from Study 1 are also summarized for comparison.

Table 8-2

Relative Success of Less Lethal Force: Cross Validation Study

Category	Study 1		Study 2		Combined	
	N	Success	N	Success	N	Success
Less Lethal	23	13%	20	50%	43	30%
Beanbag etc.	5	0%	15	53%	20	40%
Pepper Spray	13	23%	4	50%	17	29%
Taser	2	0%	0		2	0%
Baton	3	0%	1	0%	4	0%
Nonlethal	13	69%	2	50%	15	67%
Negotiation	16	13%	7	29%	23	17%
Comparison	21	0%	11	0%	32	0%
Excluded	70	0%	22	9%	92	2%
Total Incidents	143	10%	62	24%	205	14%

Note: Cases involving multiple tactics are categorized by the more forceful tactic (the one listed first).

The "Excluded" category refers to all those cases in which neither nonlethal, less lethal, nor negotiation was used and there did not appear to be any reasonable opportunity to have used less lethal force.

The major difference from the original data (Table 8-1) was the frequency with which beanbags and other less lethal bullets were used: 12 incidents involved beanbags, and an additional 3 involved rubber or plastic bullets. This difference (15 of 62 vs. 5 of 143) is highly significant (Chi-square 21.21, df 1, $p < .001$), and no doubt reflects the increased availability of and training with beanbags.

Of the 15 new cases involving beanbag (or rubber or plastic) bullets, it would be difficult to pick a representative case. If there is any generalization to be made, it is in the diversity of the various incidents. In the eight successful incidents, three times the subject surrendered, and five times he was overcome by the police after dropping a weapon. Twice, beanbag use followed the breakdown of negotiations; one successful use was combined with a Taser, one with pepper spray. The eight subjects who were successfully handled with beanbags presented police with a variety of weapons: two had knives, one a pitchfork, one a large kitchen fork, one a 4-foot pipe, one bluffed having a gun, one was suspected of having multiple guns, and one brandished a handgun.

The seven unsuccessful cases do not appear much different. Only one subject had a gun, a shotgun. One had a knife and drove his vehicle at officers. Four others were armed with knives. One subject charged police while swinging two shopping carts. In one case the failure was due to human error rather than the technology: using rubber bullets, a deputy loaded the wrong type of shell and the subject was killed. In every other case, it appeared that at least one beanbag round hit the subject and he kept coming.

It could be speculated that the main determinants of beanbag success, as well as of other less lethal weaponry, are the subject's degree of determination to die and his pain tolerance. Pain tolerance, in turn, seems affected by drugs or alcohol and emotional arousal. These factors, of course, are not variables that police could reasonably hope to assess during most incidents. Furthermore, there were also cases where out-of-control subjects seemed to be "sobered up" by being hit by a beanbag or doused with pepper spray.

It should be pointed out that there were several cases of multiple tactics in Study 2. Thus, although never used by itself, the Taser or stun gun was used three times; it was associated with a successful use of beanbag bullets, and twice it was unsuccessful in combination with both beanbags and pepper spray.

Conclusions and Implications

As indicated by Tables 8-1 and 8-2, a variety of police tactics, including less lethal and nonlethal force, were associated with differences in the outcome of SbC incidents. As stressed throughout, there is not enough information to allow for any causal inferences here. The conclusions that follow, therefore, should be considered hypotheses for further investigation.

Nonlethal Force. Overall, in the two studies combined, nonlethal force—generally tackling the subject—was the most successful tactic. The main problem with this approach has already been mentioned: there appears to be a significant increase in risk to the officer involved. Also, its high success rate may have more to do with the fact that officers recognized a lack of commitment or dangerousness on the part of the subject.

The nonlethal category had the greatest reduction in use in Study 2. While sampling differences may account for this, it is also likely that police training, which stresses containment rather than confrontation with disturbed persons, is starting to overcome some officers' preference for quick action (cf. Panzarella & Alicea, 1997). Perhaps the wider availability of less lethal technology has also reduced reliance on nonlethal force. While less lethal technologies were introduced to reduce use of deadly force, a corresponding reduction in nonlethal force is not necessarily a bad thing, given the unpredictable nature of nonlethal force.

Negotiation. The data pertaining to the effectiveness of negotiation are problematic in a number of respects. First, there was not enough information to evaluate the quality of the negotiation. Especially in Study 2, the negotiation was likely conducted by a trained member of a special response team, but there was little information as to the negotiator's approach, let alone the degree to which the subject entered into any sort of dialogue. Second, some attempt at negotiation was often involved in the incidents involving less lethal force. It is not clear whether these outcomes should be considered failures of negotiation or partial successes. (In one case, the distraction created by the negotiator allowed for less lethal force to be deployed and the subject to be successfully overcome.) Third, the type of scenario that lends itself to negotiation differs considerably from those in which negotiations were not attempted; thus any comparison of outcomes is confounded by too many other variables. What needs further study here, then, is not *whether* to negotiate, but *what approach* to negotiation works best. With disturbed persons threatening suicide, for example, many negotiators prevent family members from talking directly to the subject, while others have had some success by using family members (cf. Lord, 2001). Certainly more research needs to be done on this issue.

Less Lethal Force. For the two studies, less lethal force had a combined success rate of 30%. Exactly what this figure should be compared to is problematic. For one thing, failure to have used less lethal force would have meant either retreating and thus creating a standoff, or using nonlethal force (typically at great risk), or using or threatening deadly force. The very low success rate in the Comparison and Excluded cases–only 2 successes in 91 cases–suggests that less lethal force is much better than the alternative. However, sampling bias should be kept in mind here; cases in which the officer simply ordered the subject to put his weapon down, perhaps pointing a gun at the subject, and the subject complied, would not be likely to come to our attention.

Both pepper spray and beanbags showed promise of being able to control some suicidal persons. Risk of escalating the situation was present, though there were no clear cases where the subject might not have advanced on police anyway. Officer error in use of the technology, or injury directly from the technology, remains a problem. If courts conclude that beanbags are risky enough that they should only be used in deadly force situations, rather than in trying to prevent something from becoming a deadly force situation, this would obviously have a chilling effect on the technology (cf. Leonard, 2002). This could be unfortunate, since Table 8-2 indicates a trend toward more frequent and successful use of less lethal bullets.

Finally, the appropriateness of a response in any particular incident should not be judged by simply looking at the outcome. Simply because the subject dies does not mean that the wrong approach was used, nor does it mean the right approach was used if the subject survives. Given a large sample of relatively similar cases, it may be possible to make broad recommendations as to tactics that will minimize various risks. Even the best tactic, however, is likely to fail on occasion. And, from the data reported here, certainly no particular tactic leaps out as preferable, either in general or under any given circumstances.

It is also important to emphasize that even the tentative findings reported above only apply to SbC situations. Perhaps more than anything, the results of this research bring out the complexity of studying the effectiveness of police tactics. Questions about the effectiveness of any particular tactic or less lethal technology will have to specify the type of subject (gender, age, build, evidence of drugs, alcohol, or emotional disturbance, suicidality, etc.), the type of threat the subject poses (gun, knife, hostages or bystanders, etc.), the relative cover of police and subject, the training of the police involved, and so forth. The data and vignettes presented above are sources of hypotheses rather than conclusions.

References

Anonymous (2001, September). IACP's less lethal force options course. Law & Order, 49 (9), 95-99.

Bailey, W. C. (1996). Less-than-lethal weapons and police-citizen killings in U.S. urban areas. Crime and Delinquency, 42, 535-552.

Button, P. D. (2001). Less-Lethal Force Technology. Toronto, Canada: Toronto Metropolitan Police Commission.

California Commission on Peace Officer Standards and Training (1999). Student Reference Manual for Suicide by Cop Telecourse (aired July 22, 1999 and August 26, 1999). For information contact: Training Program Services Bureau, 1601 Alhambra Boulevard, Sacramento, California 95816-7083.

Desmedt, J. C. (1984). Use of force paradigm for law enforcement. Journal of Police Science and Administration, 12, 170-176.

Dorsch, D. (2001, September). Opened door for lawyers, burden for officers. Law & Order, 49 (9), 102-103.

Garner, J., Schade, T., Hepburn, J., & Buchanan, J. (1995). Measuring the continuum of force used by and against police. Criminal Justice Review, 20, 146-168.

Geberth, V. J. (1993, July). Suicide-by-cop: Inviting death from the hands of a police officer. Law and Order, 41 (7), 105-108.

Geis, G., & Binder, A. (1990). Non-lethal weapons: The potential and pitfalls. Journal of Contemporary Criminal Justice, 6, 1-7.

Geller, W. A., & Scott, M. (1992). Deadly Force: What We Know. Washington, D.C.: Police Executive Research Forum.

Hayeslip, D., & Preszler, A. (1993). NIJ Initiative on Less-Than-Lethal Weapons. Washington, D.C.: U.S. Department of Justice.

Heal, S. (2001, September). Special report II. Less lethal: An evaluation of less-lethal munitions. Law & Order, 49 (9), 88-93.

Homant, R. J., & Kennedy, D. B. (2000a). The effectiveness of less than lethal force in suicide by cop incidents. Police Quarterly, 3, 153-171.

Homant, R. J., & Kennedy, D. B. (2000b). Suicide by police: A proposed typology of law enforcement officer assisted suicide. Policing: An International Journal of Police Strategies and Management, 23, 339-355.

Homant, R. J., Kennedy, D. B., & Hupp, R. T. (2000.) Real and perceived danger in police officer assisted suicide. Journal of Criminal Justice, 28, 43-52.

Hopper, J. A. (2001, November). Less-lethal litigation: Departments and the courts react to less-lethal standards. Law & Order, 49 (11), 87-91.

Huntley, S. (2002, June 8). Resolving conflict without force: Denver police learn techniques to bring calm to confrontations. Rocky Mountain News, City Desk/Local, 1B.

Hutson, H. R., Anglin, D., Yarbrough, J., Hardaway, K., Russell, M.,
Strote, J., Canter, M, & Blum, B. (1998). Suicide by cop. Annals
of Emergency Medicine, 32, 665-669.

IACP (1998). Police Use of Force in America: Research in Progress
Report on the IACP National Database Project. Alexandria, VA:
International Association of Chiefs of Police.

Kaminski, R. J., Edwards, S. M., & Johnson, J. W. (1998). The
deterrent effect of Oleoresin Capsicum on assaults against police:
Testing the velcro-effect hypothesis. Police Quarterly, 1, (2): 1-20.

Kennedy, D. B., Homant, R. J., & Hupp, R. T. (1998, August). Suicide
by cop. FBI Law Enforcement Bulletin (8), 21-27.

Leonard, J. (2002, June 3). Police dropping beanbags as too
dangerous. Los Angeles Times, Part A Main News; Part 1; Page
1 (Metro Desk).

Lord, V. B. (2000). Law enforcement-assisted suicide. Criminal
Justice and Behavior, 27, 401-419.

Lord, V. B. (2001). Law enforcement-assisted suicide: Characteristics
of subjects and law enforcement intervention techniques. In D. C.
Sheehan & J. I. Warren (Eds.), Suicide and Law Enforcement (pp.
607-625). Washington, D. C.: U.S. Department of Justice.

Miller, N. (1995). Less-than-lethal force weaponry: Law enforcement
and correctional agency civil law liability for the use of excessive
force. Creighton Law Review, 28, 733-794.

Nislow, J. (2000, December 15-31). Psych job. Law Enforcement
News, 26 (545/546), 1-3.

Noesner, G. W., & Dolan, J. T. (1992, August). First responder
negotiation training. FBI Law Enforcement Bulletin (8), 1-4.

Oyster, C. K. (2001). Police Reactions to suicide by cop. In D. C.
Sheehan & J. I. Warren (Eds.), Suicide and Law Enforcement (pp.
647-652). Washington, D. C.: U.S. Department of Justice.

Panzarella, R., & Alicea, J. O. (1997). Police tactics in incidents with
mentally disturbed persons. Policing: An International Journal of
Police Strategies & Management, 20, 326-338.

Parent, R. B. (1996). Aspects of Police Use of Deadly Force in British Columbia: The Phenomenon of Victim Precipitated Homicide. Master's Thesis, Simon Fraser University, July, 1996.

Parent, R. B., & Verdun-Jones, S. (1998). Victim-precipitated homicide: Police use of deadly force in British Columbia. Policing: An International Journal of Police Strategies & Management, 21, 432-448.

Robin, G. D. (1996). The illusive and illuminating search for less-than-lethal alternatives to deadly force. Police Forum, 6, (2): 1-20.

Scott, R. F., & Copeland, M. P. (2001). Technological innovation and the development of less-than-lethal force options. In M. J. Palmiotto (Ed.), A Reader for the 21st Century (pp. 276-290). Upper Saddle River, NJ: Prentice Hall.

Scoville, D. (1998, November). FYI: Getting you to pull the trigger. Police (11), 36-44.

Trostle, L. (1990). The force continuum: From lethal to less-than-lethal force. Journal of Contemporary Criminal Justice, 6, 23-26.

Van Zandt, C. R. (1993). Suicide by cop. The Police Chief, 60, 24-30.

Cases Cited

Bell v. Irwin, Case No. 00-CV-4078-JPG. U.S. District for the Southern District of Illinois, 2002).
Chew v. Gates, 27 F.3d 1432 (9th Cir. 1994).
Clem v. Corbeau, 284 F.3d 543 (4th Cir. 2002).
Deorle v. Rutherford, 272 F.3d 1272 (9th Cir. 2001).
Headwaters Forest v. Humboldt, 240 F.3d 1185 (9th Cir. 2000; Amended 2001).
Medina v. Cram, 252 F.3d 1124 (10th Cir. 2001).
Monday v. Oulette, 118 F.3d 1099 (6th Cir. 1997).
Omdahl v. Lindholm, 170 F.3d 730 (7th Cir. 1999).
Robinette v. Barnes, 854 F.2d 909 (6th Cir. 1988).
Robinson v. Solano, 278 F.3d 1007 (9th Cir. 2002).
Saucier v. Katz, 121 S.Ct. 2151 (2001).

Chapter 9

COMPARISON OF STRATEGIES USED IN BARRICADED SITUATIONS: SBC AND NON-SBC SUBJECTS

Vivian B. Lord, Ph.D. and Sergeant Leonard Gigante

Introduction

As defined by Amendola, Leaming and Martin (1996), a barricaded situation is any incident in which one or more armed or potentially armed persons fortify themselves within a location (building, house, vehicle, bridge) with or without hostages and refuse to surrender to the police. These situations often begin as domestic disputes, suicide attempts, or crimes. Once the police are called and then more specifically special response teams, the subjects barricade themselves, often taking hostages.

Unlike other crimes such as burglaries and larcenies, barricaded incidents and hostage takings occur infrequently. In the early 1990s, Los Angeles averaged 40 hostage/barricaded incidents annually; New York averaged 92 annually. In 1996 the police agency in the current study began keeping centralized records for incidents in which its special response team was called out. At that time they averaged about 20 calls per year that could be classified as hostage/barricaded situations.

Although Suicide by Cop (SbC) situations occur in a variety of circumstance quite often surprising the uniform officer who expects to answer a simple domestic dispute, it is from those calls to which special tactical teams and negotiators respond that information can be gleaned about SbC subjects. It is the task of this chapter to provide an understanding of SbC subjects and their interactions with police officers by comparing them within the larger context of barricaded subjects. In other words, although the universe of SbC cases extend well beyond barricaded incidents, there is an extensive subgroup of SbC incidents that are within the subgroup of barricaded incidents (See Figure 1: SbC Incidents within Barricaded Incidents.)

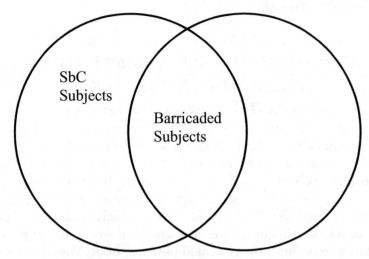

Figure 1. SbC Incidents within Barricaded Incidents

Barricaded/Hostage Situations

While there is fairly extensive literature on international terrorism and related hostage taking, little has been written on domestic barricade/ hostage situations. We know little about the individual, events that precipitate the situation, or the subject's behavior. Interestingly, more has been written about negotiation and negotiation techniques, but not necessarily related to categories of subjects who initiate the act.

Offenders

According to Crelinsten and Szabo (1979), there is a triangular aspect of hostage-taking; the hostage is the means by which the hostage-taker gains something from a third party. The passive victim (the actual hostage) is a means to an end, an intermediary in an exchange between the offender and active victim (the individual who can meet the hostage-taker's demands). The relation between the two victims is critical. If the active victim feels no great concern about the passive victim, then he or she is unlikely to yield to the demand and avert the threat. The active victim can choose to act alone or to involve other parties, such as superiors, police, friends, relatives, who then become part of the process. A feedback mechanism is set up whereby the response of the active victim and those whom he or she calls into the cases feed back to the offender who then alters either the threat or the demand or both.

Whether or not a hostage is involved is a critical factor in how much power and control the subject has and therefore greatly influences the officers' response. Although the officers' goal is to bring a peaceful resolution to the incident, if there is no hostage, there are a number of options available to officers in addition to negotiation. Turning off the electricity, using chemical agents, and even resorting to tactical entry and assault can be considered.

The FBI examined 245 incidents of barricade/hostage taking and concluded that well over half (145) of the perpetrators were suffering from a mental disorder or experiencing emotional turmoil from personal or family problems. The disorders most likely to be involved in violence were mood or cognitive disorders such as depression, bi-polar, and paranoid schizophrenia (Soskis & VanZandt, 1986).

In order to facilitate the negotiation process, Fuselier (1986) placed barricaded/hostage-takers into three categories: severely mentally disturbed, domestic disputants, and individuals interrupted in the course of criminal acts. He argues that the approach that negotiators take should differ for each of these categories. For those individuals who are mentally ill, the negotiators should work hard to establish rapport rather than attempting to address their delusional problems, because the subjects will not be able to interact rationally. Individuals involved in a serious domestic dispute will also have some emotional issues, but if the negotiators communicate support and understanding, they will be able to move the subjects to a more cooperative mode. Those individuals involved in criminal activity can be addressed more directly. Negotiators can address factual issues and focus on exchange of items for hostages.

Donohue, Ramesh, and Borchgrvink (1991) compare hostage negotiations to normative bargaining, and although they admit that there are substantial differences, the goal is to move the hostage-taker off a coercive stance to a cooperative stance. They argue that the two key relational issues are control and distance. In a coercive stance, the subject will reject any need to develop a relationship in order to expand his/her right to achieve their ultimate goals. Distance considers both physical and psychological use of space. The extent the subject comes to trust the negotiator will determine the distance, both psychologically and physically, between the two parties. The researchers used Fuselier's categories of criminal offender, mentally disturbed individuals, and domestic disputants and then examined the common form of negotiation behaviors for each category.

Criminal offenders followed the pattern described by Fuselier. They began in a competitive mode that escalated, but then dropped into more normative bargaining once the initial crisis phase diminished. Toward the end of the incident, there were brief periods of competition as the subject felt some degree of anxiety in releasing hostages and/or surrendering.

Individuals who were mentally ill were less predictable. They convert quickly into the cooperative phase, but then they return to the competitive mode, and remained entrenched in that crisis orientation until the situation is resolved through either surrender or suicide. Donohue and his colleagues note that Fuselier cautions negotiators on the situations in which individuals who are mentally ill may appear cooperative to deceive the negotiator into thinking they will do whatever the negotiator wants,

Donohue found that domestic hostage-takers take longer to become cooperative than the criminal type. Similarly to the criminal subject, as terms of surrender are discussed, there is a second crisis period that will put the domestic disputant back into a competitive mode.

Precipitators

Fuselier, VanZandt, and Lanceley (1991) grouped antecedent events that influence the subject into the three areas of financial, family, and social pressures, noting that the pressures often become multiple. In addition many of the perpetrators come from a background in which male dominance is encouraged, so when their perceived ability to be a man is threatened, negotiation may become more difficult. They also note that these situations can be planned or unplanned. Planned hostage-taking goals include freeing a prisoner, forcing political or social change, or publicizing a cause or perceived wrong. Planned incidents can be particularly dangerous, because these subjects may be willing to die for their cause. Most barricaded situations are not planned. They begin as a crime that suddenly goes wrong, a fight between significant others that escalates when the police arrive or one disputant tries to leave, or an emotionally unstable person who is delusional.

Situational Factors

There are a number of situational factors that play into the interaction between the subject and any hostages he or she might have, as well as between the subject and the negotiators. Weather, time, media, use of alcohol or drugs, and bystanders are just a few beyond the previously mentioned precipitating issues. So the situations involves not only physical factors such as weather, media, by-standers, and the structure in which the subject is barricaded, but also the physical and emotional state of the subject him or herself.

Time is critical, and of particular importance is the duration of the incident. Reducing tension is an important early objective for negotiators. Head (1987) concluded that the first half hour is the most critical because the subject is most likely to be unclear of his or her plans. Kupperman and Trent (1979) claim that the first three to four hours are most dangerous, noting if nobody is killed by then, there is a good chance that none will be. The actual time in which these situations occur compares favorably with other forms of violent crimes. The evening hours in which significant others are likely to spend time together and perhaps imbibed in a few drinks appear to be the most frequent. The time of the year plays a role in the situation and how quickly it is resolved. There are certain times of the year that are emotionally more volatile. Similarly to suicide rates, early spring, late December around Christmas and the New Year, and the dog days of summer seem to be particularly prevalent. Negotiators are able to use extreme temperatures, especially the cold, to help them influence the process. It is not uncommon to cut off the barricaded subject's electricity when there appears to be an impasse in the negotiation process.

The media is often seen as a constraint, although some negotiators have learned means to use it to their advantage. Media often will give too much information to the subject who may be actually watching him or herself on television. It also will frequently draw a crowd who must then be controlled. Of course it can interfere physically with the police actions. Negotiators have learned to actually use the media as their voice to the subject. If they believe the subject may be watching television, they will be interviewed and speak about the subject in as positive terms as is possible to help build rapport. For example, they may note that the subject is dealing with a number of problems, but seems to want to do the right thing by his family.

Bystanders, especially family members, are always seen as an impediment to the officers' actions. As will be noted in a number of cases in the current study, bystanders are an audience for the offender who is particularly of a grandiose nature; they provide more ammunition for the subject who wants to "leave in a blaze of glory." A new development is the use of cell phones to communicate with friends and family members.

In one of the current cases, the police finally began to confiscate family members' cell phones, when they realized the family was telling the subject where the tactical officers were stationed. This new development is in addition to the normal family advice, pleas, and retorts. In all cases, bystanders are an additional responsibility for the officers; they must be protected at all costs.

While subjects who are under the influence of alcohol may become more impulsive (Beck, Weisman, & Kovacs, 1976), use of hard drugs (such as the stimulant, cocaine) was found to be more lethal to the perpetrator in a study conducted by Lord (2000). Monahan's results (1992) support the relationship between substance abuse and violence. He found that the prevalence of violence among persons who had been diagnosed as abusing drugs was 16 times that of a person who had not received such a diagnosis.

Negotiation Approach

Hammer and Rogan (1996) have developed an excellent set of negotiation models that are particularly useful in the crisis situations that most of the barricaded situations fall. They argue that the basic Bargaining Negotiation approach based on the Social Exchange theory can rarely be used. They also think the Expressive Negotiation approach that primarily focuses on the emotional level of the subject is limited, so they have developed a third model called the Communication approach that combines the best from each of the other approaches.

The Bargaining Negotiation approach conceptualizes crisis negotiation in terms of instrumental issues, related and substantive demands of each party. Based on the Social Exchange theory, negotiation is viewed in terms of efforts by each party to dictate or clarify the terms of an exchange of resources. According to the Social Exchange theory, conflicts involve rewards and costs for each party; the negotiation behavior involves the exchange of some object or commodity in return for other objects or commodities. Overall effective negotiation is the result of rational discourse between the contending parties. Donohue et al. (1991) and Fusilier (1986) would argue that the negotiation with the criminal offender would benefit from this approach.

In terms of barricaded subjects, the Bargaining Negotiation approach would have the hostage taker work for everything he or she gets, but get something in return for each concession given. The negotiators would use time to their advantage and not give in too much too soon. Most types of crisis situations law enforcement encounter don't match the requirements of Bargaining negotiation. Most situations involve elevated levels of anxiety and uncertainty with pronounced emotional excitation. These subjects often find themselves in barricaded situation as the result of mental and/or emotional inability to cope with life's stressors, so they are unlikely to possess the ability to rationally bargain.

The Expressive Negotiation approach focuses on the impact of emotion and relationship. The Expressive Negotiation model is built on three corollaries. The first premise is that if there are hostages, they rarely have instrumental value so don't function as a bargaining chip to achieve specific instrumental outcomes, but rather as expressive acts of the subject to demonstrate his or her ability to control others. Second, the interest of both the perpetrator and negotiator is to prevent the situation from escalating to injury or death. The third premise is that the high emotional level during a crisis situation can negatively impact a negotiated outcome. Emotion is such a central element that the likely response is fight or flight rather than problem-solving. Relationship and trust building are viewed as critical factors in the resolution of crisis incidents.

Hammer and Rogan modified the two approaches mentioned above and developed the communication-based negotiation approach. They conclude that negotiations are interactive processes wherein negotiators and the subjects react to one another's message behavior. Parties in conflict pursue three functional interaction concerns which impact on conflict escalation/de-escalation:

1. Instrumental interactions focus on substantive issues, as well nonsubstantive issues,
2. Relationship building is still a concern with power, trust and affiliation as the core elements. Power concerns dominance and submission on the part of the negotiator and the subject. Trust revolves around the degree to which each party is willing to accept the premise that a future act by the other will not be detrimental to one's self. Affiliation is the degree of interpersonal immediacy and distance between perpetrators and negotiators.
3. Identity concerns are based on the two dimensions of Tajfel's Social Identity Theory (as cited in Hammer and Rogan, 1996). Personal identity is based on an individual's perceptions of his/her own attributes, while social identity consists of those characteristics and their emotional significance attached to one's membership in social

groups. Saving face is a principal component of Hammer and Rogan's work.

Saving face varies along three dimensions: locus of a communicator's interest directed at oneself or other; face valence, the face message behavior serving to attack or mitigate threats to the subject's face; and a temporal dimension that relates the message behavior functions to proactively protect against potential future threats to face or to retroactively restore perceived loss of face.

These three dimensions are combined to produce the following six types of face message behavior:

1. Defend self's face—behaviors are self directed messages, designed to protect one's self-image to guard against future attack or loss of face.
2. Attack self's face—directed against one's own self-image: "I have nothing to live for."
3. Restore self's face—"I'm not as crazy as you think."
4. Restore other's face—"you have lots of people who care about you."
5. Defend other's face—protect other's face from future attack or loss: "I think you are really a strong person for how you've handled this situation so far."
6. Attack other's face—traditional, more limited view of face attack behavior: "you're jerking me around."

The authors' premise is that if the negotiator listens to which dimension the subject is communicating, the negotiator will be able to interact effectively with the subject. The authors found that restoring other's face was primary face behavior used by negotiators while restoring self's face was used by perpetrators.

Suicide by Cop Incidents

As cited in Chapter 1, Suicide by Cop (SbC) are those incidents in which individuals who, when confronted by law enforcement officers, either verbalize their desire to be killed by law enforcement officers and/or make gestures, such as pointing weapons at officers or hostages, running at officers with weapons, or throwing weapons at officers. They are usually defined as SbC by the officers who must interact with these particular perpetrators. In a few cases, the perpetrators themselves will verbalize their desire to be killed by the police. No literature at this point has examined those SbC incidents that could also be classified as barricaded and/or hostage-taking situations. The few studies that have been conducted on the SbC topic examine SbC incidents as a whole, or within deadly force studies including those SbC incidents in which deadly force was actually used by the officer or the perpetrator.

Current Study

Amendola, Learning, and Martin (1996) studied 80 barricade and/or hostage incidents that occurred in a large Eastern city between 1990 and 1995. As with the present research, the 80 incidents were cases in which the special response team, consisting of negotiation and tactical personnel, was dispatched.

The current study examined 30 barricade and/or hostage incidents that occurred in a moderately large southeastern city (population: 600,000) beginning in 1998 and continuing through 2001. Before 1998, centralized information about the special response team's call-outs was not available.

Amendola, et al.'s study details empirically many of the characteristics of the incident itself, the perpetrator, and the officers involved. It will provide the baseline from which the current study can spring, first comparing the 30 cases with Amendola and colleagues' cases and then comparing the current general barricade incidents with the current situations categorized as SbC. These two comparisons will allow the reader to develop a more generalized picture of barricade perpetrators and incidents and then compare those subjects whose intent may have been death by a police officers' weapon.

Although there are seven sets of tables, the information is divided into perpetrators' characteristics, situation specific information, and finally interaction between perpetrators and officers.

Perpetrator Characteristics

The first tables describe types of incidents; precipitating events; the subjects' personal characteristics such as gender, ethnicity, age, employment and marital status, and psychological, substance, and criminal history; and factors that directly influenced the incident such as weapon, use of alcohol or drugs during the incident, and evidence of planning.

General barricade situations: The current and Amendola's studies are similar in the percentage of cases in which hostages were taken, but the differences in categories make it difficult to draw comparisons beyond the general hostage-taking frequency. The current study has almost an equal division among suicide attempts, domestic disputes, mentally illness, and crime-related. The city studied by Amendola and colleagues appeared to have cases that were primarily suicide attempts or bungled criminal cases. The differences could be completely arbitrary based on the definitions utilized. For example, a number of the threatened suicide cases identified by Amendola could have been individuals with a history of mental illness and/or were also involved in conflicts surrounding significant others (Table 9-1: Type of Incidents: Total Incidents).

Current study: Within the same classification system of the current study, some interesting differences can be found between those cases that are considered SbC and those that are not (Table 9-1A: Type of Incident: Total Incidents). SbC subjects are more prevalent in the categories of suicide attempts and domestic violence; however, they are less likely to have hostages. Since their intent is to die, the higher percentages in threatening suicide is not surprising. In addition, the antecedent event of domestic conflict may reflect the sense of loss they are feeling, or a form of manipulation. It may be that they believe that they can only regain control of their significant others with an exhibition of death at the hands of law enforcement. In other words, their intent may not be death, but rather a grandiose show to regain the affection and/or control of a significant other. The lack of hostages is revealing. Following Crelinsten and Szabo's reasoning (1979), the hostage is a means by which the hostage taker gains something he or she needs or wants from a third party. Most people are aware that approaching law enforcement with a lethal weapon, showing the intent to injure one or more officers, is sufficient to be shot. Although there are infamous cases in which individuals intent on death by officers' weapons have included hostages in their plan, these cases appear to be exceptions. Hostages would be more useful to those who are attempting to negotiate a demand such as freedom.

What are not SbC cases is also revealing. As it will be noted in Table 9-4A, several of the SbC subjects had a history of mental-health treatment, but the incident which initiated a response from the special response team was not mental illness. In other words, SbC subjects quite often have been diagnosed with depression and personality disorders, but rarely with psychosis-related illnesses. Those individuals who are psychotic and are actually in a psychotic episode can be dangerous

(Monahan,1992), but are less likely to be considering death by police officers.

Table 9-1

Type of Incident: Total Incidents

Type	Amendola n=80	(%)	Current n=30	(%)
Threatened Suicide	41	(51.0%)	9	(30.0%)
Domestic Disturbance	5	(6.3%)	8	(26.7%)
Crime-related	31	(39.0%)	6	(20.0 %)
Mentally ill	not listed		7	(23.3%)
Other	2	(2.0%)	0	
Hostage Taking	23	(29.0%)	6	(26.7%)

Table 9-1A

Type of Incident: Current Study Grouped by SbC

Type	SbC n=8	(%)	Not SbC n=22	(%)
Threatened Suicide	3	(37.5%)	6	(27.3%)
Domestic Disturbance	3	(37.5%)	5	(22.7%)
Crime-related	2	(25.0%)	4	(18.2 %)
Mentally ill	0		7	(31.8%)
Hostage Taking	1	(12.5%)	7	(31.8%)

General barricade situations: The events that precipitated the barricade incidents are very similar between Amendola and colleagues' study and the current study (Table 9-2: Antecedent Events). Issues surrounding the loss of a significant other or other family problems appear to be the most prevalent reasons for these incidents. Clearly many of these incidents begin as unplanned crisis events and evolve into subjects fortifying themselves. Although Amendola classifies many of her cases as criminal related, only 15% of her reported incidents began as crimes, which is similar to the current study.

Current study: There are some distinctive differences between the SbC and non-SbC cases in the events leading up the actual barricaded incidents (Table 9-2A: Antecedent Events). Those perpetrators who are not SbC are much more diverse in their precipitators while the SbC precipitators load on relationship terminations and multiple problems. Over a third were in the process of losing a significant other, while another third were primarily losing a significant other plus dealing with other issues. For example one individual took his wife hostage on the second-year anniversary of the miscarriage of their baby. He and his wife had been separated for nine days after he had lost one of numerous jobs he had tried to hold.

Table 9-2

Antecedent Events

Type	Amendola n=20 (%)		Current n=30 (%)	
None	Not listed		3	(10.7%)
Termination of Relationship	12	(60%)	9	(32.1%)
Other Family Problems	Not listed		5	(17.9%)
Money Problems	1	(5%)	1	(3.6%)
Mental Illness	Not listed		2	(6.7%)
Criminal	3	(15%)	4	(14.3%)
Multiple	Not listed		4	(14.3%)
Other	4	(20%)	2	(6.6%)

Table 9-2A

Antecedent Events

Type	SbC n=8 (%)		Not SbC n=22 (%)	
None	0		3	(13.6%)
Termination of Relationship	3	(37.5%)	6	(27.3%)
Other Family Problems	1	(12.5%)	4	(18.1%)
Money Problems	0		1	(4.5%)
Mental Illness	0		2	(9.0%)
Criminal	1	(12.5%)	3	(13.6%)
Multiple	3	(37.5%)	1	(4.5%)

General barricade situations: As would be expected, a majority of perpetrators are male and more than half are African American and between the ages of 25 and 39 for both studies. Employment and marital status can not be assessed from Amendola's study because of missing data, but the current study reveals a high percentage of unemployment and unmarried subjects. Both the issues surrounding employment and relationships are critical, and the ability to assess both these factors would be critical to the negotiation (Table 9-3: Offenders' Demographics, Employment and Marital Status).

Current study: Again, some interesting differences appear between SbC and non-SbC. SbC subjects are younger and more likely to be white and unemployed. All perpetrators are primarily unmarried males (Table 9-3A: Offenders' Demographics, Employment and Marital Status).

Table 9-3

Offenders' Demographics, Employment and Marital Status

Demographic	Amendola n=98	(%)	Current n=30	(%)
Gender				
Male	78	(78.6%)	26	(86.7%)
Female	8	(8.1%)	4	(13.3%)
Missing	14	(13.3%)	0	
Ethnicity				
White	23	(22.5%)	12	(41.4%)
African American	55	(55.5%)	16	(55.2%)
Other	22	(22.0%)	1	(3.4%)
Age				
Under 25	36	(36.5%)	6	(22.2%)
25-39	52	(51.5%)	16	(59.3%)
40-59	12	(12.0%)	5	(18.5%)
Employment				
Unemployed	8	(8.16%)	14	(46.6%)
Employed	2	(2.04%)	8	(26.7%)
Missing	88	(89.8%)	8	(26.7%)
Marital Status				
Married (Including Common Law)	19	(19.4%)	6	(20.0%)
Not Married	20	(20.4%)	23	(76.7%)
Missing	61	(60.2%)	1	(3.3%)

Table 9-3A

Offenders' Demographics, Employment and Marital Status

Demographic	SbC n=8	(%)	Not SbC n=22	(%)
Gender				
Male	8	(100%)	18	(81.8%)
Female	0		4	(18.2%)
Ethnicity				
White	4	(50.0%)	8	(36.4%)
African American	2	(25.0%)	14	(63.6%)
Other	2	(25.0%)	0	
Age				
Under 25	3	(37.5%)	3	(13.6%)
25-39	3	(37.5%)	13	(59.0%)
40-59	1	(12.5%)	4	(18.1%)
Unknown	1	(12.5%)	2	(9.0%)
Employment				
Unemployed	6	(75.0%)	8	(36.4%)
Employed	2	(25.0%)	6	(27.3%)
Missing	0		8	(36.4%)
Marital Status				
Married (Including Common Law)	2	(25.0%)	4	(18.2%)
Not Married	6	(75.0%)	17	(77.3%)
Missing	0		1	(4.5%)

General barricade situations: There is too much missing information to compare criminal histories between Amendola's and the current study; however, the vast differences between previous mental health problems is worth noting. Almost half of the current study's subjects had identified mental health problems, while only 16 percent of subjects in Amendola's study had such identified problems. On the other hand, more than twice as many subjects in Amendola's study had previous suicide attempts (Table 9-4: Perpetrator Criminal and Psychological History).

Current study: Another interesting measure that was included in the current study was prior police contacts that might or might not have led to arrests (Table 9-4A: Perpetrator Criminal and Psychological History). A majority of perpetrators had more than one previous police contact or no police contacts at all with very few having had only one police contact. The non-SbC subjects' police contacts ranged from no to several contacts.

More than half of all the perpetrators had no criminal record with no
differences between SbC and non-SbC subjects. The main difference was
a drug or alcohol abuse history with half of the SbC subjects identified
as substance abusers.

Table 9-4

Offender Criminal and Psychological History

History	Amendola n=98	(%)	Current n=30	(%)
Criminal				
Record	24	(24.49%)	9	(30.0%)
No Record	3	(3.06%)	16	(53.3%)
Missing	73	(72.45%)	5	(16.7%)
Psychological History (known)				
Previous Suicide Attempts	28	(28.57%)	4	(13.3%)
Previous Drug/Alcohol Abuse	30	(29.59%)	10	(33.3%)
Previous Mental Health Problems	16	(16.33%)	12	(40.0%)

Table 9-4A

Perpetrator Criminal and Psychological History

History	SbC n=8	(%)	Not SbC n=22	(%)
Prior Police Contact				
None	2	(25.0%)	7	(31.8%)
One	1	(12.5%)	2	(9.0%)
More than One	4	(50.0%)	9	(40.9%)
Missing	1	(12.5%)	4	(18.1%)
Criminal				
No Record	4	(50.0%)	12	(54.5%)
DWI	1	(12.5%)	1	(4.5%)
Domestic	0		1	(4.5%)
Property	2	(25.0%)	3	(13.6%)
Personal	0		1	(4.5%)
Missing	1	(12.5%)	5	(22.7%)
Psychological History (known)				
Previous Suicide Attempts	1	(12.57%)	3	(13.6%)
Previous Drug/Alcohol Abuse	4	(50.0%)	6	(27.3%)
Previous Mental Health Problems	3	(37.5%)	9	(40.9%)

General barricade situations: For Amendola's study and the current study, use of drugs and alcohol during the incidents was not always evident. Most of the current study records did not include post-incident interviews, so unless the subject was obviously under the influence of a substance, the officers were unable to ascertain substance use. There did seem to be more awareness of drug use in Amendola's study, while there was almost an equal division between no substance use and alcohol-only use in the current study (Table 9-5: Other Factors Related to the Perpetrator). Influence of alcohol and drugs is an important factor to be considered when decisions are made tactically. In most cases, it is important to keep the situation going, the perpetrator talking so that he or she might sober up. In other cases, it was found useful to let the subjects drink until they became too tired and drunk to continue. For example, one female was drinking in a bar until the bartender refused to serve her any more drinks. She went out to her car and returned with a gun, taking the bartender and several patrons hostage. She would only scream at the negotiator, stating that the bartender had refused to sell her drinks and that her children had been taken away from her. As she continued to drink and the night wore on, she became tired. The negotiator kept phoning her, keeping her awake. Finally she let the bartender and the customers go and then came out herself. Although it might appear risky to let an individual continue to drink, any alternative tactical strategies could have gotten the hostages hurt or killed.

Planning does not appear to be a factor in a majority of the current study incidents. This lack of planning is reflected in the lack of pre-incident suicidal comments, such as communicating to others their desire to die or predicting that the police would kill them, as well as, actual identified planning steps, such as buying a weapon or designing a devise to look like a weapon.

Current study: Overall both SbC and non-SbC subjects were similar in other factors related to the perpetrator. As noted earlier, either the subject's use of drugs or alcohol were not obvious or alcohol only was the main substance used. SbC subjects did appear to be more likely to make comments to others about their suicide desires, but actual indicators of planning were not evident in either categories. Guns were most likely to be used by both; however, weapon use is the one place Amendola mentions SbC. In those cases that they were attempting to have officers kill them, she notes that subjects did not always have their own weapons, or at least not real weapons. (Table 9-5 - Other Factors Related to Perpetrator)

Table 9-5

Other Factors Related to the Perpetrator

Factors	Amendola n=80	(%)	Current n=30	(%)
Use of drugs/alcohol during event				
None	0		14	(46.7%)
Alcohol only	4	(3.75%)	12	(40.0%)
Drugs	15	(15.0%)	0	
Missing	43	(43.75%)	4	(13.3%)
Pre-incident suicidal comments	not listed			
No			20	(66.7%)
Yes			6	(20.0%)
Missing			4	(13.3%)
Signs of planning	not listed			
No			20	(66.7%)
Yes			10	(33.3%)
Weapons used				
None	28	(27.5%)	4	(13.3%)
Gun	52	(51.75%)	17	(56.7%)
Knife	13	(13.75%)	5	(16.7%)
Other	5	(5.0%)	0	
Missing	0		4	(13.3%)

Table 9-5A

Other Factors Related to the Perpetrator

Factors	SbC n=8	(%)	Not SbC n=22	(%)
Use of drugs/alcohol during event				
None	4	(50.0%)	10	(45.5%)
Alcohol only	4	(50.0%)	8	(36.4%)
Drugs	0		0	
Missing	0		4	(18.1%)
Pre-incident suicidal comments				
No	4	(50.0%)	16	(72.7%)
Yes	4	(50.0%)	2	(9.0%)
Missing	0		4	(18.1%)
Signs of planning				
No	5	(62.5%)	15	(68.2%)
Yes	3	(37.5%)	7	(31.8%)

Factors	SbC		Not SbC	
	n=8	(%)	n=22	(%)
Weapons used				
None	1	(12.5%)	3	(13.6%)
Gun	6	(75.0%)	11	(50.0%)
Knife	1	(12.5%)	1	(4.5%)
Missing	0		4	(18.1%)

Summary: Overall the Amendola and current studies reveal similar results. Loss of significant others was the main antecedent event occurring before the incident. The perpetrators were primarily African American males armed with guns. The differences may have been more around what was measured by each study; however, the subjects in the current study were more likely to have a mental-health history, but fewer past suicide attempts.

As would be expected, more differences were found between those subjects whose intent was to be killed by a police officer's weapon and those subjects who barricaded themselves for other reasons. Although almost all the subjects were unmarried, had more than one previous police contact, but no criminal record, the SbC subjects were younger and more likely to be white and unemployed. Although few of the subjects in general planned the incident, the SbC subjects were more likely to have multiple issues with which they had problems coping, more likely to have a history of substance abuse, and had made pre-suicidal comments. Guns were more likely to be used by all the perpetrators, but SbC subjects were less likely to take hostages.

Situation Specific Factors

The time of year and time of day are under the control of the perpetrator; however, the duration of the call is influenced by a number of different factors. They include: the subject's state of mind, the influence of drugs and alcohol, weapon availability, potential danger to the public and other extraneous circumstances, and the officers' strategic and tactical mindset (McMains & Mullis, 1996).

General barricade situations: The time of day that barricaded incidents appeared to be most prevalent is similar to other forms of violent crimes. For both studies, 1700 to 2300 hours (5 p.m. to 11 p.m.) are the busiest hours with the hour or so on either side of this peak time period as the next most frequent.

The two studies did differ in time of year: early spring contained the most barricaded situations in Amendola and colleagues' study, while deep winter was the prime time for barricades in the current study. Because of the differences geographically, they may not be that dissimilar as far as weather, but different events would need to be considered. The current study has a number of incidents surrounding Christmas and New Year holidays with all of their emotional, family gatherings, and substance abuse ties. In the suicide literature, early spring is considered a high-risk time for suicide attempts as individuals struggle with the dark days of winter and their personal lack of fulfillment that spring promises. (Table 9-6: Incident Time Frame)

The duration of the incidents in the current study were substantially longer for domestic disputes, criminal offenses and mentally ill-related cases. As noted earlier, the uniqueness of each case and the complexity of the interaction between offender, situation, and officers makes it difficult, but important to interpret these differences. For example, an incident in the current study involved a young Asian male who was being investigated for automobile theft. When the detectives arrived at his house, they first talked to his grandmother, with whom he lived. The young man came out of his room with an assault weapon. The detectives grabbed the grandmother and retreated. The subject first only screamed and yelled at the officers. He fired out the window several times, and it was considered that the tactical team might need to go in to safeguard the community. At one point when he fired over the head of a sniper, the sniper fired back hitting near the subject's head. When the negotiator called back, he first said the sniper couldn't shoot, but it was the last time the perpetrator shot his weapon, and he started to become more compliant and negotiate terms. The incident lasted for more than 10 hours before the boy came out.

McMains and Mullis (1996) notes that time increases basic human needs, and the negotiator can be placed in a position to fill those needs. As the subject gets hungry, the negotiator can manipulate the fulfilling of his or her hunger need to gain trust and reduce anxiety. The subject will be concerned with his safety so the negotiator must be able to help the subject work through the consequences of his or her actions. Usually the perpetrators believe their actions are more serious and the consequences much worse than they really are, so the negotiator can minimize them to some extent. Beyond these two needs, the negotiator can then address the real issues, fulfilling the perpetrator's social and self-esteem needs.

Current study: SbC subjects' incidents appear most frequently in the dark winter months, but once overall barricade situations are controlled, the non-SbC incidents are more spread out among the seasons. The winter months with their accompanying holidays are still the most frequent for all incidents, but spring and summer also are common.

Interestingly, SbC subjects don't appear to have a particular time of day while the non-SbC cases follow the popular evening hours. Finally, the SbC incidents lasted much longer than non-SbC cases no matter what kind of call they were. It is possible that once the response team realizes that it has an individual who is armed and possibly wants to die, then the negotiators must work harder and longer to find a negotiation point. If an individual wants to live, the officers would have more negotiation leverage than with a subject who just wants to die (Table 9-6A: Incident Time Frame).

Table 9-6

Incident Time Frame

Time	Amendola n=98	(%)	Current n=30	(%)
Time of Year				
Feb.-Apr.	31	(31.25%)	5	(16.7%)
May-July	19	(18.75%)	6	(20.0%)
Aug.-Oct.	27	(27.50%)	6	(20.0%)
Nov.-Jan.	17	(17.50%)	13	(43.3%)
Time of Day				
0500-1100	17	(17.5%)	4	(13.3%)
1100-1700	20	(20.0%)	7	(23.3%)
1700-2300	39	(38.75%)	10	(33.3%)
2300-0500	17	(17.5%)	4	(13.3%)
Missing	6	(6.25%)	5	(16.7%)
Duration of Incident				
(Avg. hours by type of call)				
Threatened Suicide	2.56		2.58	
Domestic Disturbance	3.57		5.34	
Criminal Offense	2.94		4.33	
Mentally Ill	Not listed		4.89	
Hostage Involved	3.80		3.44	

Table 9-6A

Incident Time Frame

History	SbC n=8	(%)	Not Sbc n=22	(%)
Time of Year				
Feb.-Apr.	0		5	(22.7%)
May-July	0		6	(27.3%)
Aug.-Oct.	2	(25.0%)	4	(18.2%)
Nov.-Jan.	6	(75.0%)	7	(31.8%)
Time of Day				
0500-1100	2	(25.0%)	2	(9.0%)
1100-1700	3	(37.5%)	4	(18.1%)
1700-2300	0		10	(45.4%)
2300-0500	2	(25.0%)	2	(9.0%)
Missing	1	(12.5%)	4	(18.1%)
Duration of Incident				
(Avg. hours by type of call)				
Threatened Suicide	4.25		1.75	
Domestic Disturbance	8.58		3.4	
Criminal Offense	0		4.89	
Mentally Ill	7.63		2.69	
Hostage Involved	5.0		3.75	

Interactions Between Subjects and Officers

General barricade situations: The last tables discuss the dynamics between the perpetrators and officers (Table 9-7: Interaction between Subjects and Law Enforcement Officers). Hammer and Rogan (1996) discuss the interactive process that occurs when perpetrators and negotiators react to one another's message behavior. Amendola notes that a great number of her cases included demands made by the subject to the police with more than half the police response being no verbal response at all. The current study found a high percentage of threats to both the police and towards one's own life with the police response highly verbal with over half the incidents including the negotiators advancing to the point of discussing the perpetrators' problems. If couched in Hammer and Rogan's terms, the current study's subjects "attacked their own self's face," as well as "attacking other's face."

For example, a juvenile male with a minor criminal and drug record was upset because his girlfriend was in the process of being adopted by a relative who was placing more constraints on her life and his ability to see her. The boy broke into the house, hit the father with the butt of a gun, and shot out the television. The family ran out, including the girlfriend. The boy began very aggressive, "attacking other's face," with statements of "Just kill me. That's what you want anyway. I'll not come out alive." The negotiators worked on "restoring other's face" by getting him to talk about his feelings for his girlfriend and his need to take care of himself. The boy would catch himself lowering his aggressive response and would begin to threaten, or "attack other's face." He also wanted to get messages to his girlfriend that could be interpreted as "restoring self's face." These messages included that he loved her and was sorry that he had attacked her family. The negotiators in return used messages of "defending other's face." These messages were that he had been trying to help his girlfriend and take control of the situation. The cycle continued for several hours until the boy finally agreed to come out.

In some cases controlling the scene is difficult for the police. The subjects are on bridges or in a parking lot. If they are contained in a building, then in a majority of cases a perimeter can be established to keep the subject in one area and the public safe. Cutting the electricity which limits the subject's access to comfortable temperatures and television has been found to be useful. In a surprisingly few cases, any form of gas was used or tactical teams forced their way in. Smith (1993) found that injuries were most common in situations in which the special response teams decide to forcibly enter. The two studies here would support Smith's findings. Only one perpetrator was killed in Amendola's study and none in the current study. Most of the perpetrators were either arrested or committed to a mental health facility.

Although SbC subjects' intent is to be killed, a higher percentage of non-SbC perpetrators threatened suicide; however, a higher percentage of SbC subjects threatened the police which may have been their form of suicide threats. Interestingly, a higher percentage of SbC perpetrators made demands or requests of the officers, although many of these requests were to see significant others. The only confession to a crime was by a SbC subject (Table 9-7A: Interaction between Subjects and Law Enforcement Officers).

Individuals who attempt suicide are usually seen as ambivalent; they don't see any way out of their problems or life except death; however, if they can be shown realistic alternatives, they often can be talked out of death. Overall the negotiators were able to discuss the subjects' problems with them, but it is particularly true with the SbC subjects.

Scene-control tactics were spread fairly evenly among the less forcible strategies. Perimeters were established and electricity was stopped. In only two non-SbC situations did the special response team forcibly enter the barricaded building.

Arrest was the main outcome of all the cases, although a higher percentage of non-SbC subjects were committed to a mental health facility.

Table 9-7

Interaction between Subjects and Law Enforcement Officers

Interactions	Amendola n=98	(%)	Current n=30	(%)
Perpetrators' Verbal Behaviors				
Made Demands/Requests	38	(38.8%)	9	(40.9%)
Confessed to Crimes or Events	12	(12.5%)	1	(4.5%)
Suicidal Threats	0		18	(81.8%)
Asked for Suicide by Police	6	(6.25%)	8	(36.4%)
Threatened Police	6	(6.25%)	9	(30.0%)
Delusional	0		4	(13.3%)
Just stated "Was not Coming Out"	0		4	(13.3%)
Verbal Intervention				
None	54	(53.9%)	4	(13.3%)
Attempted, but Never Connected	Not listed		5	(16.7%)
Dealt with Weapon Only	3	(3.75%)	2	(6.7%)
Build Rapport	12	(12.5%)	3	(10.0%)
Discussed Problem	12	(12.5%)	16	(53.3%)
Scene Control Tactics used				
None	18	(18.4%)	6	(20.0%)
Perimeter Containment	Not listed		14	(46.7%)
Cut Electricity	7	(7.5%)	5	(16.7%)
Gas	5	(5.0%)	1	(3.3%)
Forcibly Entered Building	2	(2.5%)	2	(6.7%)
Less than Lethal Force	Not listed		1	(3.3%)
Final Outcome				
Left Alone	0		1	(3.3%)
Committed to Mental Health	39	(40.0%)	13	(43.3%)
Arrested	17	(17.5%)	13	(43.3%)
Injuries/Killed	1	(1.25%)	0	
Suicide	0		2	(6.7%)

Table 9-7A

Interaction between Subjects and Law Enforcement Officers

Interactions	SbC n=8	(%)	Non SbC n=22	(%)
Offenders' Verbal Behaviors				
Made Demands/Requests	4	(50.0%)	5	(22.7%)
Confessed to Crimes or Events	1	(12.5%)	0	
Suicidal Threats	2	(25.0%)	11	(50.0%)
Asked for Suicide by Police	8	(100%)	0	
Threatened Police	5	(62.5%)	9	(40.9%)
Delusional	0		4	(18.2%)
Just stated "Was not Coming Out"	1	(12.5%)	3	(13.6%)
Verbal Intervention				
None	0		4	(18.1%)
Attempted, but Never Connected	2	(25.0%)	3	(13.6%)
Dealt with Weapon Only	0		2	(9.1%)
Build Rapport	0		3	(13.6%)
Discussed Problem	6	(75.0%)	10	(45.5%)
Scene Control Tactics used				
None	2	(25.0%)	4	(18.1%)
Perimeter Containment	2	(25.0%)	12	(54.5%)
Cut Electricity	3	(37.5%)	2	(9.1%)
Gas	0		1	(4.5%)
Forcibly Entered Building	0		2	(9.1%)
Less than Lethal Force	1	(12.5%)	0	
Final Outcome				
Left Alone	1	(12.5%)	0	
Committed to Mental Health	2	(25.0%)	11	(50.0%)
Arrested	4	(50.0%)	9	(40.9%)
Injuries/Killed	0		0	
Suicide	1	(12.5%)	1	(4.5%)

Summary: The current study in general has some interesting differences from Amendola's study, as well as some similarities. The similarities centered around the perpetrator. The incidents all primarily occurred in the evening, although the seasons were somewhat different, and all the offenders included demands as part of their verbal behavior. The negotiators in the current study were more likely to take longer and discuss the subjects' problems with them even as the subjects threatened the police and threatened to take their own lives. The outcomes of both studies were similar with the current study including more arrests.

What was concluded about the current study in general seemed to be particularly true about the SbC cases. They lasted longer; the perpetrators threatened the police, and made more demands than the non-SbC subjects; however, the non-SbC subjects threatened suicide more. Arrests were the most likely outcome of both SbC and non-SbC subjects, although a larger number of non-SbC subjects were committed to mental hospitals. This outcome decision probably was influenced by the suicide threats.

Conclusion

Overall, barricaded subjects across studies were similar with differences most likely due to measurement differences. SbC subjects also were more similar than different than barricaded subjects. Although SbC subjects did seem to possess more multiple stressors and abused drugs and alcohol more than non-SbC subjects, the main difference seemed to be the officers' response. The duration of SbC incidents was much longer. There is a great need to conduct more single case studies in which the dynamics of the negotiation process and the interactions between the negotiator and subject are assessed. In addition, more information needs to be gathered during the incident, as well as, post-incident about the subject. Such pertinent information as marital status and other support people, employment, and the subject's history of abuse and current use of drugs and alcohol is critical for the negotiators during the incident. Post incident information is vital to increase effectiveness in future barricaded incidents.

References

Amendola, Karen, Leaming, Marj, and Martin Jennifer. (1996). Analyzing characteristics of Police-Citizen Encounters in High-Risk Search Warrant Issuances, Domestic Disturbances, Hostage and Barricaded persons Incidents, and Encounters with Fleeing Felony Suspects. (Grant 92-IJ-CX-K019). Washington D.C.: Police Foundation.

Beck, A. T., Weissman, M. A., & Kovacs, M. (1976). Alcoholism, hopelessness and suicidal behavior. Journal of Studies on Alcohol, 37, 66-77.

Crelinsten, Ronald. D. & Szabo, Denis. (1979). Hostage-Taking. Lexington, Mass: Lexington Books

Donohue, W., Ramesh, C. & Borchgrevink, C. (1991). Crisis bargaining: Tracking relational paradox in hostage negotiation. The international Journal of Conflict Management, 2 (4), 257-274.

Fuselier, G. (1986). A practical overview of hostage negotiations. FBI Law Enforcement Bulletin, 55 (4), 1-4.

Fuselier, G.D., VanZandt, C.R., & Lanceley, F.J. (1991). Hostage/barricade incidents: High-risk factors and the action criteria. FBI Law Enforcement Bulletin, 60 (1), 6-12.

Hammer, Mitchell, R. and Rogan, Randall G. (1996). Negotiation models in crisis situation: The value of a communication-based approach. Edited by Rogan R. G., Hammer, M. R. and Van Zandt, Clinton. R. Westport, Conn: Praeger 9-24.

Head, W. (1987). The hostage response: An examination of U.S. Law enforcement practices concerning hostage incidents. (Dissertation) State University of New York at Albany.

Lord, V. (June, 2000). One use of victim precipitated homicide: The use of law enforcement to commit suicide. Criminal Justice and Human Behavior 27 (3) 401-419.

Kupperman, R. and Trent, D. (1970). Terrorism: Threat, reality, response. Stanford: Hoover Institution Press.

McMains, M. J. (1996). Crisis negotiation: Managing critical incidents and hostage situations in law enforcement and corrections.
Cincinnati, Ohio: Anderson

Monahan, J. (1992). Mental disorder and violent behavior: Perceptions and evidence. American Psychologist, 47, 511-521.

Smith, D. (1990). Caught in the crossfire. Center to Prevent Handgun
Violence, 1-8.

Soskis, D. & VanZandt, C.R. (1986). Hostage negotiation: Law
enforcement's most effective non-lethal weapon. Management
Quarterly, 6 (4), 1-10.

Chapter 10

ANTECEDENT (PRE-DEATH) BEHAVIORS AS INDICATORS OF IMMINENT VIOLENCE

Barry Perrou, Psy.D, Founder
Public Safety Research Institute

Introduction

Increasingly a police emergency, suicide has become a more widely acknowledged and accepted practice of coping with a myriad of real or perceived personal problems. According to the National Institutes of Mental Health (2003), 775,000 people attempt suicides annually. Certainly not all of these are "in-progress" attempts, but there seems to be an increase of "public view" suicide incidents. With the advent of the emergency 911 telephone system, law enforcement officers have become the 24-hour emergency mental health outreach, since other government service providers, including mental health professionals, usually maintain Monday through Friday work schedules. Even when a suicidal individual is part of a treatment population, police officers are often the first on the scene; however, in cases where non-police responders or crisis interveners arrive first, these non-tactically trained individuals may pose a greater danger to the overall operation.

The shift in responsibility from the mental health outreach system to law enforcement crisis response has occurred gradually and undetectably. Law enforcement and public safety* personnel now take the majority of responsibility for attempt suicide and suicide-in-progress response. Consequently, police and public safety agencies have also assumed the danger inherent in these situations.

Law enforcement personnel as first responders usually are not trained or prepared to deal with the suicidal individual. Once on scene, officers typically make efforts to verbally engage suicidal individuals. Too often, an inverse relationship develops between the effectiveness of the officers' intervention efforts and their safety as officers successfully engaging with suicidal persons. This "rescue" dynamic, perceived by officers as a product of the "last-resort" nature of their efforts, exerts greater pressure on officers not to "fail" in their rescue efforts. The author, a former full-time Crisis Negotiation Team commander, has made observations of many suicide-in-progress situations, suggesting that over the course of the incident, first-responder/crisis intervener

---

* *Suicide and Law Enforcement:* 365-372 (2001), Reprinted with permission of the publisher, Behavioral Science Unit, FBI Academy, Department of Justice

police officers will typically shift from a police perspective that emphasizes tactics, to a less guarded mind-set indifferent to their own safety. The officers often will become secretly thankful to the patient for not committing suicide during their effort to rescue. This tends to suggest a form of Stockholm syndrome. For the officer who verbally engages the patient, sometimes jeopardizing personal safety, the question of "When do I fail and will I cause the death?" always looms in the officer's mind.

The experience of the author, in handling hundreds of suicides in progress, suggests suicide interventions that conclude successfully are usually preceded by the following indicators:

> Less interactive tension
> Lowered voice
> Less anger
> Less profanity
> Diminished aggressive body language;
> Increased non-aggressive body language
> Diminished threats of violence
> Less hopelessness and helplessness
> Greater willingness to listen to the officer's suggestions

Solicitation of situation outcome promises and safeguards, such as "No handcuffs, no press and if I surrender you will ..."

Compliance with Surrender

For the patient who is not connecting with the intervening officer, the officer's verbal intervention may be annoying. Often, as in "jumper" situations or voice-to-voice (non-telephonic) communication, the patient cannot escape the officer's presence–absent death. The patient who cannot be rescued may sometimes exhibit physical predeath indicators/behaviors momentarily before the violent terminal act. The officer who tries extremely hard to get the patient to surrender, but cannot make the connection is typically perceived by the suicidal patient as annoying. Absent failure (death), the officer will try even harder, which translates into greater annoyance to the patient. The issue of disengaging with the patient and the implication of tacit approval by the rescuer for the suicide to occur remains unresolved. Indicators of an imminent violent act (predeath behaviors) consist of those behaviors that enable the patient to develop a psychological momentum, a cadence, in order to commit suicide. No known research specifically defines or explains this phenomenon, but video documentation has captured the behaviors of individuals instantly before their suicide or attempted suicide.

Methodology

Twenty open-ended interviews with crisis interveners, police officers and crisis negotiators who have responded to suicides in progress provided the data. Additionally, the author viewed 12 videotapes made by witnesses of completed suicides or attempted suicides in progress.

Observations

Specific behaviors seen or heard during suicides in progress portending imminent life threatening action are as follows:

Hyper-vigilance (scanning)

At the conclusion of a crisis intervention, the ground-level patient who cannot be diverted from an actual suicide attempt exhibits symptoms of hyper-vigilance. Visually scanning (approximately from shoulder to shoulder) is common. At that moment, the patient seems to calculate circumstances negatively, remaining hopeless in perspective. Rather than acknowledging the presence of caring intervention rescuers, the patient maintains a fatal attitude. The presence of emergency personnel, rescue equipment and life-support systems does not change the patient's self-destructive intent.

Change in Respiratory Rate 1) periodic very deep breaths; 2) repeated very deep breaths

This is usually detectable (visually, audibly, or both) as the last act before death. However, the breathing pattern is not always pronounced; sometimes, it is so subtle that it can be seen only by an observer specifically looking for such behavior. Typically unaddressed, this behavior is beyond reconciliation; the death act will instantly occur if it is not interrupted. The author has observed this behavior with individuals shooting themselves in the head and mouth.

Counting Down/Up (Stereotypical Behavior)

Jumpers poised to commit suicide have demonstrated the behavior of counting down or counting up or beginning and relying on a cadence to take them to the point of release and fall. The "cadence" seems to be a rocking motion that develops momentum to the point of release. Patterns learned in childhood and adolescence are quite prevalent in the form of "On your mark, get set, go" or "On the count of 3: 1, 2, 3 . . ." Such preparatory efforts are also observable by those taking pictures of others waiting to be photographed ("Say cheese" or on 3, ...).

Case Examples

Case 1: Police Officer Suicide: Scanning, Hyperventilation (periodic very deep breaths)

A police officer murdered his estranged wife and continued to hold a loaded and cocked semiautomatic handgun. Subsequent crisis negotiations failed. Hyperventilation and scanning were detected two minutes prior to his fatal shot to the head. These actions became more pronounced, just moments before the terminal act.

Case 2: Armed Suicidal Man: Scanning, Hyperventilation (repeated very deep breaths)

After firing his .22-caliber semiautomatic handgun into the air while sitting in the middle of a vacant lot, a man made two separate attempts (approximately 15 minutes apart) to shoot himself through the mouth into the brain. In both instances, the man performed scanning motions. After placing the weapon into his mouth, he began hyperventilating. The behavior was repeated in both attempts. The man was rushed by officers after the weapon misfired on both attempts.

Case 3: *Bridge Jumper: Stereotyped Countdown*

A woman climbed onto a freeway overpass outside the 9-foot fence restricting pedestrian traffic. After protracted negotiations with police negotiators, the woman subtly rocked her head and upper torso three times and then jumped to the freeway below.

Case 4: *Stalker Suicide: Hyperventilation*

After stalking a woman for a period of time, a man sent her a bomb through the mail, intending to kill her. He planned to meet her in the afterlife. He videotaped his own suicide. Just prior to shooting himself in the head, he hyperventilated (repeated very deep breaths), taking 24 deep breaths immediately before pulling the trigger.

Case Examples: Police Officers as Crisis Negotiators

In actual crisis situations, the identification and subsequent interruption of the antecedent behaviors has successfully diverted individuals away from suicide, ultimately bringing the person to surrender. Police officers, as crisis negotiators, have reported both visually and audibly observing antecedent behaviors and, where possible, have changed their tactic from one of calmly soliciting cooperation to one of making loud and forceful demands, thus rudely diverting the person's attention and momentum away from the suicide disconnect. As an example, a police officer is in negotiations with "Anna." She is suicidal and on the telephone holding a gun to her head. The officer can hear her start the predeath behavior of hyperventilating (repeated deep breaths). At this point, the police officer loudly and forcefully interjects words to the effect "STOP WHAT YOU'RE DOING....I CAN HEAR WHAT YOU ARE DOING AND I AM TELLING YOU TO STOP IT RIGHT NOW. STOP! TALK TO ME, DON'T DO THAT....."

On two occasions during "jumper" situations, negotiators, who were in close but safe proximity to the suicidal subject, observed them hyperventilating in preparation to jump. In each instance, the negotiators loudly and demandingly raised their voices, ordering them to stop their behavior eventually frustrating the subject's intent to suicide causing them to surrender. In yet another case, by using a specialized police telephone system, police crisis negotiators were negotiating with a suicidal woman who was inside her vehicle holding a gun to herself. During the incident, negotiators could hear her begin to hyperventilate, and they forcefully and loudly interjected demands of the woman to stop. After using this interruptive technique, negotiators broke the momentum that would have led to a violent act, so she surrendered.

Discussion

The suicide and attempted-suicide processes must be of specific concern to police officers, law enforcement crisis negotiators, firefighters and mental health crisis interveners as first responders. It also must have importance to incident commanders tasked with the safety of all parties involved in the rescue, most specifically frontline interveners. The exact point in the suicide process in which the intervener engages the suicidal patient is generally unknown and concern for the rescuer must be the paramount issue. Recognizing predeath behaviors, crisis interveners can evaluate danger either before engagement with the patient, at the point of approaching the patient, at the point of engaging the patient, or during the process of the intervention. Application of this knowledge can also dictate officer safety tactics. The knowledge can also suggest to the intervener a change of tactics that will break the momentum of the patient moving to suicide and possibly prevent suicide. Crisis negotiators from numerous police departments have reported that when they could hear the suicidal patient start hyperventilating during the intervention, they would respond by yelling at the patient, thus breaking the intensity of concentration moving toward self termination. Further applications of the information is in situations where crisis interveners have become too close to the patient, and there is a potential for injury to that rescuer if the patient should fire a fatal shot into and through their head, leaving the projectile still traveling possibly in a deadly path. This misfortune has previously occurred to one police officer, who did not suspect that the patient was about to commit suicide. That police officers injury was not fatal.

Law enforcement officers assigned as "long gun" and "long-gun spotters" in hostage-taking situations also have reported behavior that suggests the person is about to commit a violent act against a hostage or others. Recognizing this behavior as a pre-violent behavior directed toward another lends justification for the consideration of deadly force to save the life of the hostage. Arguably, knowingly harming another in the presence of a SWAT team or police containment team would indicate a willingness to realize certain consequences and thus would be a form of Suicide by Cop. In certain critical non-SWAT situations, incident commanders may assign "designated shooters," specifically identified individuals who will use deadly force if necessary. These individuals are placed to have maximum observational positioning and avoid the possibility of cross-fire injuries. For these personnel, recognizing predeath behaviors and acknowledging them as warning signs should raise their state of alertness to the highest degree and make them even more prepared to use deadly force if necessary in the protection of others.

Recommendations

Individuals poised to commit violent acts are dangerous to themselves and others. Knowing when to safeguard themselves and others (hostages, bystanders) is one of the many responsibilities assigned to police because of the element of danger. Crisis interveners and crisis managers of all professions should be familiar with this information so they can knowingly act on the cues provided by the dangerous party and better manage a safe resolution of the incident without added injury to others. Application of this information should assist in deciding when to retreat or abort a rescue operation and for police long-rifle personnel, in deciding when to use deadly force to save the life of a hostage. This information may further assist in the legal arena by articulating the points leading to the decision to use deadly force.

Conclusion

This research provides an overview of different indicators people use when about to commit violent acts. Just as cocking the hammer of a loaded revolver indicates the weapon may soon be fired, these antecedent (predeath) behaviors indicate people may harm themselves. Whether intentionally or unintentionally, these actions may also harm others. Recognizing these behaviors can help interveners in close proximity become more vigilant about their own safety and assist by identifying a critical few moments to use interruptive tactics with suicidal subjects, disrupting the momentum of self termination.

References

National Institute of Mental Health, April, 2003 from
http://nimh.nih.gov/research/nimhsuicfact.cfm

Chapter 11

OFFICER-INVOLVED SHOOTINGS: CASE MANAGEMENT AND PSYCHO-SOCIAL INVESTIGATIONS

Barry Perrou, Psy.D. and Brien Farrell, J.D.

Recognizing that SbC situations are lethal traps designed to place police officers in a no-option situation, it is important to capture all aspects of the subject's psychological "being" and "existence" at the time of the shooting, and collect evidence of their psycho-social mind set in the days and possibly weeks leading up to the encounter. SbC situations are emotionally charged investigations. For the public, the media, your agency, the District Attorney's Office, and defense attorneys representing the law enforcement agency and the officers involved, an immediate and comprehensive investigation is critical. Simply stated, this aspect of the investigative should focus on: *"What was the individual's state of mind at the time that he or she precipitated this shooting, and how did he or she live in that state of mind prior to the shooting?"*

Details that need to be collected for this type of an investigation are somewhat outside the range of information typically gathered in officer involved shootings. Investigators should look beyond how the death occurred and focus intensely on the issue of *"Why?"* This is vital in developing an understanding of the motivation, plan, and intent (pathology) of the suicidal individual. Additionally, *timeliness is critical.* Witnesses, family members, friends, and co-workers become less cooperative as hours pass. Emotions such as anger coupled with confusion may foreclose meaningful interviews at a later time. Investigators must be **appropriately** persistent and respectful in the collection of this information. Much of the most important information can only be captured in the immediate investigation.

The following provides an investigative checklist:

1. Suicide

- Any suicidal notes or messages left with anyone (written, telephone, answering machine, tape recorders, etc.)
- Statements as to suicidal ideas or statements of shooting it out with the police or wanting to be killed by the police
- Anything that would suggest morbidity, or preoccupation with death

+ Giving away personal property
+ Para-suicidal or high risk behavior (sky diving, bungee jumping, street or track motorcycle racing, unannounced disappearances, etc.)
+ Any fortification inside subject's residence

2. Mental Health and Medical Records

+ Public mental health records
+ Private mental health records
+ All physical health medical records
+ List of all medications ever taken
+ List of all medications found in the house and location
+ List of medications found in bedroom night stand
+ Information regarding family (parents, siblings, children) mental illness
+ Scars relative to self-mutilation or cutting of wrists
+ Questionable gunshot wounds or scars

3. Criminal/Scene Investigation

+ Photos of everything
  + autopsy (clothing on and clothing off)
  + position of fallen body
  + subject location
  + aerial photo
  + trajectory of shots fired
  + subject's residence with emphasis on a death "shrine," weapons, death wishes, or indicators of preoccupation with death
+ Police event index (E.I.) search
+ Computer aided dispatch search (Computer Hazard Warnings)
+ Rap Sheets (all states)
+ Statements by witnesses and friends regarding family relationships, work, death, violence, future, despair, etc.
+ Check for weapons restrictions
+ Neighbors statements of subject's behavior for the seven days before shooting (raging, angry, loud, banging, slamming doors, crying, sad, depressed, resigned, etc.)
+ Examination of gunshot residue on hands
+ List and photos of all weapons including guns, knife collections or crossbows or hunting bows
+ Full photos inside subject's home or residence
  (Note: Where "photo" is indicated, a photo and a video should be taken.)
+ Full photos inside subject's vehicle

- Photos and information re: injuries sustained by spouse or significant other (domestic partner) or family member
- Close-up photos of bedroom areas especially anything suggesting that the subject was feeling melancholy, photo albums of a past "better" time...photo albums of children, etc.
- Camouflage attire
- Photos and information re: favorite hangouts
- Photos showing lighting at the time of shooting if at night. If necessary, photograph the following night
- Any video or recordings
- Any videos taken before incident of subject or family
- Any juvenile victim history/cases (i.e. child/sexual abuse cases)
- Any juvenile suspect history/cases (arson, run away)

4. Civil

- All civil court filings involving subject and immediate family (family law, bankruptcies-federal court, collection matters, small claims, etc.)
- Eviction notices
- Restraining orders
- Notices of repossessions

5. Marital/Relationship Information

- Statements by friends, neighbors, co-workers, spouse or significant other about domestic matters (divorce, separation, violence, etc.)
- Both subject and/or spouse's extra-marital affairs/issues

6. Employment History

- Employment history including personnel records (discipline, job search, etc.)
- Financial information

7. Alcohol/Controlled Substances

- Drug and alcohol history
- Blood alcohol and all drug toxicological reports
- All self-medicating history and behavior (check local liquor store)
- Favorite alcohol
- Drug paraphernalia

8. Miscellaneous

- Driving history(reckless and high speed driving)
- Military history
- Military occupational specialty (MOS)
- Tattoos (get clear photos)
- Bumper stickers on all vehicles (looking for a reference to death)
- Anything that would suggest paranoia (guns hidden throughout house, gun hidden under the mattress)
- Organizational affiliations
- Type of dog and dog's name
- Other pets (cats, snakes, etc.)
- Biological parents married or divorced? If divorced, when?
- Parents deceased? If yes, when? (exact date)
- Any children predecease them? If yes, who and when? (exact date)
- Any sexually explicit videos of subject or of subject with others
- Any sexually explicit photos of subject or of subject with others
- Photos of t-shirts with slogan that could be pre-morbid suggesting a death wish, violence, or anti-authority or anti-social
- Photos of baseball caps with slogans
- All recent writings, letters to others, diaries, etc.
- All "doodles" on paper lying around...look near telephone
- Photos of inside of the car, hidden weapons, quick draw positioning (Note: Confer with the District Attorney's Office regarding the right to collect specific documents, photographs, or other evidence.)

Investigators need to balance the search of shooting-specific evidence with the collection of the above information that will greatly help with case preparation and evaluation in the likely event of litigation against the police agency, the municipality and the officer. As the above solicited information may not appear necessary at the time of the shooting investigation, it is absolutely essential in defining the actions of the subject/suspect, the dynamics of the incident and helps with advising and/or defending the department in the event of a lawsuit.

References

Hutson, H.R., Anglin, D., Yarbrough, J., Hardaway, K., Russell, M., Strote, J., Canter, M., & Blum, B. (1998). Suicide-by-cop. Annals of Emergency Medicine, 32 (6), 665-669.

PART FIVE

THE IMPACT OF SBC INCIDENTS ON LAW ENFORCEMENT OFFICERS

Chapter 12

DYNAMICS IN RESPONDING TO DEPARTMENTAL PERSONNEL

Scott W. Allen, Ph.D

Introduction

Many of the previous authors have discussed the dynamics and ramifications of suicide-by-cop (SbC) on a more systems or law enforcement/community approach. This chapter will encompass the reactions of individual law enforcement officers who have been involved in a SbC confrontation. The law enforcement department's responsibilities and responses to the officers will also be discussed.

Suicide by Cop Overview

Gerberth (1993, p.105) apparently was the first to formally define SbC as any "incidents in which individuals, bent on self-destruction, engage in life-threatening and criminal behavior to force the police to kill them." Over the years, SbC , as a definitive construct, has remained with the operative focus on the motivation and personological dynamics of the subject rather than upon outcomes.

The first professional references to SbC were published by FBI agents of the Behavioral Sciences Unit. Noesner and Dolan (1992), and Van Zandt (1993) presented SbC as a significant risk that law enforcement officers are confronted with as a situation which may require deadly force. Van Zandt developed a 16 indicator profile of a typical SbC individual. Van Zandt also concluded that law enforcement officers involved in SbC shootings exhibit post-trauma symptomatology, most notably, feelings of guilt. Lord (1998, 2001) provided further specification of a typical SbC individual as usually unemployed, with some alcohol or drug usage at the time of the encounter, and little or no evidence of any premeditation for the confrontation with law enforcement. Perrou (2001) described antecedent behaviors indicative of imminent violence, inclusive of SbC which may increase the vigilance of law enforcement officers in these potential deadly force situations.

Suicide by Cop Incidence

Although the criteria to define a SbC incident can be problematic (Keram, 2001), the frequency of SbC is substantial enough to provide a potentially demoralizing impact upon a law enforcement agency. According to Parent (2001), approximately 400 individuals are killed by law enforcement officers each year. Of this total, it is estimated that at least 10% of these shooting fatalities can be considered as SbC. Utilizing stricter criteria (a stated wish to die and asking police to kill them, evidence of written or verbal suicidal communication to a friend or family member, possession of a lethal weapon or what appeared to be such and evidence of intentional escalation of an incident or provocation for officers to shoot them), Perrou (1999) and Hutson et al (1998) found higher frequencies of SbC incidents. These studies found fatal SbC shootings ranging from 25% to 28% of all police involved fatal shootings. Pyers (1999) found 50% of police shooting fatalities as instances of SbC. As such, SbC can be considered both a high frequency event, and a high intensity event that impacts the individual officer(s), their families, the law enforcement agency, and the community. The psychological impact upon the law enforcement participants can be demoralizing and potentially career ending even following unequivocal shootings.

The Psychological Consequences Following a SbC Incident

The agency or departmental response to an officer involved in a SbC use of force incident should be the same as any other police-officer involved shooting. Generally speaking, there are two consistent themes which influence traumatic reactions. First, an officer is typically unprepared for the emotional and physiological reactions of a particular event. Second, the officer usually is not afforded the opportunity to verbalize and emotionally ventilate these emotional and physiological reactions which could defuse and ultimately ameliorate profound post-trauma consequences. In fact, the actual causative factors are the continual, rigid re-creation of the traumatic stimuli which were experienced in the actual time and space of the traumatic confrontation. The psychological effects of a traumatic incident vary but often consist of emotional withdrawal, sleep disturbances, anxiety/fear, poor concentration, hypervigilance, substance abuse, survivor's guilt, and an overall feeling of being out of control. This list is certainly not exhaustive but expresses the most frequently occurring reactions to a traumatic event. Additionally, and most specifically, in a SbC traumatic incident, the law enforcement officer is compelled to confront the emotional responses of grief, guilt, and anger. Initially, a law enforcement officer experiences a numbing disbelief over the reality that he/she was forced to use deadly force in a situation in which mediation was the primary, driving strategy for resolution of the critical event. This emotional dichotomy is not easily reconciled without an immediate response which provides psychological support on a systems level. Support systems are composed of people an individual can rely upon in times of crisis. Such support systems within the law enforcement community include family, friends/co-workers, mental health professionals, pastoral members, and benevolent organizations.

Mental Health Professional's Response

A mental-health professional's response to a SbC incident should be inclusive of the following components; immediacy, proximity, expectancy, brevity, and accessibility (McMains, 1986, Allen, 1986).

Immediacy involves the initiation of an intervention as soon after the traumatic event as possible. The most efficacious response would be an immediate intervention, while it is recommended that no intervention should be undertaken more than 24 hours after the shooting. A protracted interval of time allows the involved officer to emotionally withdraw and develop a fully-entrenched denial system.

Proximity is generally a function of immediacy. An immediate response will allow for the interaction between the involved shooter and the mental-health professional at the scene of the shooting or at another optional location which is determined at the scene by the mental-health professional and the chain of command of the involved shooter.

Expectancy is the most integral philosophical component of the intervention dynamic. It is incumbent upon the mental-health professional to articulate at the onset of the intervention (it is strongly suggested that this on-scene intervention be termed psycho-educational to further assuage any confidentiality issues) that whatever emotions and cognitions the involved shooter is experiencing are normal. It is the event that is atypical and outside the realm of usual human experience. Therefore, any disquieting symptomatology is a normal response and the management of these symptoms will be within his/her control in the near future.

Brevity in that intervention is conceptualized as short-term with the goals of education, minimization of disabling symptoms, and the quick return to full duty status. Accessibility compels the mental health professional to establish a system of contact for the involved shooter and/or family members on a 24-hour per day availability.

Intervention Stages

From two decades of clinical experience, it is my view that an optimal intervention program would proceed through six stages (Incident, Investigation, First Week, One to Six Weeks, Three to Six Months, One-year Anniversary). As previously mentioned, at the time of the incident, it is suggested to respond expeditiously to the scene.

Incident. At the scene, the mental health professional has the opportunity to assess the emotional reactions of the involved shooter(s) and any other witness officers to the shooting. Frequently, witness officers are similarly traumatized as are the officer(s) directly involved in the shooting. Next, a contact is made with the involved shooter(s). Immediately following introduction with the officer, the responsible and ethical mental health professional will inform the officer of the confidentiality of the interaction, as well as any limits to the confidentiality of their interaction. On the scene, unless absolutely dictated by clinical exigency, this interaction should be only psycho-educational in content. Therefore, during the on-site interaction, the responsibility of the mental health professional is to assess the emotional reactions of both directly involved shooter(s) as well as witness officers, an explication of confidentiality and its limits to those officers professionally contacted, initial evaluation of contacted officers, and a psycho-educational description of the post-trauma symptomatology most likely to be experienced by the officer in the next 24-48 hours. In a SbC shooting, the involved shooter rapidly begins to respond to the emotional dichotomy of the shooting. For the entire career of the law enforcement officer, there has been a clear edict of protect and serve the community. Superimposed upon this cognitive-behavioral preamble is the initial reality of the event which was, as a first responding officer, to assist the individual whom was soon there after a recipient of reactive lethal fire from the officer. This emotional dichotomy is not easily reconciled without immediate psychological support. The officer is clearly relieved that he/she has survived the confrontation. However, there is a rapid onset of frustration and anger towards the individual who compelled the officer to fire. Along with this affective response, there is a more temperate cognition regarding the departmental and legal ramifications of the shooting. It is at this point, that the officer begins to emotionally withdraw from others. Therefore, it is incumbent upon the mental health professional to clearly state to the officer that the most deleterious reaction to a SbC shooting is emotional withdrawal and he/she is to select at least one person who the officer will seek out and share his/her feelings regarding the traumatic shooting.

Investigative phase. The second stage is comprised of the following components; the emotional responses of anger towards the SbC subject and potential emotional withdrawal, and the cognitive/emotional responses to the departmental investigation and the mandatory provision of a sworn statement. Other dynamics that may be present in some SbC shootings are the potentially deleterious effects of intrusive media attention and overtly negative reactions from community members. During this period, intervention should be directed towards providing the officer strategies which will lower stress and allow him/her to provide an accurate statement to the homicide detectives.

First week intervention phase. This period is extraordinarily critical, as well as being multifaceted. During this phase, the mental health professional is expected to provide services to a potentially broad array of clients. Obviously, the mental health professional will continue to be available to the shooting officer. Interactions with the officer will consist of symptomatology assessment, cognitive restructuring exercises, and possible systematic desensitization sessions. These strategies will allow for a consultation with the involved officer's chain of command if the officer requires more than the established departmental administrative relief from duty (which for most departments is a range of one to three days). During this time frame, the shooting officer has already given a statement to the homicide unit, and there usually is a profound sense of relief that this stressful undertaking has been completed. With this administrative hurdle completed, the officer tends to refocus upon his anger and frustration toward the deceased individual. The responsibility of the mental health professional is to subtly guide the officer from anger, to frustration, and finally to a point of empathic compassion for the victim. This process is typically facilitated by the mental health professional providing concrete information regarding the victim's suicidal intent while concurrently praising the officer for his/her success in preventing any further injuries of police officers and civilian onlookers. It is also suggested that the mental health professional should schedule an appointment to visit with the law enforcement officer and his/her family at their home to assess the emotional status of the officer's significant other and any children. Frequently, the affected police officer receives significant and helpful intervention, however, family members are not always provided with any form of assistance. Specifically, the mental health professional involved in the trauma response should provide information regarding the dynamics of trauma response and the symptomatic reactions to the traumatic event of a SbC shooting. Children of the affected officer should also be seen to ascertain their reactions to their parent's traumatic event. Oftentimes, children of a parent who is involved in a police-involved shooting experience a significant degree of cognitive dissonance. A child of a law enforcement officer interacts with his parent on the level as a benevolent mother or father. Following a shooting in which their parent has shot and killed someone, the child is confronted with the reality that his/her parent literally has the ability to kill someone. This is stark contrast to the parental image the child possesses toward his/her parent. The responsibility of the mental health professional is to intervene to explain the role responsibilities as well as role differences between their parent as a law enforcement officer and during family time as a mother or father. A final responsibility of the mental health professional during this period is to determine if any other law enforcement officers and/or the shooting officer's squad would benefit from a group-debriefing process. This form of intervention will be discussed later.

One to six week intervention phase. This later period is a time in which the mental health professional facilitates the law enforcement officer's ventilation of emotions and perhaps further phobic desensitization, if necessary. The primary goal of this phase is to initiate the process of recovery toward the pre-incident level of emotional stability and appropriate behavioral interaction with the environment. Specific criteria which the mental health professional will be assessing is the return of typical sleep patterns for the officer, emotional investment with others, the initiation of a reconciliation process which will lower the distressing periods of anger/frustration, and a lessening of hyper-vigilance. As the affected officer establishes levels of progress in these areas, the disposition of full-duty status (ability to return to the original assignment with no restriction of firearms nor arrest powers) becomes a viable probability.

Three to six month stages. During these periods, the mental health professional is available to the officer for follow-up assistance. There may be lingering emotional issues (anger/frustration), or there may be a transient exacerbation of an emotional response or phobic reaction. Another frequently occurring dynamic during these time frames is the emergence of other symptoms not necessarily related to the SbC but are nonetheless triggered by the traumatic event. The most frequently reported issue is marital/family discord which became intensified by the emotionality of the SbC trauma. Another frequently occurring behavior which is typically exhibited during these time periods is manifested by the officer either on- or off-duty. The potentially lethal behavior is known as indirect self-destructive behavior. This constellation of risk taking behaviors will be discussed later.

Anniversary stage. The final stage in the SbC post-shooting trauma response program arrives at twelve months, which generally entails the mental health professional initiating a contact with the law enforcement officer. During this contact, the mental health professional evaluates the officer's typically heightened emotions over the one to three weeks prior to the anniversary of the SbC incident. The officer is evaluated for intensity of sequelae inclusive of post-trauma symptomatology, survivor's guilt, indirect self-destructive behavior, any residual couples, marital, or family problems, or any individual coping (dissonance) issues by the child/children of the law enforcement officer(s).

Group Debriefing of Officers Involved in a SbC Shooting

A group debriefing is a clinical response that is highly recommended for most SbC shootings. While this intervention can clearly be helpful to the shooting officer, it is also extremely beneficial to the other officers (as well as other departmental members who may have become involved peri- or post-event) who were directly involved in the shooting or who witnessed the incident. For all members who take part, the debriefing, allows for the ventilation of emotions, clarification of the incident's chronology and participants' behaviors, emotional bonding, and an understanding of the symptoms following a traumatic event.

A group debriefing is a confidential psycho-educational process to mitigate the impact of the trauma and to assist in the recovery of those individuals who may be experiencing normal reactions to a highly unusual event. Therefore, a debriefing should be scheduled within the first eight- to 72-hours following the shooting incident. If the shooting officer is attending the debriefing, it is absolutely requisite that the meeting occur only after the shooting officer has provided his/her final, official statement to the homicide shooting team as well as the state attorney. All personnel who were impacted by the event are invited to the debriefing. The debriefing is undertaken under the edict of strict confidentiality although it must be remembered by all participants (especially if the debriefing is facilitated by peer counselors) that confidentiality is not an absolute guarantee. For instance, a judge in any future court proceeding could waive the confidentiality of the group debriefing.

The Stages of Group Debriefing

The suggested stages of a group debriefing follow the general formats articulated by Mitchell (1983), and Solomon (1989).

Stage 1 is a statement by the mental health professional (or peer counselor) of the levels of confidentiality, the purpose and ground rules for the debriefing, and an introduction of the group debriefing facilitator, preferably by a senior staff member of the law enforcement agency (who then promptly leaves following the introduction).

Stage 2 begins with an introduction of the participating group members. This is followed by each member providing a brief, general recollection of the traumatic event–their initial thoughts regarding what was transpiring during the trauma.

Stage 3 is another round of each member describing his/her emotional reactions during the traumatic event–most specifically, what was their most comfortable emotion (peaceful, soothing), and what was his/her most uncomfortable emotion (fear, panic). This stage is obviously the most critical as it relates to how each member has emotionally reacted to the traumatic event. It is incumbent upon the mental health professional or peer counselor to facilitate the processing of these emotional reactions on an individual level, as well as upon a group level. It is also recommended to allow for the processing of these emotions of the group members by the group members themselves. This strategy establishes a dynamic for the establishment of strong affective bonds among the group members. By hearing all of the participants' experiences of fear, anger, grief, and mourning of loss (to mention just a few of the myriad of affective responses), each individual will be more likely to understand that his/her emotional reactions are typical responses. With this normalization of post-trauma symptomatology, the participants will be able to accept their feelings. Further, each participant will be more able and willing to assist other group members who may be experiencing greater degrees of unresolved loss.

Stage 4 is the final stage and involves an overall review by the mental health professional or the peer counselor of symptomatology and affective reactions which have been discussed during the previous four stages of the group debriefing. Summary statements regarding grief and loss are particularly powerful and helpful for the participants. A concluding statement regarding the power of peer support is particularly recommended. Finally, a broad and general statement providing referral sources for those individual members who may benefit from more in-depth, or specialized follow-up intervention is presented to the group.

Indirect Self-Destructive Behavior and Suicide Prevention

As the variables for suicide within the law enforcement community are multiple and the maintenance of reliable statistics related to suicidal behavior is dubious, the orientation toward rates of suicide should be replaced by the behaviors of suicide. However, there is a basic consensus among researchers in the field that police work is a high-stress occupation. These job-related stressors are related to the dangers of violence and peer pressure, organizational and authority conflicts, as well as, personal problems, such as, marital and family dynamics, substance abuse, and psychosocial affects of depression, frustration, and feelings of powerlessness.

At present, suicidal behavior can't be easily incorporated into current psychological theories, and certainly no single theory can account for all suicides. Regardless of theoretical orientation, suicide is widely agreed by professionals to be an extremely intricate complex of behaviors. Therefore, a definitive approach may ultimately provide a clearer understanding of suicidal behavior and suicide potential. Baechler (1979) defines suicide as a behavior in response to the demands of life. Suicide is neither a disease nor a force, but rather a behavioral solution. Lester and Lester (1971) defined suicide as a complex set of behaviors aimed at improving a hopeless situation or in the hope of preserving a threatened self-image. It is specifically, this latter dynamic which can compel the law enforcement officer involved in a SbC to contemplate suicide (or, at the least, engage in suicidal ideation). The affective component of self-concept in a law enforcement officer is deeply ingrained, primarily, the concept of protect and serve. Some SbC law enforcement officers, especially those involved in an equivocal shooting, or, a shooting in which the victim possessed an unloaded or fake firearm, quickly react to this seeming contradiction between protecting the general public, but shooting and killing an individual within the public. Since the self-image of the competent, protective law enforcement officer is profoundly challenged, the SbC involved shooting officer is at high risk to become actively suicidal.

Suicide as a behavior is infrequent, occurring in a small proportion of any given sample of a population. However, there is a tendency for individuals, especially law enforcement individuals toward self-injury, self-defeat, and self-destruction (Allen, 1986). Farberow (1980) termed such behaviors as indirect self-destructive behavior (ISDB). As defined by Farberow, ISDB occurs when the individual develops a plan for indirect self-destruction (suicide) that is more socially acceptable than suicide. Secondly, ISDB is an insidious progression of risk-taking behavior, which ultimately exceeds the boundaries for safety, and survival. Some examples of ISDB manifested by police officers are; working road patrol without wearing a bullet-proof vest, "jumping" (responding inappropriately quickly) a two-officer call as a one-officer unit, consistently taking overly aggressive risks while working, and developing new hobbies which clearly incorporate risk-taking behaviors (skydiving, motorcycle riding without a protective helmet, ultralight flying). According to Farberow and Achete (1980), these behaviors are initiated in response to an emotional need for punishment. For law enforcement officers, risk-taking behaviors become ISDB when there is objective evidence of depression or guilt. Symptoms most often associated with ISDB are the feelings of hopeless and helplessness which precipitate an overall lack of self-esteem. Therefore, it is the responsibility of the mental health professional to provide information relevant to the process of ISDB to line supervisors, as well as police friends and partners of the law enforcement officer involved in a SbC shooting. The mental health professional should assess any work-related behaviors exhibited by the officer so as to realize the early identification of any potential ISDB patterns.

Regardless of the underlying motivator (sudden shame, guilt, ISDB), the law enforcement officer involved in a SbC incident may be at risk for some dynamic of self-destructive behavior. The goal for this form of crisis intervention is to assist this law enforcement officer to effectively contain or control the physical expression of the internal turmoil manifested as suicidal ideation and behaviors. Following the initial responses to a SbC incident by the mental health professional (individual and/or group assessment and intervention), the final stage of the intervention process is a follow-up or aftercare. Berent (1981) believed this stage prevents premorbid cognitions, affects and behaviors from returning. Follow-up care strengthens the law enforcement officer's capacity to cope with stress by reinforcing creative problem-solving techniques. Follow-up further develops mastery over complicated interpersonal or family relationships, as well as sustaining sobriety in those cases where substance abuse has been identified as problematic.

Suicides within the law enforcement community are not tragic acts committed in isolation, but, rather, an intent that is communicated by the SbC law enforcement officer within their psychosocial environment. Suicide is neither a disease nor a psychotic violent act, but in fact, a complicated problem-solving behavior. Therefore, the progressive law enforcement agency will optimally consider the provision of training to its members to understand the underlying processes and consequences of suicide, as well as the stages of response within the crisis intervention process (Allen, 2001). Every law enforcement agency must consider the establishment of nonstigmatizing and nonpunitive policies related to the management of the law enforcement officer, including confidentiality during on-scene psychoeducational contacts, group debriefings, and if necessary, throughout any direct clinical intervention inclusive of hospitalization. Finally, every law enforcement agency should develop and support nonpejorative return-to-work policies and procedures for law enforcement officers who experienced significant emotional reactions following a SbC incident.

Conclusion

Post-trauma reactions ranging from minor, transient vegetative responses to suicidal behavior (inclusive of ISDB) following a SbC incident are typical, high-frequency events. Mental health professionals intervening with a law enforcement officer involved in a SbC incident must provide immediate intervention which is incisive and pragmatic. As the phenomenon of SbC is unlikely to decrease, mental health professionals should provide intervention which is consistent with critical incident response except allowing for an emphasis upon anger resolution.

Most SbC incidents benefit from psychological debriefings. However, it is important to realize that the factors of timeliness and appropriateness are critical. Not all law enforcement officers are responsive to debriefings immediately after the event, nor do all officers benefit from a group process. Therefore, it behooves the mental health professional to be cognizant of these dynamics and optimally, be involved with the department prior to a critical event. In this way, the mental health professional can ascertain accurately the timing for the debriefing, which officers will best benefit, which officers should be scheduled for individual intervention. Finally, the mental health professional should provide both consultation to the command staff and training to law enforcement officers. Consultation with command staff provides the departmental imperative by establishing an administrative rationale that insulates law enforcement officers from potential punitive action following post-trauma intervention. Training will delineate accurate information regarding departmental policy and provides practical information regarding appropriate responses to deadly-force situations, especially SbC encounters. Departmental training will offer pragmatic information related to suicide that inculcates individual responsibility for competent identification, understanding, interaction, intervention and referral for law enforcement officers involved in, or witnesses to a SbC incident. Finally, ongoing, departmental training will allow the mental health professional to become professionally and personally involved with the law enforcement officers. This process can only facilitate the integral dynamic of trust when providing intervention within the law enforcement community.

Suicide by cop is a profound, critical event to the law enforcement officer. It is imperative that the mental health professional does not further usurp the sense of control from the officer, but rather facilitate the transition from hypercritical shooter to a competent, emotionally-intact person.

References

Allen, S. W. (2001). Suicide prevention training: One department's response. In D. Sheehan & J. Warren (Eds.), Suicide and Law Enforcement (pp.9-15). Washington, DC: U.S. Government Printing Office.

Allen, S. W., Basilio, I., Fraser, S. L., Stock, H. V., Garrison, W. E., Cohen, L. M., Stephens, P. J., & Cornell, L. M. (1994). Proximate traumatic sequelae of Hurricane Andrew on the police family. In J. Reese & E. Scrivner (Eds.), Law enforcement families: Issues and answers (pp.143-154). Washington, DC: U.S. Government Printing Office.

Allen, S. W. (1986). Suicide and idirect self-destructive behavior among police. In J. Reese & H. Goldstein (Eds.), Psychological services for law enforcement (pp.413-417). Washington, DC: U.S. Government Printing Office.

Achete, K. A. (1980). The psychopathology of indirect self-destructive behavior. In N.Farberow (Ed.), The many faces of suicide (pp. 127-162). New York: McGraw-Hill.

Baechler, J. (1979). Suicides. New York: Basic Books. Berent, I. (1981). The algebra of suicide. New York: Human Sciences Press.

Bongar, B. (1992). The suicidal patient. Washington, DC: American Psychological Association.

Farberow, N. L. (1980). The many faces of suicide. New York: McGraw-Hill.

Gerberth, V. (1993). Suicide-by-cop: Inviting death from the hands of a police officer. Law and Order, 108, 105-109.

Chapter 13

CRISIS MANAGEMENT TRAINING
FOR
LAW ENFORCEMENT AND FIRST RESPONDERS

Barry Perrou, Psy.D.
Founder, Public Safety Research Institute

Introduction

This chapter consists of content that should be included in training material for law enforcement officers and other first responders. As the reader will realize, this information should be taught by a psychologist or professional who is experienced and trained to work with people in suicidal crisis and people in suicidal crisis at the point of action or conclusion.

For the purpose of this chapter, the term "suicide-in-progress" (SiP) means anyone poised or at the point of using deadly force in an effort to kill themselves..."self terminate." The term "classic suicide" is used to describe in general terms suicide by anyone, not specific sub categories such as suicide-by-cop (SbC) or suicide of police officers. The term "suicide-by-cop" has been defined by other authors in earlier chapters of this book, but a panel of "subject matter experts" for the California State Commission on Police Officer Standards of Training (P.O.S.T.) has defined suicide-by-cop as "a situation in which an individual engages in behavior that poses an apparent risk of serious injury or death with intent to precipitate the use of deadly force by law enforcement personnel" (Cal. P.O.S.T., 1999).

Nearly any "classic" suicide-in-progress (SiP) can become a potential suicide-by-cop confrontation when police are summoned. Suicide-by-cop is an attempt to trap officers in deadly confrontations that by design removes the possibility of a tactical retreat, the use of less-lethal (non-lethal) options by police officers engaged in these situations, thereby necessitating the use of deadly force.

Training should provide understanding about the phenomenon of classic suicide, about "classic" suicidal subjects, the phenomenon of suicide-by-cop, about suicide-by-cop subjects, profiles of all incident types, and especially identifiable behaviors leading to suicidal confrontations.

This training should also provide students with more than a one-dimensional, didactic explanation of facts and prepare the student to observe, recognize and articulate the potentially deadly components of human behavior that create the trap of suicide-by-cop.

Trainers should challenge police officers conventional thinking (and denial) about suicide; that being, there are only single motives behind human behavior, learning to anticipate alternative actions causing other unpredictable behaviors and outcomes. Additional objectives for training should include: review and update of traditional tactics or lack of tactics deployed by law enforcement personnel and the creation of awareness of precipitator/suspect profiles based on past events and research. There are many recorded video events that are very useful to help trainers identify and index aberrant behavior suggesting unpredictable outcomes.

Training and comprehension must be provided to everyone who might come in contact with these types of incidents, including but not limited to: dispatchers, line officers, field supervisors, incident commanders, command level personnel and municipality legal staff and risk managers. Training, possibly in an abbreviated manner, must also be provided to department executives, Employee Assistance Program (EAP) staff and/or Psychological Assistance Units, so they may also understand the sensitivities of the victim officers and their families, the precipitant subject and their families, the impact on the department, and the impact to the community.

Classic Suicide

According to the National Institute of Mental Health, in the year 2000, suicide occurred 29,350 times (N.I.M.H. April, 2003). Over the years of data collection, this number has remained fairly constant with a slight dip in the past two years. The impact of suicide is not singular, but typically affects six others who were in someway connected to the suicide subject. These individuals are respectfully referred to as survivors. If suicide had "energy," and it does, it is suggested that the suicidal energy in some content is transferred to the survivors upon completion of the death act. Of course this is not a scientific finding, but the profound emotions of the survivors is very powerful and is consistently represented as a common theme. Officers who have contact with survivors should remember to be sensitive to the feelings and emotions that follow such tragic events.

There are differing attempt ratios depending on age. For ages up to 17 years, there are 100 attempts for every one completed; adult, 20 attempts for every one completed; and elderly, four attempts for every one completed. Two-thirds of all high school students have had some suicidal ideation (thoughts). With the major mental illness of Bi-polar Disorder (manic-depressive illness), 15% of those with this diagnosis will commit suicide. Suicide is the eighth leading cause of death in the United States, and the second leading cause of death for youth after accidents. Based on the attempt to completed ratio, approximately 800,000 attempt suicides occur annually. For law enforcement agencies, these are not all in-progress events, but instead, some are reported to the police after the fact. However, many of those are in-progress with an increase of "public-display" attempts (as cited in Firestone 1999).

Of those who commit suicide, some facts about the phenomenon are as follows:

Gender: Males are three times more likely to complete the act of suicide than females.

Race: White subjects are two times more likely to commit suicide than non-whites.

Marital status: Divorced individuals are the most likely, and married subjects are the least likely to commit suicide.

For every 10 suicides:
    8 are men
    9 are white
    7 are white men
    2 are white women
    1 is non-white, most likely a male

Gender by suicide method:

	Men	*Women*
Firearms	65%	42%
Hanging	16%	13%
Inhaled gases/poisons	6%	7% (Car exhaust, natural gas in house)
Ingested poisons	6%	27% (overdose, drain cleaner, poison)
All other means	7%	11%

(N.I.M.H, April 2003)

As a trainer of police officers about suicide and suicide related matters, the discussion of "police officer suicide" is always raised and discussed. When asked how many have known a police officer who has committed suicide, approximately two-third of the students (law enforcement personnel) will respond that they have known someone in the police profession who has taken his/her own life. Admittedly, a single suicide in a small police agency will, in varying degrees, affect everyone, and the "energy" and clear remembrance is transferred to the officers. Police executives and managers need to recognize that sworn **and** non-sworn employees are impacted and should be afforded the opportunity to participate in Critical Incident Stress Debriefings (CISD). See the Teaching Module for additional information (The Psycho-Social Investigation of Shooting Investigations and Case Management).

The National P.O.L.I.C.E. Suicide Foundation Inc. has found that comparing line of duty deaths to officer suicide, police officers die more frequently at their own hands than in violent deadly confrontations. According to the Foundation, (The Bridge, August, 1999), a police officer dies in the line of duty every 57 hours. Contrastingly, a police officer commits suicide every 22 hours. In either circumstance, this is a tragic loss of life, possibly avoidable with good recognition training and prevention programs.

Suicide is a social problem. When alerted to an in-progress event, the problem and outcome becomes that of the police agency and police officers. To reiterate, suicide in our society is a social problem, and as a part of the social service system, police officers, where possible, should disseminate and support the local suicide crisis line or the National Hopeline Network hot line at 1-800-SUICIDE (1-800-784-2433). The National Hopeline Network will connect the caller anywhere in the United States to counselors certified by the American Association of Suicidology who are a part of the nationwide Hopeline Network. The caller is connected to the nearest crisis center and if busy, the call will be automatically routed to the next nearest available crisis center. The important fact is that there is someone skillfully trained to accommodate the caller and attempt to manage the situation before it becomes a death or a law enforcement crisis call for service.

Following the medical model of treatment, the best-trained person in a particular area of expertise should be utilized for diagnosis and/or treatment (corrective intervention). Analogizing an injury situation, once the patient is medically stabilized, specialists are summoned to lend their expertise. This concept should also apply to police agencies where crisis counselors are available. This is a valuable resource and, if applied in a preventative posture, accomplishes the intervention task hopefully moving to a life-saving conclusion. If the poised suicide event is one of public display, e.g. "jumpers" or barricaded subject with a gun in a car in a public place, then community safety and subject welfare further draws the police agency into the equation. But where subjects are legally inside their home and suicidal, crisis counselors can be a valuable resource and diminish the drain of personnel assigned to a crisis while still demonstrating care and compassion for the subject and safety to the community.

Police Management of a Suicide-in-Progress Incident

From the police perspective, an individual poised to commit suicide is someone who probably meets the requirements of an involuntary psychiatric hospitalization, or "hold." This would suggest that this individual is in need of mental health intervention more than law enforcement engagement. However, the reality is that there are few mental health outreach programs that have assigned staff trained to respond to suicide-in-progress situations. This puts the responsibility squarely on the law enforcement agency, and is an area of police training as "first responders" that is traditionally overlooked.

In suicide-in-progress situations, a police officer's fundamental urge is to "rescue." That is the charge of law enforcement: to approach where others won't. However, rescuing typically causes a rapidly escalated risk of injury to the officer and may precipitate the suicidal act. Also, dispatching police officers to a suicide-in-progress brings weapons as an optional means of suicide (suicide-by-cop).

In managing a suicide in progress event, police officers must first acknowledge that suicide is a violent act. Webster (Mish, 1994) defines "VIOLENCE" as:

> *"1 Physical force used so as to injure, damage, or destroy; extreme roughness of action. 2 Intense, often devastatingly or explosive powerful force or energy, as of a hurricane or volcano. 3 a) Unjust or callous use of force or power, as in violating another's rights, sensibilities, etc. b) The harm done by this. 4 Great force or strength of feeling, conduct, or expression; vehemence; fury."*

Clearly the act of suicide meets this definition.

Webster defines "HOMICIDE" as "*homicidium*, manslaughter, murder: to cut, kill: any killing of one human being by another."

Webster's definition of "SUICIDE" is:

> *"1 The act of killing oneself intentionally. 2 Ruin of one's interests or prospects through one's own actions, policies, etc. 3 A person who commits suicide."*

By Webster's definition, the action of both events, suicide and homicide, is violent. The serious issues in managing a SiP or SbC situation are: 1) who is the action directed towards; 2) how can that action be interpreted or mis-interpreted leading to the deadly event; and 3) how do police officers avoid escalating the suicide-in-progress or precipitating a suicide-by-cop situation? Suicidal people poised to commit a violent act towards themselves can be extremely intense. There are no known statistics, but somewhere between suicide and safe surrender, there are known incidents of accidents. For example, the person who decides to surrender the firearm to a police officer/crisis negotiator may in fact accidentally discharge the weapon possibly killing or hurting him or herself or others. The "jumper" who is poised to jump at the edge of a building but instead agrees to go to the hospital may slip and fall to his or her death while trying to retreat to safety and surrender. Accidents can occur and police officers have a tendency to "overextend" themselves in an effort to show good faith, compassion and caring.

Society and police officers are all too familiar with "homicide-suicide" situations. These tragic incidents have specific characteristics and are usually raging acts of violence saving the act of suicide for the last death or serious injury. However, as reported by the Associated Press (Naples Daily News, October 15, 1999), an "accident" occurred in Jacksonville, Florida.

The article reads:

> *"Single bullet kills 2 men in Florida" Jacksonville, Fla.—Two Florida men killed when the same bullet struck them in the head, police said. William Barton, 31, and Dean McGraw, 35, were at a Jacksonville home when Barton began playing with a 9mm semiautomatic pistol, said Lt. Mark Foxworth of the Jacksonville Sheriffs Office. Barton put the gun to his head and pulled the trigger. "We don't know if it was accidental or a suicide," Foxworth said. The bullet passed through Barton's skull and struck McGraws in the head. Both were later pronounced dead at the local hospital.*

Suicide-homicide...accidents can occur, and during such intense moments of intoxication, depression, psychosis, or surrender, tragedy can occur. **Officer safety must be the priority beyond anything else, including rescue.**

A suicide-in-progress (SiP) is high drama in slow motion. Typically, first responding officers rush to rescue and too frequently place themselves and the suicidal person in greater peril. Crisis managers have developed a simplistic pattern of "C's" as a guide for on scene incident commanders to follow. The C's are as follows:

Command: Someone must take responsibility for the overall event

Coordinate: That same person must coordinate responding officers, paramedics, ambulances, and other resources

Communicate: The same officer in command must communicate all efforts involved in handling the situation, make assignments, and if necessary, order the initiation of tactical/action plans.

Contain: The command officer must assure that the suicidal subject is loosely (and safely) surrounded and that there is no option of escape, or escalation of risk/danger unless as prescribed in a tactical plan.

Control: This is where the circumstances surrounding the event are "stable." Control typically comes after accomplishing the preceding 4-C's. In medical reference, this is where the patient is "stable," although not out of critical condition. Control does not suggest that the situation is concluded, but instead merely a safer place in time to implement a plan of action.

Contingency: This is the development of secondary plans (typically a physical rescue) by the officer in command, and those assisting in this rescue effort. Some situations may suggest that more than one contingency plan may be necessary. It is important that these plans be documented and thoroughly discussed with all involved police officers to avoid surprises.

Critique: "Critique" is the after-action, no-fault discussion of what happened, what worked well and what aspects of the operation needed enhancement. Most police officers don't have a great frequency of "SiP" situations and therefore don't have as much opportunity for improvement through repetition. Incident commanders or field supervisors should be responsible for assuring that everyone attend the critique, especially if there was a fatal or injury outcome.

The Precipitating Triad (Action Imperative)

When managing a situation where a suicidal subject is poised at the "edge" of death, the rule of the **cause and effect** relationship is intensified. This is most demonstrable with "jumper" subjects when approached or encroached upon by rescuers. As the rescuers close distance between the subject and themselves, the **window of opportunity** starts to close. By the **power of proximity**, the subject responds to the rescuers' movements, and as the subject anticipates that he or she may be grabbed, they are left with few options. Do I surrender or jump? For others: Do I surrender or plunge the knife? Do I surrender to the "entry" team making entry, or do I pull the trigger? At that highly charged and impulsive moment, the subject may jump, impale, or act dangerously which would suggest that the best intentions of the rescuers have actually precipitated the subject's death. Law suits are increasing where suicide rescuers failed to ask the simple question: "Did the rescuers deploy appropriate tactics to save a life or did they create the "action imperative" for the death act?

An incident commander is responsible for the well-being of his/her personnel. The others present to assist should follow orders; non-planned independent or heroic actions in a planned event are counterproductive. Not only do such actions increase the level of dangerousness, but also catch others in containment off-guard and reactive. In SiP events, rescuers initially have very little control of the outcome. If the subject is so intent on suicide, then it is better conducted at his/her own hands, rather than drawing in police officers to unsuspectingly and unintentionally assist in his or her death. This is part of the sad reality surrounding suicide. Incident commanders also need to keep their emotions in check. A suicide-in-progress situation is very seductive. Everyone who can see or hear the situation unfold has an immediate "connect" with that person. A personal investment to "save." It is vital for someone to take charge as the Incident Commander and emotionally disconnect with the subject. This doesn't mean an absence of caring, but rather an application to a more global responsibility. The larger picture is everything else that must be managed and coordinated in a professional and thorough manner, having a greater impact on a successful outcome than repetitive dialogue that each of us might have in our own heads with that suicidal person if we were there with them. Suicide is interesting; it is high drama; it is tragically memorable;...it is seductive.

The fatal action of suicide is usually an impulsive act, an impulsive micro-second. Getting to that suicidal precipice usually occurs over a longer period of time, but where someone is poised to pull the trigger, it usually becomes impulsive at that very instant. That "trigger pull" action is accomplished with vehemence and fury as suggested in Webster's definition of "violence." As police officers know, a bullet has no friends or enemies, and in managing a suicide in progress, suicidal subjects in such states of emotional distress and compression rarely take into account safety issues of others. Their despair is so great that post-action consequences are rarely calculated. For people contemplating suicide, the act is not where they are going, but more accurately from where they can escape. Not what starts, but what ends, the cessation of the emotional pain and anguish. The action is a "death disconnect."

Suicide-by-Cop (SbC)

Suicide-by-cop (SbC) frequently happens in a residence. As police officers know too well, the "family dispute" call is a highly charged emotional confrontation of inconsequential behavior upon the part of the "disturbing party." An review of all officer-involved shootings investigated by the Los Angeles County Sheriff's Department was conducted seeking quantifiable data about the SbC phenomenon (Hutson, Yarbrough, Hardaway, Russell, Strote, Canter, and Blum, 1998). Researchers reviewed 437 officer-involved shootings for a 10-year period looking for four definable criteria specific to the behavior and mental state of the SbC subject. (It should be noted that upon request, the Sheriffs Department will investigate officer-involved shootings of other police departments in Los Angeles County.) The criterion were as follows:

- A wish to die and ask police officers to kill them
- Evidence of written or verbal suicidal communications to a friend or family member
- Possession of a lethal weapon **or** what appeared to be such
- Evidence of intentional escalation of the incident or provocation for officers to shoot them (the outrageous act)

Researchers found that 12.5% of the officer-involved shootings met SbC criteria; however, in the final year of the study while the reviewers were actively collecting the current data, they found that 28.3% of the officer-involved shootings met criteria. Possibly, questions and inquiries by investigators at the direction of the researchers became more specific so that the forensic pathology was more deeply explored, presenting a truer picture of the phenomenon during the final year. Of the 46 incidents that met the criteria of SbC, the following is a breakdown of quantifiable data that provides "profile" and "circumstantial" data that can be incorporated into training protocols. These are incident "identifiers" that should be considered before the officer(s) get to the scene and are unwittingly pulled into the "confrontational" trap. These identifiers are:

1. *Gender:* Males are more predominant.
2. *Ethnicity:* Whites are more predominant.
3. *Weapons:* Firearms or firearm replicas are primarily used, followed by edged and blunt instruments. The firearms are usually operable and often loaded.
4. *Associated factors:* Asked to be shot or killed by police, prior arrests, psychiatric history, substance-abuse history, domestic violence history or another precipitating event.

According to the Los Angeles' study, 72% of the shootings occurred at or in a residence. This coincides with interviews of attempted SbC survivors, who suggested that the residence belonged to them, and any intervention by law enforcement was an invasion of their territorial rights. By defending their territory, they were justified to act defiantly, escalate, and engage in a violent confrontation. Officers armed with this "identifier" or "profile" information are better mentally and tactically prepared for the unknown when they respond to a call, suggesting suspicious behavior.

Brien Farrell, City Attorney for the city of Santa Rosa, California, who has defended numerous Santa Rosa police officers for use of deadly force, articulated the following key points about SbC (June,1998):

1. A suicidal person can and may kill. Therefore, these incidents are dangerous, high-risk events that demand sound officer tactics.

2. Some suicidal persons want officers to kill them and may harm others to make it happen.

3. These events are increasing in frequency and magnitude.

4. Officers are often surprised by the behaviors of the precipitator in these situations.

5. The event often involves a precipitator who is armed and violent and whose **behavior is irrational, threatening, non-compliant, and defiant.**

6. The actions of the precipitator are intended to remove the non-deadly force option available to the officer.

7. The event often involves a planned or spontaneous "trap" created by the precipitator to manipulate the officer into using deadly force against them.

8. The violence and extreme dynamics of these situations and the resulting publicity and lawsuits increase the potential for adverse psychological impact on the officer and other involved law enforcement personnel.

9. In a "suicide-by-cop" incident, the officer is truly the victim, although the incident is often incorrectly portrayed by the media as the result of excessive force or improper tactics.

10. Thorough investigations are crucial in revealing the truth about the incident.

Outrageous Act. A vital component that acts as the catalyst for SbC confrontations is the presence of an outrageous act. This equates to a socially unacceptable behavior that needs investigating by the police. For example, a SbC subject might walk into his front yard and commence firing bullets into the air. Another example would be to shoot the neighbor's pet or physically abuse a domestic partner provoking him/her to call the police. Another emerging practice is to lead police officers on a lengthy pursuit establishing an action "limit line" when either the car runs out of gas, or the subject has a typically open view chance to stop and engage police by pointing a weapon at them. Another emerging practice is that of individuals repeatedly committing greed crimes such as armed robbery, enjoying the rewards of their efforts until they are identified and put into a near-capture situation. They then cause an officer-involved shooting ultimately, suicide-by-cop. As one deceased suspect said right before pointing his empty 9mm firearm at the Swat Team, "Prison's not a pretty place and I ain't going back."

Police dispatchers. Dispatchers are vitally important and too frequently ignored. They are the first line of defense at gathering critical information, especially when the information collected suggests abnormal circumstances or behavior. They should identify behavior based on the information collected in the previous mentioned studies and ask specific questions better defining the circumstances and profiling the volatility of the person and circumstances. Dispatchers need to ask a series of specific questions (see below) that eliminate loose interpretations by the person calling to report the event. These questions have been assembled based on research and the experience of police officers who have handled these types of calls. These questions are intended to identify behavioral history, current intent, level of volatility and the degree of risk.

Since this is legally discoverable, and could be evidence in litigation, all of the questions should be asked of the caller and recorded as 'Y'=yes, 'N'=no and 'U'=unknown. The more 'Y' answers received by the dispatcher, the higher degree of danger and the probability of engagement likely to occur. As information is gathered from the target location, dispatchers should be updating responding personnel on a dedicated radio frequency.

The questions are:

About the caller:
    Are you safe? If not, can you get to a close safe location and call back on 911? (Most 911 dispatch systems accommodate call transfer and conferencing if necessary.)

About the SbC precipitator:
    Has he/she been drinking today?
    Has he/she taken any drugs or medications today or yesterday? If so what?
    Has he/she ever been in a psychiatric hospital or treated for a mental disorder?
    Has he/she ever made any prior attempts at suicide?
    Does he/she have any guns, knives or other weapons now? If so, what?
    Has he/she pointed a weapon at anyone today?
    Has he/she ever made any threats to kill or be killed by the police?
    Are there any family problems that he/she is feeling sad about?
    Has he/she ever been in prison?
    Has he/she been screaming or yelling with extreme rage during this incident?

Police first responders. For police first responders, the tactics to approach these situations are similar to those of a bank robbery in progress. A coordinated response should be initiated by the officer handling the call or the field supervisor. Officers should not independently approach the location until enough assisting units are present and safely deployed. An offsite staging area for plan development should be identified, and personnel should gather there for assignments. Once a plan is developed, officers should set up containment on the location and for neighborhood/community safety purposes, possibly consider evacuations. (Of course, if acts of violence or deadly threats to others is occurring, then established department policies for handling hostage situations or violent crimes-in-progress should be followed.)

Once officers are in position, the dispatcher or a designated containment officer should call into the target location and request the subject to exit the location through a pre-designated door in a prescribed manner assuring officer safety. Typically this is shirt off and hands raised above the head, holding nothing. If the subject complies, officers can safely detain the person and make those evaluations (clearing the location) necessary to conclude the call. If the individual refuses to exit the target location, an evaluation of circumstances must be considered (see Situational Assessment). If no crime has occurred, there must be a legal basis and a **common sense** evaluation made before escalating the situation. If a crime has occurred, those documents of "judicial review" such as warrants should be obtained. If "exigent circumstances" can be clearly articulated, then officers may need to take those life-saving rescue efforts that are necessary keeping officer safety as the highest priority.

If the subject comes out of the house armed and/or pointing a weapon at officers, then department policies governing deadly force situations are relevant. The degree of response is largely dictated by the equipment and resources officers have available to them such as less-lethal armament, and the degree of deadly threat presented.

Situational assessment. In situations of barricaded suicidal subjects, there should be serious evaluation for the need to escalate and engage. These types of police calls for service provide too great a risk to "act" causing a common circumstance of officer-involved shooting, and too frequently a suicide-by-cop.

The 4th amendment to the U. S. Constitution clearly defines the protections afforded people and increases common-sense safety parameters for police officers. The 4th amendment states:

"The right of people to be secure in their persons, houses, papers, and effects, against unreasonable searches and seizures, shall not be violated, and no warrant shall issue, but upon probable cause, supported by Oath or affirmation, and particularly

describing the place to be searched, and the persons or things to be seized."

In the protection of all people, this section does not exclude persons who may be suicidal or those with mental disorders. They are afforded the same protections. One of the exceptions to the 4th Amendment is "exigency"; however, exigency must be well **articulated** and an evaluation for the need to act or rescue be made. With increasing frequency, men are barricading themselves in their homes and threatening suicide. Seemingly, they are protected under the 4th Amendment until such time a crime occurs. The facts are: 1) someone who does not care about living is legally inside their home, and 2) they are usually legally in possession of a firearm, (2nd Amendment to the U.S. Constitution, the right to bear arms). Tragically, law enforcement is now faced with the dilemma of putting these facts into the standard resolution equations available to police officers. Too frequently this does not work, and too frequently these situations, when forced or escalated, are deadly.

In as much as police officers genuinely want to save lives, we must accept that sometimes by legal constraint, the matter is beyond their control. In the situation of a barricaded suicidal subject where no crime has occurred, no hostages are being held, and there is no articulated medical emergency, police officers are frequently frustrated by the limitations. To their advantage, these limitations also prevent them from trying to control a situation that needs to de-energize. Forcing the confrontation, although in an attempt to rescue, typically escalates the engagement into a deadly resolution. Police officers should not die at the hands of someone who has little or no regard for human life. Usually at this point in the event, officers are well aware of the deadliness. The questions that police officers should ask themselves, their peers and respectfully their supervisors about these "standoff" situations before taking action are:

Why?
Why now? (Don't create the action imperative)
Is the action legal? (2nd, 4th Amendments and "exigency")
Is the action risk effective?

Too frequently the explanation of exigency is answered as a "rescue operation" when making a warrantless entry into a home. In *People v. Poulson* (1998 69 Cal. App 4th Supp.1), exigency must be articulated and meet the guidelines given as examples by U. S. Supreme Court Justice Warren Burger who stated, "A warrant is not required to break down a door to enter a burning home to rescue occupants or extinguish a fire, to prevent a shooting or bring emergency aid to an injured person. The need to protect or preserve life or avoid serious injury is justification for what would be otherwise illegal absent an exigency or emergency" (p.5).

When applying the **common sense** component of the above questions to the barricaded suicidal situation, "Is the action risk effective," the question becomes, "Why run at a person holding a gun, knife or deadly weapon and threatening to use it against the police officer, especially in an attempt to save them when they are resistant to being helped?" If the rescuing police officer should be killed or injured during the rescue attempt, the outcome historically is one officer killed or injured, and one subject killed, less likely injured. Tragically, in these scenarios, police officers may have accommodated or possibly precipitated a suicide-by-cop situation, which could result in officers and citizens being injured or killed. As much as they wish, police officers can't save everyone. As written earlier, suicide is a social problem. For obvious reasons, it is unwise to allow emergency response personnel to dictate the conclusion of a suicidal standoff. A possible solution to these situations may be walking away.

Walking Away (A Limited Response)

In 1991, the Los Angeles County Sheriff's Department, after great deliberation and with safeguards in place, experimented with new tactics. In past events, the harder patrol deputies tried to save someone barricaded in his/her home, often intoxicated and suicidal, the more likely he/she was to precipitate a deadly shooting. Instead, the Crisis Negotiations Unit would respond to "suicide calls," usually a despondent barricaded suicidal male. Instead of doing more and gaining less, the Crisis Negotiations Unit would coordinate patrol efforts to do less and get more (better results). The purpose was to avoid a suicide-by-cop situation and keep the lives of all concerned safe. Additionally, the focus shifted from what they were going to do with the suicidal subject versus what they were not going do with the subject (as long as he or she was not harming anyone). Instead, greater emphasis was placed on protecting the surrounding community while the incident was unfolding and or concluding. If the subject did anything to place others at risk, the situation would revert back to a more substantial incident requiring more personnel. A baseline assessment was behavior towards others, typically acts beyond the doors and walls of the subject's residence or implied or verbalized intent to acts of violence external to the location. At a minimum in these situations, a "limited" containment of patrol officers was placed around the target location while crisis negotiators attempted to negotiate the person through his or her crisis with unknown expectations. In most situations after the protocols were put in place, there was usually no need to call the SWT team to the incident. The Crisis Negotiations Unit found that people who place themselves in these situations were generally intoxicated, depressed, and feeling abandoned. The hour of the incident usually started about 11 p.m., and as the process of intoxification and rage-to-energy diminishment occurred, the subject would fall asleep or pass out. Along with that, the explosive and impulsive energy to suicide that gathers as alcohol and believed causative reasons blend, passes or diminishes as the person "sleeps it off." In the early morning, around dawn, someone from the crisis team or the station would call back into the target location and generally find the subject apologetic, cooperative and willing to come outside.

A "limited" walkaway containment is a tactical deployment of personnel at points of egress from the target location. Officers' vehicles are blacked-out so not to create a target. This demonstrates care and concern for the community refocusing the solution from "getting" the subject to protecting the community. If there is family discord, when the estranged person is directed to find a relative or friend to stay with or stay in a motel.

The Sheriff's Department has had great success with these tactics and has used these procedures in hundreds of situations. Other police agencies throughout California are also following the same concept and have found great success. For police managers, this new tactic lessens the drain on staff, reduces overtime from a full incident "call-out" to minimal personnel, and diminishes liability by leaving the destiny of the incident with the subject. Of specific note, control of the incident is never surrendered by law enforcement, instead, "selecting the right time and place for battle" rule is applied.

SbC Outside Residences

Suicide-by-cop doesn't just occur in static situations such as residences. In examining officer-involved shootings in other circumstances such as police pursuits, information is abundant about precipitating behaviors as indicators leading to the violent engagement.

This suicidal subject presents himself in an ambivalent manner. According to Schneidman and Mandelkorn (as cited in Getz, Allen, Myers, & Lindner, 1983), there are 10 common characteristics of people who have committed suicide or are about to commit suicide. Of those characteristics, Dr. Schneidman defined ambivalence as "How will this individual announce or draw attention to the suicide." For police officers, this information (like above in static situations) must be put into a workable and observational process so that officers can observe the behaviors, ask the salient questions of danger, and develop procedures and/or tactics for officer survival.

Over time, police officers develop an instinctive nature. They become experts at recognizing human behavior when it relates to a subject's reaction of right, wrong and police presence. Sometimes this instinct is called a police officers "six sense" or "gut" instinct. As police officers know, their invaluable "six sense" or "gut" reaction is sometimes a suspicion not fully definable, but certainly worth pursuing to the limit of the law or until the suspicion abates. By all accounts, this is good police work. However, sometimes behaviors are not recognized and therefore not qualified as suspicious or possibly dangerous beyond what is apparent on the surface. For the police officer, a suspicious person drawing of a weapon triggers a fight reaction, whereas a suspicious person with the intent to draw a weapon may not be so easily detectable. There are some less-obvious behaviors that may require the pairing of behavior and explanation for optimal learned recognition.

As a broader example, we know that it is against the law to rob a bank. Loosely defined, this behavior is abnormal. It is wrong. Robbing a bank is not what law-abiding citizens do. The assumption about someone who robs a bank is that he or she will take the money and possibly spend it on a lavish lifestyle or support a drug habit. What about the individual who robs a bank and when being chased by responding police officers in their police vehicles, slows to 25 miles per hour? Or, the traffic violator who maintains a 25 mph slow-speed "pursuit" while police become aggravated at the persons for non-compliance to their authority. The serious question is what is the behavior?, and is it consistent with others placed in this similar situation? If the behavior is not consistent, then the action of robbing a bank and not attempting to get away is "abnormally abnormal." Most police officers have been put into a position to identify and anticipate what a suspect/perpetrator might do next. The question that they may ask or have probably asked of themselves or their partners is "What is this guy up to?" This must be seen as the internal "red flag." This is where police officers must listen to their "gut" instinct. They also need to recognize that as they get close and create the "precipitating triad," the chance for engagement is enhanced.

Situations may change rapidly into SbC. Some indicators of the "Rapid Onset" are as follows:

- Abnormally abnormal behavior
- Slow speed pursuit

- Lone occupant in a fleeing car
- Very obvious and outrageous behavior
- Provoking behavior when confronted
- Deadly threat in plain view creating a full and open target
- Vacillation from homicide to suicide (pointing gun at officers then self repeatedly)
- Officers' "gut" instinct or "six sense" about their observations

The "with indicators" subject is defining a stage for the engagement that can be established for any reason: a clear target for the police, the location that the fleeing vehicle runs out of gas, a place of full display, a positioning for television cameras and reporters to gather "news" about his/her experienced life injustice, etc.

The training component in examining these situations is that "catch" and "capture" are at a time of highest risk. Many times these events become protracted situations requiring crisis negotiators where available, but typically, the sequence of events is the following: (1) the person is at a point of suicidal intent, (2) suicide-by-cop is a considered option, (3) an opportunity presents itself to utilize police officers for suicide, and (4) the rule of ambivalence is present and the behaviors associated with staging a SbC situation are put in place and acted out.

*Rapid onset **without** indicators.* Officers report that suicidal subjects have forced them to use deadly force in a perceived or real threat to the officer or community safety. When these situations occur without warning, the officer is placed in a position to respond. The engagement is defined as follows:

- Going down **now**
- In your face
- Police defensive response
- Lethal force is justified
- Subject "driven" outcome
- Police reflexive action
- Police self defense
- All other survival options removed
- Kill or be killed

This individual is typically an opportunist who engages an unsuspecting police officer. These situations as described above are not police officer contacts initiated by a call for service or a traffic stop, but more typically they occur without warning and without any behavioral indicators.

Pursuit

For police officers, "pursuit" is a very powerful word. It evokes emotions of win or lose; however, in SbC situations, typically someone being followed by police officers at 25 mph is more likely being **followed**, and the persons behavior is "failure to yield" (or obey) with possible alternative intent. This does not remove the seriousness of the situation, but instead should serve as a "red flag" that something abnormal is happening. Police officers must recognize that the term "pursuit" is closely associated with high speed chases. In SbC situations, officers must examine behaviors cautiously and not act in a way that causes them or others to close in on an arrest until control, however loosely, is established. If during this "control" effort, the subject confronts officers, then the appropriate force necessary (less than lethal to deadly force options) may be required.

Conclusion

Suicide by any method is a violent act. Law enforcement agencies across the nation are faced daily with large numbers of these events on an in-progress basis. Whether the person is poised to commit suicide by jumping, self-stabbing, self-shooting or suicide-by-cop, these situations represent an obvious threat to the safety of the officers leaving a large impact to the subject's family, the community and very importantly the suicidal subject. Law enforcement agencies need to consider specific training leading to the development of some protocols, procedures and tactics based on the premise of safety first. This may supercede the old paradigm of "rush to rescue," which too frequently results in injury to one or all of the above, or psychological and emotional impact on many, but especially of those with the best intentions...the rescuer...the police officer.

References

Blankenstein, A. (1998, August 24) . Some Seek "Suicide by Cops," Study Finds. The Los Angeles Times, p. B1.

Blankenstein, A. (1998, November 25). "Suicide by Cop" Shootings Rise, Study Says. The Los Angeles Times , p. B6.

California State Commission on Police Officer Standards of Training (July, 1999). Telecourses, Inservice Training for Law Enforcement. Suicide By Cop, Part I. (Reference 99-07)

Firestone, L. (1999, March) . Suicide: What therapists need to know. Paper presented at the California Psychological Association Convention, San Diego, CA.

Getz, W., Allen, D., Myers, K.R., & Lindner, K.C. (Eds.) (1983). Brief counseling with suicidal persons. Lexington, MA: Lexington Books.

Hutson, H. R., Anglin, D., Yarbrough, J., Hardaway, K., Russell, M., Strote, J., Canter, M., & Blum, B., 1998. Suicide-by-cop. Annals of Emergency Medicine, 32(6), 665-669

Mish, C. F. (1994). The Merriam-Webster Dictionary, New Edition. Springfield, Massachusetts: Merriam-Webster, Incorporated

Naples Daily News, October 15, 1999, Two men die of head wounds from same bullet, http://naplesnews.com/today/florida/d14566la.htm

National Institute of Mental Health, April, 2003 from http://nimh.nih.gov/research/nimhsuicfact.cfm

The National P.O.L.I.C.E. Suicide Foundation Inc., August, 1999 from http://www.psf.org/media.htm

INDEX

Notes

Notes

Notes

Notes

OTHER TITLES OF INTEREST
FROM LOOSELEAF LAW PUBLICATIONS, INC.

Use of Force
Expert Guidance for Decisive Force Response
by Brian A. Kinnaird

Deadly Force
*Constitutional Standards, Federal Policy
Guidelines, and Officer Survival*
by John Michael Callahan, Jr.

Defensive Living
*Attitudes, Tactics and Proper Handgun Use to
Secure Your Personal Well-Being*
by Ed Lovette & Dave Spaulding

Handgun Combatives
by Dave Spaulding

**Essential Guide to Handguns for Personal Defense and
Protection**
by Steven R. Rementer and Bruce M. Eimer, Ph.D.

The Retail Manger's Guide to Crime and Loss Prevention
*Protecting Your Business from Theft, Fraud and
Violence*
by Liz Martinez

**Identity Theft First Responder Manual for Criminal
Justice Professionals** – *Includes Free Victims'
Assistance Guide*
by Judith M. Collins, Ph.D. and Sandra K. Hoffman, B.A.

Police Management Examinations
by Larry Jetmore

Police Sergeant Examination Preparation Guide
by Larry Jetmore

Advanced Vehicle Stop Tactics
Skills for Today's Survival Conscious Officer
by Michael T. Rayburn

Advanced Patrol Tactics
Skills for Today's Street Cop
by Michael T. Rayburn

Path of the Warrior
An Ethical Guide to Personal & Professional
Development in the Field of Criminal Justice
by Larry F. Jetmore

The COMPSTAT Paradigm
Management Accountability in Policing, Business
and the Public Sector
by Vincent E. Henry, CPP, Ph.D.

How to Really, *Really* Write Those Boring Police
Reports
by Kimberly Clark

The New Age of Police Supervision and Management
A Behavioral Concept
by Michael A. Petrillo & Daniel R. DelBagno

Effective Police Leadership
Moving Beyond Management
by Thomas E. Baker, Lt. Col. MP USAR (Ret.)

Powerful Pocket Guides - the Lou Savelli Series
Gangs Across America and Their Symbols
Identity Theft - Understanding and Investigation
Guide for the War on Terror
Basic Crime Scene Investigation

(800) 647-5547   www.LooseleafLaw.com